D0848997

Instaurations

D. S. CARNE-ROSS

Instaurations

Essays in and out of Literature
Pindar to Pound

INSTAURO: "To renew, repeat, celebrate anew . . . *sacrum diis
loci*, to offer, perform . . ."
(Lewis and Short, *A Latin
Dictionary*).

INSTAURATION: "1. . . . Restoration, reno-
vation, renewal. 2. Institu-
tion, founding, establishment. Obs." (OED).

UNIVERSITY OF CALIFORNIA PRESS

BERKELEY   LOS ANGELES   LONDON

University of California Press
Berkeley and Los Angeles, California

University of California Press, Ltd.
London, England

Copyright © 1979 by The Regents of the University of California
ISBN 0-520-03619-0
Library of Congress Catalog Card Number 77-91772

Printed in the United States of America

1 2 3 4 5 6 7 8 9

TERESA

meorum
finis amorum —
non enim posthac alia calebo
femina

CONTENTS

In pity for the hardships of man's condition, the gods have established their recurrent festivals as a respite from labor, granting him the Muses and their master Apollo and Dionysos as fellow-celebrants, that he may be corrected and restored. And the nourishment afforded by these festivals man shares with the gods: this too they have granted.

Plato, *Laws* 653d

Holidays are days when we celebrate. The word signifies first an intermission of everyday activity, a suspension of work. . . . But a holiday, in the strict sense, is something other than the empty space of an interruption. Of itself the suspension of work involves a holding back of ourselves and this may be its determining aspect. Through this holding back we come to ourselves. But not as though we were drawn back to our own self-centered ego. Rather, this holding back thrusts us forth into a scarcely known region where our essential being is determined. From this, wonder arises, and also fear, and awe. Man starts each time to reflect: something opens around him. The reality to which everyday life has accustomed us cannot however hold open the open region. Only what is unaccustomed can clear the open region, to the degree that the unaccustomed has its hidden measure in a rare simplicity where the reality of that familiar real is concealed. The unaccustomed cannot be directly encountered or grasped in what is customary. It opens, and holds open the open region, only in poetry (or, separated from it by an abyss and in its own time, in "thinking"). To celebrate a holiday is to become free for the unaccustomed of the day that stands apart from the lackluster, troubled everyday: the clear day.

Heidegger, "Andenken,"
Erläuterungen zu Hölderlins Dichtung

PREFACE

Introducing a book of this sort is like showing a prospective buyer around a house that has grown slowly and come together in bits and pieces. "Mind these stairs. They're a little rickety, I'm afraid, but we like the view from the top. Now this room started life as a study, then the end wall was knocked down and it turned into a kind of loggia." This book is subtitled "Essays in and out of Literature": "in," because the six central essays are literary studies; "out of," because the two endpapers, though grounded in literature, range well beyond it. The central essays, too, often come up against larger, extraliterary issues. What this means is that someone opening the book at random may find that one page deals with Pindar's way of narrating a myth or Góngora's dislocation of the fixities of everyday syntax, another with the consequences of discovering that our sources of energy are finite or with the new educational forms that may have to replace the academy. I had better try to explain the approach to literature which allows this rash sweep of engagement.

First, I do not see the text as existing within a distanced aesthetic sphere. Certainly it is "framed" and thus set off from the surrounding welter, and yet literary experience may not be so sharply distinguished from the rest of our experience as we have been led to believe. It follows that a good deal of what others must take as in some sense metaphorical is for me more nearly literal. Such a view restores to literature its old didactic function. The text does not simply give pleasure or enlarge sensibility; it teaches. Second, though I deal for the most part with writing from the past, my approach is not in the usual sense historical. I try not to impose modern preoccupations on the work of earlier ages; on the other hand, I do not believe that you have to lodge yourself in, or "go back" to, the past in order to hear what it is saying. The old text is made new as it comes to present understanding. And present understanding, as it questions and is questioned by the old text, becomes not old but *dépaysé*, estranged, even alienated, from its own time and place.

Or freed from their stranglehold. Literature is the tale of the tribe, in the phrase Pound liked, and the student of literature who makes full use of the resources open to him has firsthand access to other, alternative visions of the world, models of a reality other than the reality our society imposes on us as reality itself. He can hope to stand in what Trilling called a place beyond the reach of culture, beyond the grip of the present phase of culture. From this vantage point he may be able to discern certain permanent aspects of the human situation and also see contemporary issues in a special way. For even an ancient text, if we let it speak out, can speak powerfully to questions of the day. Does this mean that the attentive reader of Sophocles knows something about the dangers threatening our environment which the agronomist doesn't? In an important sense, yes, it does. I am aware that such a view will not commend itself to most students of literature (who sensibly prefer to stick to their lasts), while to others it is likely to appear the idlest nonsense. I am not attempting here to defend this view, merely to describe as briefly as possible the position from which I write. The defense must be left to the book itself. If Sophocles and Góngora and the rest, read as I read them, can throw light on our present condition, then there may be something to be said for my blend of rather detailed literary stuff (God is in detail) with amateur forays into matters that, though they surface on a popular level in the newspapers and concern everyone, are thought to belong to their own special disciplines. But can war be left entirely to the generals?

Not all good literature possesses this power, or not in equal measure. The work that still bulks largest in our humanistic syllabus was written by Christians and though the academy is reluctant to face this possibility, the classic and predominantly Christian literary achievement of the last half-dozen centuries may be a good deal less accessible now than we like to suppose. If true, this is lamentable for it would mean that another large piece of cultural memory is going to fall away. But there is one great compensation. As the nearer past recedes, chronologically remoter regions offering fresh sources of nourishment are coming into focus, and among these recoveries I include that of Greece, not the familiar "classical" Greece of our tradition but the earlier Greek world, "la Grèce sacrale d'avant le rationalisme naissant, toute pleine encore de la présence des dieux, telle que l'ont pressentie Nietzsche et surtout Hölderlin."[1]

This is the place to confess to a bias or conviction that runs through my book and may be found disconcerting, a conviction about the peculiar importance of Greek. Not simply ancient Greek literature and thought, but the ancient Greek language. There have been those who attributed a privileged ontological status to Hebrew, believing that it preserved traces of the speech of Eden in which word and thing were congruous. Something of the same *Mystizismus* colors or infects my view of Greek. More than any other language, to my ears, it says what is: what has been, is now, will be. It holds permanent human possibilities that, as Heidegger would say, may be retrieved or, as Pound would say, made new. So that when I try to imagine some renewal of our estate, a revival of Greek plays a large part in it. The reader who finds that my Hellenic excavations have brought up no wisdom not available on ground level may dismiss all this as so much *Gräkomanie* and thankfully resume his proper studies.

Renewal is one of the meanings of the word I have chosen for the title of this book. The Latin verb *instauro* can however also mean "celebrate," and my title, with the epigraphs from Plato and Heidegger, is intended to suggest a conception of poetry as celebration, rather than exploration of the self and its various entanglements. Celebration of what? Perhaps Peter Brook can answer, or explain our present inability to answer: "We do not know how to celebrate, because we do not know what to celebrate."[2] And yet poetry still celebrates.

An instauration is also a founding or establishment, the sense Bacon had in mind when he called his program for the advancement of natural science *Instauratio Magna.* Three and a half centuries later, we may be coming to the end of the great movement at whose beginnings Bacon stood, or at least see that it is going to end. If so, the question that faces us all is: What comes next? What new founding is possible? This book looks forward to another instauration, one to which poetry will have more to contribute. For poetry, "the last of our verbal expressions which remain impervious to the scientific world view,"[3] remembers much that has been forgotten elsewhere and may once again become central.

All that remains is to thank those friends past and present who helped me in various ways and offered advice, which I have not always taken: William Arrowsmith, Morris Fry, Sherry Gray, C. J. Herington, Alberto de Lacerda, William Mullen, Donald Sheehan, George Steiner, Geoffrey Waite. And although he has had nothing to do with the gestation of this book and may not relish being too closely associated with it, I will set down too, for my own pleasure, the name of an old friend in letters, Ian Fletcher.

I

CENTER OF RESISTANCE

The academy is agreed to be in poor shape. From one angle it can look like a costly device for keeping distracted children amused and providing momentary enthusiasts with anything that will turn them on. From another, a place where card-carrying technicians train the young, some of whom are retrievable, to become technicians in their turn. More grandiosely, one can even see it as the very headquarters of cultural betrayal. The situation looked more hopeful a few years ago during our time of troubles when the large questions were at least raised. They were raised, debated briefly, and then set aside as the campus grew quiet once again. Professors have homed back to their ruts, students want a good education to get a good job. The campus is quiet but all is far from well.

Even so, we cannot despair of the university. What else is there? We should be able to say of our particular institution:

> A serious house on serious earth it is,
> In whose blent air all our compulsions meet,
> Are recognised, and robed as destinies.[1]

A serious house, because it shelters something essential that is not found elsewhere. I propose to call this something *literacy*, letting the word draw on whatever is still valid in the Roman concept of *humanitas*, both the humane and the humanistic (in the old educational sense, not the modern pseudophilosophical), and on the Greek concept of *paideia* which in Plato's hands ranges from instruction to general culture and beyond that to an

1

awakening and redirection of the spirit. Literacy is learned, very slowly, from that old constellation of humane disciplines which puts literature at the center and ranks round it the other *artes liberales:* the arts that liberate, one might translate today.[2] For these arts—we may have to turn them into arts of resistance— provide an area of freedom where the largest questions can be kept open, in forms not dictated by society or intellectual fashion. Questions about man's mode of being, the earth he lives on and the social and political worlds he creates. Questions, too, about what Pound calls the gods. The arts, and literature most articulately, afford a region of meditative openness which is at the same time a vantage point from which to look, with a necessary detachment from immediate needs and goals, at what our society does and the way we find ourselves behaving inside the reality it proposes: the lives we lead within that commanding structure, the deaths we die there. Arts of resistance, also arts of remembrance: for they carry the past into the present and mitigate the constrictions of a time that knows only the present. They preserve, as David Jones has put it, our *signa:* "They show forth, recall, discover and re-present those things that have belonged to man from the beginning."[3]

These arts, the liberating arts of literacy, have taken refuge in the university. That is what makes it a serious house. Our sacred precinct, Philip Rieff calls it.[4] What can the poor man have been thinking of?

1

"What is comprised under the word literature," wrote Matthew Arnold in 1871 when the move to put English at the center of things was afoot, "is in itself the greatest power available in education." Where classics, the philological grind, had failed to constitute a true training of mind and heart, the best literature in one's own language might succeed: provided that English avoided the vices that had brought classics down. The first thing an ordinary person says when he hears talk of a modern literature school, remarked a Balliol tutor in the 1880s is "For heaven's sake don't let us murder Shakespeare etc., by treating them as we treat Aeschylus and Sophocles."

The English department has not murdered Shakespeare etc.

2

Yet it would be fair to say that somewhere along the line the Arnoldian vision of literature as the central civilizing force has dimmed. No doubt it was bound to. Something is inevitably lost when a passion becomes a profession, when the spirit's fine commerce with an author is turned into an academic discipline. There is no need to be frightened of this, yet the procedure has its dangers. For its own proper purposes, the academy transforms whatever it studies into an object of knowledge and in so doing distances it. This distance is the condition of the objective knowledge it pursues. The historian could not study a historical period if he stood as close to it as the Christian believer tries to stand to the time of Christ's life on earth. What makes the academic study of literature problematic is that literary experience is more like the Christian's experience than it is like the historian's. When the naive reader (the good reader, that is) comes first on a major poet, he feels as though some elemental force has burst into his life. Everything looks different; as he goes about chanting the sacred syllables, he finds himself transported into a new more vital world.

The head-on encounter with a great text cannot be institutionalized. It may come as the by-product of classroom work but it cannot be directly aimed at there. To put the point in different terms: the academic treatment of literature comes to seem inadequate only if we take the claim Arnold made for it very seriously indeed, and take it a good deal further than Arnold did. The argument of this essay, and of this book, is that literature matters more than it has ever done before because it is the strongest, even the sole, remaining witness to much that mankind has always known but is now in danger of losing. To approach literature in this way need not mean treating it as something other than itself (as religion, for example), nor does it mean asking of literature something it cannot give. Such an approach does mean that we need to find ways of reading unlike those practiced in the academy, ways that have their own rigor even though they cannot be institutionalized. Neither scholarly research nor the concept of literature as a source of disinterested aesthetic pleasure will serve if we hope to see it as a witness.

Since the English department has never professed to see literature as a witness (whatever this term may prove to mean), there is no point in complaining that it fails to do so. Let me instead put to the department a question about something that concerns

3

it very much: How far, in its teaching of literature, does it pro-
mote literacy? Literacy, in the old sense, was learned primarily
from Latin, from concentrating slowly and often painfully on
the way words are put together. *Nunc et latentis.* Someone, in
the genitive, now hiding. *Proditor.* Something, modifying the
subject, not yet stated, which betrays or conceals. *Intimo.* (In?)
the innermost. *Gratus.* The something that reveals is charming.
Puellae. A girl's. So a girl is hiding. *Risus.* A girl's laugh, revealing where she is hiding. *Ab angulo.* From the corner—the shadows at the edge of the evening piazza. And suddenly, from this
dense linguistic medium, a picture stands out sharp and clear:

> Nunc et latentis proditor intimo
> gratus puellae risus ab angulo.

No English poem needs to be read quite as hard as these lines of
Horace. The sheer difficulty of construing has I think a positive
value. English attracts a lot of people who are not, as we say,
strongly motivated; they want a light rinse of humane letters and
suppose that the English department is the least disagreeable
place to get it. The briefest exposure to Horace would send these
people packing. And there is something else. No doubt the student did not always profit from the old philological grind, but
one thing it did impress upon him. It forced him, at however
crude a level, to be conscious of the phenomenon of language.
With English or American literature, the student too readily feels
that he can take the language for granted and pass directly to
what interests him, the "content." He does not much regard the
verbal medium, though he watches dutifully for the images or
symbols that may be planted there.

The medium is the message, I tell students in beginning Greek,
to discourage them from thinking of this difficult language as a
can opener that, once mastered, will allow them to get at the
contents of Greek literature. We come to our studies from a culture where the instrumental view of language is dominant. At
best, language is our means of expression; for the ordinary purposes of life, words are tools, often throwaway tools, which we
use for this or that purpose. No, it is the other way about, Heidegger says: language uses us. When I hunt for the right word,
the initiative is with the word. It comes (or does not come) of its
own volition, opening up a situation or problem in a way I

would never have thought of. Language discloses a world of which I am part.

Language also discloses worlds of which I am not part, or not without effort. Early on in his career the student should be told: "When you take a word in your mouth you must realize that you have not taken a tool that can be thrown aside if it won't do the job, but you are fixed in a direction of thought which comes from afar and stretches beyond you."⁵ In reading an old book, something from the past comes into my mind. A rough-and-ready and not very accurate description, for this foreign presence is changed by the words and forms of thought in which I talk about it. Changed, but not into something quite different: much remains constant. Nor is this presence really foreign, for it has been carried down by a tradition in which I too stand. My mind and world also change, to receive this past presence, but not into something quite different. I am still standing in my own world but it has been enlarged and does not look the same. What happens here is that past and present fuse, and point into the future. The whole life of tradition and culture depends on this fusion. It is a linguistic fusion: only language allows it to happen.

Language speaks primarily through everyday utterances, but at present, since it is under attack from many quarters, it speaks there only faintly, concealing more than it reveals. Our words move about on the surface of language; they do not go down into its depths. Conversation is the exchange of ready-made verbal packages. It is in literature and only in literature that language retains its full power to speak. Linguists, for their own purposes, have reversed the old view that saw the written language as purer, nobler, than ordinary speech. From my quite different position I retain the old view though not for the old reasons. The difference between written and spoken is not crucial (does it matter if Homer recited his poems, or dictated them, or even scratched them down himself?), nor am I concerned with any distinction between "literature" and "life" since I do not see literature as belonging to some separate aesthetic realm. What concerns me is language's power to speak and the openness to language which literature requires. Though we tend to forget this, our literary studies preserve whatever is left of the special attention we once paid to our sacred texts, Hebrew texts that spoke God's word, Greek and Latin texts that traced the paths of thought and provided the exempla of civil living. It was the task

5

of the clerisy to live inside language held to be charged with highest meaning, to purify the dialect of the tribe by keeping open and uncorrupt the linguistic sources of truth and wisdom. These are cultural forms that have passed; our clerks have other things to occupy them. Yet we continue to live inside language, well or badly, and will do so till the world ends. It is our element, the ancestral home into which we are born.

The nearest thing we have today to sacred texts are the classics of literature studied in college, and the special attendance they demand I am calling literacy. The English department, which should be the home of literacy, if it has one, serves its texts in a variety of ways. At the bottom level it must do battle against the sturdy forces of postliteracy. One notch up, its large overviews of literature ensure that the future citizen-consumer has heard the names of Homer and Shakespeare and some more recent worthies. It offers the would-be poet instruction in the rudiments of his craft, and entertains the radical contemporary who likes to read a book now and then but can't be bothered with anything written more than ten minutes ago. It takes care of some representative foreign masterpieces abandoned by the modern languages department, teaching them in translation (those "faithful" translations which professors trust and which, keeping faith with the letter of the original, kill the spirit stone-dead). It promotes the view of literature as a source of aesthetic pleasure and as a means of enlarging your sensibility and becoming a full human being. There are also graduate seminars where scholarship is maintained and truth pursued. But the scrupulous attention to difficult language which a classical text requires, the kind of reading that creates literacy: this the English department does not teach, or all too rarely. It does not have to. What appears as the great advantage of English studies (no messing about with foreign languages!) proves to be their gravest defect: Language does not stand guard over literature there, hence the department cannot claim to teach literacy in the old sense, nor does it teach the new literacy we may have to develop.

2

Herodotus noticed that the Egyptians used two kinds of written character, a sacred and a demotic (2.36). The young Mallarmé expressed the desire for "une langue immaculée," as unyielding to the casual eye as a musical score: "Des formules hiératiques dont l'étude aride aveugle le profane et aiguillonne le patient fatal."⁶ Despite the mannered diction, this is less obscurantist than it sounds. The trouble with literary studies based on English is that they make literature look far too easy. No elaborate training in literacy is called for, apparently; bring the texts your common humanity and a reasonable diligence and they will grant their riches. Does "the greatest power available in education" really require no more than this? One would expect something more arduous to be needed—and I do not mean merely scholarship. Anything worth studying initially repels, by its difficulty, and at the same time attracts, partly through the sheer challenge of overcoming the initial difficulty, partly by the beckoning promise of what is felt to lie ahead. If the study of literature is to be defended; if we are to create, within the confusions of our society, enclaves where the life of the mind is ordered around exemplary texts, around the canon of sacred texts that every true culture requires: then a far more stringent, far more dedicated, form of study has to be developed. One that will never attract the crowd; there are areas where everything must depend on the few. The attempt to put English at the center of humanistic studies was well worth making. It brought a wider and more generous conception of literature. It is becoming clear, nonetheless, that it has not achieved what was hoped of it. We should recognize our mistake and put back at the center the difficult texts that formerly stood there: the Greek and perhaps some of the Latin classics.

Before he lays this book aside, I invite the reader to test my proposal by means of an experiment, in the classroom if he happens to be a teacher. Let him read, as intensely as possible, any play by Sophocles and then turn to a classic novel, say Henry James's *The Portrait of a Lady*. In the light of that contrast I suggest he is likely to find that in James the bare forked animal has been so overlaid with the late trappings of civilization that he has almost vanished. In the well-policed, financially secure world of ceremonious manners where the great novelists spend much of their time, our primary necessities have taken such specialized forms that they are hardly recognizable. Today, when ceremony is another word for sham and the trappings have mostly been removed and, perhaps, as things fall apart, our old necessities are starting to show their face again: today, there is a real sense in which the distant world of Sophocles, where the human situation is pared down to the bone, stands closer to us than the upholstered world presented by the great writers of the last few centuries. There are many ways of being dressed, or overdressed; only one of being naked.

So much of the ground of the premodern experience has gone that many of the supposedly accessible literary classics may in reality be a good deal less accessible than they appear. We seem to understand what is said readily enough and this prevents us from realizing how remote the world from which the texts speak has become. Take a passage like this from the beginning of the third chapter of *Daniel Deronda:*

> A human life, I think, should be well rooted in some spot of a native land, where it may get the love of tender kinship for the face of earth, for the labours men go forth to, for the sounds and accents that haunt it, for whatever will give that early home a familiar unmistakable difference amidst the future widening of knowledge: a spot where the definiteness of early memories may be inwrought with affection, ... may spread not by sentimental effort and reflection, but as a sweet habit of the blood.

Living as we do now, like nomads, never staying long enough in one place to grow into it—and if we do stick somewhere, the place itself is soon bulldozed out of recognition: from our perspective, what imaginable mode of existence does a passage like this point to?

Eliot, nonetheless, is here bearing witness (in my sense) to something, to a way of living on earth which alone offers humankind its true measure of content. But she was writing at a time when such a way of life, "this blessed persistence in which affection can take root," as she beautifully calls it, had almost disappeared. (Her immediate point is that the novel's heroine lacked this background.) The industrial revolution was far into its stride. We cannot hope to understand, let alone recover, what she is talking about here—*Bodenständigkeit,* autochthony or "homesteadiness"—from its very late expression. To find out what kinship for the face of earth *means* we need to go back to its earlier forms when it meant something far stronger than even Eliot could imagine. For the great divide had already opened up.

8

Thirty years before *Deronda* was written, Dickens had described the coming of the Railway Age, the earliest of the modern attacks on the possibility of persistence—"the first shock of a great earthquake [. . . that] wholly changed the law and custom" of human life.[7]

This great divide now stands between us and the whole earlier life of man. Of course, if everything that is needed to live well is found here, on our side of the divide, then there is no need to worry. But if the past holds much that we need now and may need more urgently tomorrow, then to be cut off from the past is the gravest of dangers. In the mass society we are taught to look on the past as a junkyard of outmoded devices, at best as a quaint reservation to be visited on ceremonial occasions. The only place where the past still has a home is in the liberal arts college, our "sacred precinct" where the remembering arts are cultivated and the texts of literature studied. Literature plays an important role here. It houses the living past as nothing else (except language) can. It also warns us, through our response, when a region of the past has fallen out of memory and become inaccessible. A modern literature like English which seems to be within cultural range is not the best medium through which to face this danger. The value of classical literature (from this point of view) is that it forces us to be conscious of the divide and to ask ourselves if we still have any relation to premodern man or whether we belong to what is essentially a different species. Here there are none of the deceptively familiar landmarks that let us suppose we could make ourselves at home in Fielding's London or Jane Austen's Bath. The initial remoteness of the classical (especially the Greek) world is far greater, hence the initial effort to find a way there is far greater. But once the effort is made, something strange happens. The remoteness is found to be stimulating rather than obstructive. Thanks to the purifying, essentializing action of distance, man in Homer or Sophocles seems to be naked. We observe in him our own compulsions and perplexities not so much in a simplified as in their original or permanent form.

Greek literature is understandable (as it wasn't even a few generations ago) and peculiarly sustaining at a time of cultural nakedness when the ceremonies of civilization are falling away like leaves in autumn and we sense that we may soon have to do without a great deal that has long been taken for granted. Many

9

of us are in fact already doing without something that held life together for centuries and finds expression in countless places in Western literature. Boswell begins a sentence about Johnson with these words (*anno* 1729):

> In his march through this world to a better . . .

Unsupported by the great structure of belief which Boswell can so briskly assume, these nine words sound almost grotesque. I doubt there is anything in ancient literature which leaves today's reader feeling so totally excluded. A character in Shakespeare describes, with no special emphasis, a good woman in these terms: she,

> Oft'ner upon her knees than on her feet,
> Died every day she lived.
> [*Macbeth*, IV.iii.110 f.]

The plays of Shakespeare are among our most intimately loved possessions. And yet if this is the world they speak from, do we who live in a world that is not merely non- or post-Christian but has lost the whole sacramental sense of life: do we not find ourselves compelled, much of the time, to move there like aliens?

I have deliberately introduced the problem of belief, though I am well aware that it is not supposed to be a problem. If not exactly solved, in the academy it has been so tactfully played down that atheists contrive to make themselves quite at home with the devotional poetry of George Herbert. For the approach to literature which I am trying to present, real difference of belief separating reader from author is a fundamental problem, despite willing suspensions of disbelief and distinctions between the emotive utterances of poetry and the verifiable statements of science, despite exercises in historical sympathy, the substitution of a psychological for a theological framework, or modes of critical discourse so refined that the notion of actually believing anything seems a downright vulgarity.[8] By these means, the critics have created the Imaginary Library where the literature of all time and space is at our immediate disposal. The reader must however pay a stiff price for his admission ticket. If you bracket off the question of belief, of your own sense of life, of the text's truth, you threaten literature's power to address you. Reading

10

becomes a system of make-believe; you playact a response to views of life which outside the classroom you wouldn't entertain for five minutes.

A great work of literature cannot be approached in the objective, disinterested way proper to the natural sciences: we ourselves are at issue there. Nor does a text belong to some distanced aesthetic realm; our most intense experience of literature tells us that this is a fiction. It follows that our beliefs can never simply be set aside when we read. Where do we read *from* if not from the center of our own being? Certainly we can entertain a variety of views about the world; it is part of the task of education to enlarge our limited range of opinions. But when a book introduces us into a world of which we can only say, "No, things are not like that," even more when it proposes a view of life which we hold to be untrue, then it is very doubtful how far we can be said to read it. And what profit there is in trying to. What this means, if my account of the matter is at all accurate, is that many of the classic texts of the last six centuries or so can no longer, within a non-Christian world, occupy their central place in education.

*   *   *   *

To say that a great divide cuts us off from much of the past is another way of speaking of the loss or failure of tradition. (So long as we have language, it cannot fail altogether.) This is a topic that has been talked threadbare and offers the mind little purchase. Hannah Arendt found a fresh way to look at it:

> With the loss of tradition we have lost the thread which safely guided us through the vast realms of the past, but this thread was also the chain fettering each successive generation to a predetermined aspect of the past. It could be that only now will the past open up to us with unexpected freshness and tell us things no one has yet had ears to hear.[9]

In other words, the loss or radical fracture of tradition need not mean that the past has been lost. Rather, it has been dislocated. Where there was once an orderly territory there is now a kind of chaos. A fertile chaos, if we choose to make it so, for if whole regions have become almost inaccessible, others may lie invit-

11

ingly open. With the collapse of so much that stood massively but obstructively in the foreground, we can now see beyond the ruins to the more distant past which paradoxically has come to seem closer to us. This curious change of perspective has not gone unnoticed; it is a recognized feature of twentieth-century culture. A hundred years ago Nietzsche spoke of "mythless man" standing eternally hungry amid all the pasts, digging and grubbing for roots, "even if he has to dig for them among the most distant antiquities."[10] Prophetic words, for although the process was already under way when Nietzsche wrote, it has gone a good deal further since then. I have in mind the modern feeling for the archaic, "the resurrection of long-forgotten styles" (in Malraux's phrase)[11] and the recovery of ancient images and modes of thought, the great labor of retrieval which has brought a lost world to light and set old and new side by side. It is this that allowed Picasso to put an African tribal mask in a revolutionary modern painting, and Pound to make the poetry of half a dozen ancient cultures part of the idiom of contemporary poetry, and Heidegger to discover in a sentence of Heraclitus a statement still waiting to be made.[12]

These discoveries or recoveries have occurred in the cultural stratosphere. But new currents are being felt down on earth too. There is a vague but widespread sense that we have gone about as far as we can along one particular road and that a change of direction may be needed, although the material set of our lives holds us so tightly that perhaps only catastrophe could bring it about. No one yet knows the consequences, to a society that has taken infinite expansion for granted, of the news that our sources of energy are *finite.* This adjective, from the philosopher's word finitude, is suddenly turning up in the newspapers. When a queer new word speaks out it is well to listen to it, and there are signs that people are listening and as a result can pay attention, as they could not have done even a few years ago, to voices telling them of something called a no-growth society. What is interesting about such a concept, which directly challenges everything the modern world holds dear, is that it speaks from the same region (if unwittingly) as the high cultural movements I mentioned just now. The only model for a no-growth society comes from those archaic communities which Lévi-Strauss calls "cold," that is, static or vegetable communities (from our heated point of view) which resist modification of their structure and

12

appear to be "predominantly concerned with persevering in their existence."[13] (Hence capable, it may be, of that blessed persistence in which affection can take root.)

We cannot "go back" to the past. We may nonetheless have to learn from its forms. What prevents us from doing so and makes the very idea seem distasteful and ridiculous is our way of thinking of the past as the used up and done with. We badly need, if we are to face to future with confidence, a new sense of the past. We might find it in German theology which likes to distinguish between two kinds of past; Heidegger has taken over this distinction and made it powerful. There is the past that really is over and done with, the *Vergangenheit* or passed, and can at most be reconstructed as an object of study. (This is the region the academy has claimed as its own.) There is also the past which Heidegger calls the *Gewesenheit*, the past that has been and still is ("*ist* gewesen") and can enter fully into our lives. This past— we may think of it as a field of possibilities—does not lie inertly behind us. It stretches out ahead of us. It may be where we are going: if we choose to go in that direction.

3

Could the leadership required for so novel a direction of thought come from within the academy? It hardly seems likely, and yet there is ground there, in the liberal arts college, where such thinking might grow. And there are people there who have pretty well given the academy up and yet live by the riches it still holds; people who are repelled by most of our cultural forms and yet have not fallen into cynicism and despair. Suppose that these people came together and formed a group, and that by adroit politicking they have created a free space, an enclave, where they can pursue a rigorous program of their own devising. The word enclave ("a piece of territory entirely shut in by foreign dominions," says the *Shorter Oxford*) seems to describe their relation to the campus, and the surrounding society, rather nicely. They are conscious of being in opposition to much that is taken for granted there, so (not yet knowing quite what they mean) they call their group a center of resistance. What are they working on? Oh, studies in literacy, they say simply. With Platonic *paideia* somewhere in mind, they take literacy to involve a

13

great deal, an awakening and redirection of the spirit, a turning-about of the whole being. A regrounding, which they see as the search for a new beginning.

This does not mean beginning something altogether new. From today's resources, that would be disastrous. It means more like rebeginning or reactivating an old beginning. But that is not quite right either, for a beginning, in Greek an ἀρχή, is never old, nor is it a mere starting point that is left behind when one gets under way. It is an originating power that preserves its power all along the way. The *archē* may be, not lost but lost to sight, and function all the more powerfully from being concealed. It may be wrenched off course and reach out blindly, grow enormously, without the guiding impulsion of its originating power. (Man is the most inordinate of beings, Sophocles said. But did Neil Armstrong know that when he planted Old Glory on the moon?) The *archē* may also be recovered. This does not involve what is commonly understood as going back to the past. The past, which is not the same as the passed, holds certain possibilities which are never repeated but may be, as Heidegger puts it, *wiederholt*, fetched back or retrieved—recovered, that is, and put into play again.[14] Genuine innovation means reactivating these permanent possibilities and combining them with the new elements that every age brings.

So, with their eyes on the present and still more on the future, the members of this enclave spend much of their time trying to recover the lessons of books that speak from a region far beyond the wreckage that litters the more immediate past. Greek books, many of them, and very hard to decipher. For Greece—it is the earlier, tragic, poetic Greece that most concerns them—is still almost terra incognita. Though we speak of the "legacy" of Greece, we have in fact received very little at first hand from the earlier Greek world. What we have received has come to us indirectly, via Rome, and what Rome transmitted Rome first transformed. It is the *other* Greece that is most valuable today, the un-Roman half-unknown Greece that (unlike Rome) is unaffected by the failure of tradition since it never really belonged to our tradition. To make our way there we must first recognize that we do not know the way there, or know what to expect when we get there. In reading a Greek sentence we have to recognize how little we understand what the words mean, even though we think to translate correctly. The dictionary meanings tied to them like labels do not fit properly or offer at best misleading approximations. *Phainesthai,* "to come to light, appear," the lexicon tells us. But what if this word means that "a being assumes its radiance, and in that radiance it appears"?[15] "Entrer en dialogue avec les Grecs," writes the philosopher Jean Beaufret, "nous suppose devenus capables d'entendre la parole grecque d'une oreille grecque,"[16] and to do so we must seek to confront the Greek with the fewest intermediaries, with the least possible interposition of the tradition of classical scholarship and interpretation. For if it is thanks to this tradition that we possess any Greek at all, what has been handed down has been domesticated by the countless acts of historical understanding which are inseparable from its transmission. And in the process what matters most has been distorted or lost.

In reading Latin, in thinking about Rome, we remount the stream stage by stage. (Outside the political sphere, that is perhaps the greatest remaining value of Latin: it makes us ask how far the tradition still holds.) What Greece requires is rather a leap into the unknown, a leap that may take us directly to the sources. (Or to some cloud-cuckoo-land of our own devising. It is unavoidably a risky business). This demands a great deal. It demands an initial labor of *dépaysement;* we have to rid ourselves of all the familiar expectations, of everything we "know" about Greece. And then stand open before the texts with all the energy of attention we possess. What is needed, says Heidegger, who has done more than any man since Nietzsche to build a way to the richest Greek territory, is *die nüchterne Bereitschaft, vor dem Kommenden der Frühe zu erstaunen.*[17] The sober resolve to stand in astonishment before what comes from the early. For although Greece has been with us for centuries, it has revealed only one aspect of itself. Apart from Homer, who until the Romantic period played second fiddle to Virgil, Greece spoke mainly through the philosophers, through Plato and Aristotle. There were the poets, to be sure, but poets can hardly be said to *think.* Only quite recently did it dawn on us that the poets too thought to some effect, and in ways very unlike the philosophers. And that the "pre-Socratic" writers were not unsystematic apprentices knocking on the doors of the future philosophic schools.

To the list of our fertile exhumations from the past which I mentioned just now we must then add this, the most momentous

15

of all: the recovery of the earlier Greek world. It is not hard to see why it should have had to wait so long before it could address us. Earlier classicists approached Greece from a position of confidence, assured of the superiority of their own civilization and their own religion. Our position is different: it is need that sends us to Greece. We have no faith in our civilization and nothing that deserves to be called a religion. In early Greek poetry and thought we find not the idle or delightful fictions of paganism but a religious sense, a holy, that can speak strongly to those untouched by the transcendent deity of the Judeo-Christian tradition. In the Homeric world, a German scholar writes, "the divine is not superimposed as a sovereign power over natural events; it is revealed in the forms of the natural, as their very essence and being."[18] There are those who look to Greece from the wasteland of the present and think they discern there something that in a new form might one day be recovered, a sense of the holiness of earthly dwelling.

Putting Greek at the center of intellectual life does not mean reinstating an old, outworn discipline. It means turning to something that only recently has begun to dawn.

4

The university is sometimes criticized for being too remote from the real needs of the day. But the point can be turned and the opposite criticism made: Is not the university too much a part of society? To be consistent, should not the campus be more sharply distinguished from the marketplace, given some of the interests professed on the campus? The university takes children from the television age, from a time of instant gratification and compulsive togetherness, and has them studying works that speak only to solitary, absorbed attention, works that come, often, from distant ages when men thought of the earth as a sentient organism and lived in walled towns that closed each dusk on the gathering dark outside. Through its programs in the humanities (how harmless that sounds!) our oldest images make a ghostly return, images of the city and the wild and the heavens. Ancient terrors provide a topic for classroom discussion, and forgotten, inordinate reaches of the mind.

To step from the campus into the marketplace should be like

entering another dimension. And yet campus and marketplace interpenetrate. The university claims no extraterritorial status to license its special interests, no sequestered ground where its revenants might feel at home. For although it has its own house styles and professional modes of inquiry, it is still part of the great world outside and inhabits the same reality. What place can the revenants have in that reality; what sense do the older humanities make there? Should we not lay the past once and for all and devise a genuinely modern curriculum? Common sense suggests this, the whole temper of our time suggests it. Or reclaim the university's, the *mind*'s, extraterritorial rights? Lionel Trilling said of Freud that he "needed to believe that there was some point at which it was possible to stand beyond the reach of culture."[19] We know of no such point today. We are so confined within the terms of our age and culture that we are unable to resist their pressures or even, half the time, to realize that we are being pressured. Pressured? This is the way we live now, the way everyone lives. And yet this point beyond the reach of culture is the condition of freedom, freedom that the university should provide. It should at least be able to make room for a group of people (my imagined center of resistance) who are searching for an extracultural or extraterritorial position from which to look at the way we live now and attend not so much to what is wrong in our society (reversing admitted wrong to approved right leaves the framework intact) as to what is *missing* there.

For although our world looks spacious, there is much that it does not find space for. I mean unused or denied possibilities, possibilities in human beings and also perhaps in things: so that even a tree or a table is no longer all it might be. And yet nothing is recognized as missing. It is as if a letter had fallen out of a line of type and left no gap, for the other letters have closed in and rearranged themselves so as to make perfectly good sense, presenting a solid, almost impenetrable front. And though society is on the face of it fragmented and frequently claims to be pluralist, there is a point of view from which it looks remarkably coherent (the center holding well enough to allow the breakaway movements their antics on the periphery), and it is not hard to see that our pluralism conceals massive agreements. We have a variety of options but no radical alternatives, no form of cultural transcendence as radical as the Christian, for instance, once had. His

17

religion told him of a place or state that was altogether other, not only in the next world but in this one. Distinguishing abruptly between the city of God and the city of man, it gave him a perspective from which the good things of this world hardly differed from the bad and thus allowed, even institutionalized, a principle of absolute resistance, a vertical thrust that stood out uncompromisingly against the horizontal life of man.

The Christian *knew* (perhaps still knows) of this other. We have no such knowledge, merely the vague but obstinate sense of something "missing" in what our society proposes as reality. Is there any means of verifying this sense of an absence? And, a harder question, have we any hope of discovering *what* is absent? The only way of doing so would be by stepping momentarily outside our reality and into another one. From this vantage point we might be able to see our reality as a social construct, one among many such constructs, and thus not necessarily containing the sum of possibilities. It is always hard to do this, more so now than ever, for our Western reality has imposed itself on so much of the planet. Yet there are still a few pockets where people that until recently we called primitive manage to hold on to their own social reality. These people are coming in for some rather anxious scrutiny nowadays. Along with a number of like-minded inquirers I went some time ago to a lecture by Alfonso Ortiz, a Tewa Indian and a professional anthropologist. Professor Ortiz told us, among other valuable things, that his people think it disrespectful to lie abed when the sun is up. If their father is at work, they should be too. We listened dutifully and did our best to imagine what it must be like to live in a world where such sentiments are still possible. Some of us, it may be, very much wanted to reach out to a world graced by this natural piety. We would like to share the feelings of the Indian logger mentioned by Gary Snyder who gave up logging and sold his chain saw "because he couldn't stand hearing the trees scream when he cut into them."[20] And indeed Ortiz ended by telling us that if we want to be saved we will have to go to school to the Indians. Yet it was no use. The cultural gulf between the Indian reality he described and the reality we actually inhabit (whatever we may think of it) was too great. We *know* that trees do not scream when we cut into them. To unknow this we would have to dismantle a reality that began with the transcendental God of the Old Testament. We cannot suddenly step into a sacred universe in which man and earth are part of a great vital continuum bound together by sympathy. The pieties Ortiz held up to us could come across only as picturesquely technicolored Native Customs.

A reality is not like a costume you put off when you grow tired of it. This is something that the counterculturalists of the sixties failed to understand and something religious syncretists still do not understand. A social reality grows slowly and holds tenaciously, even when you believe you have rejected it, and an American or European cannot simply turn Indian or Buddhist because he thinks the grass greener on their side of the fence. Might it not be possible, though, to reenter our own Western reality *at some earlier phase of its development?* This after all is what we do in the humanities classroom when we assume the Elizabethan world view to read Shakespeare or the medieval world view to read Dante. The scope of these exercises, however, is deliberately limited. We visit Dante's world as historians, or tourists. We do not believe or disbelieve what he says; we merely grant it imaginative assent. Or we suppose that it belongs to some special aesthetic realm detached from our ordinary existence. In consequence, what we read has no power to question or alter our reality which is left safely outside the classroom. Approached in this way, the work of art cannot address us. But there is another way.

When I stand in the small graveyard at Monterchi before Piero's *Madonna del Parto*, I know that I am present at a sacred (not simply a Christian) event. It is quite misleading to say that I am having an aesthetic experience. It would be more accurate to say that it is having me; I seem to do little more than provide an occasion for this august event to come into being. What happens there, moreover, is wholly discontinuous with the rest of my life. Something speaks from a region outside my familiar reality.

The *Madonna del Parto* is one of the great paintings of the world, and the shock it produces may have led me to put a high-sounding interpretation on my response. Take something far slighter, this stanza from Herrick's "Corinna's Going a-Maying":

> Get up, get up for shame, the Blooming Morne
> Upon her wings presents the god unshorne.
>   See how Aurora throws her faire
>   Fresh-quilted colours through the aire:

Get up, sweet Slug-a-bed, and see
The Dew bespangling Herbe and Tree.
Each Flower has wept, and bow'd toward the East
Above an houre since: yet you not drest,
  Nay! not so much as out of bed?
When all the Birds have Mattens seyd,
  And sung their thankfull Hymnes: 'tis sin,
  Nay, profanation to keep in,
When as a thousand Virgins on this day,
Spring, sooner than the Lark, to fetch in May.

Suppose for a moment that in addition to being a poem this is a report on a certain kind of experience. (Supposing this does no harm to the poem as poem since only by first attending to its formal qualities can I discover what it is reporting.) We would find then that these graceful verses, full of gods, full of a happy natural piety, preserve on our own cultural soil at least a trace of what Ortiz was talking about. We are not of course asked to believe anything (in the sense in which we believe that Piero's Madonna is really a goddess), for Herrick himself does not believe what he says. He is playing. A Christian poet writing for Christian readers, he can admit these country rites only with this proviso. (Come, he says later, let us "take the harmless follie of the time.") And yet there is something here just on the far side of play, for the poem can draw on a rustic paganism that still survived in Elizabethan England and lingered on for several centuries more,[21] the *parva religio* of the country folk—the *pagani* or people of the *pagi*—who had not quite forgotten the local sanctities of place. Familiar ceremonies like bringing in the May tree kept them in touch with the mysteries. In responding to the poem are we too, without recognizing what we are doing, keeping in touch with the mysteries? Does the ghost of a real presence still haunt our literary, "aesthetic" response?

Herrick, I suppose, could not have granted this, for truth was elsewhere, with his true religion, just as later it was to be with science. And yet poetry is naturally, in the old sense, pagan and poets are the great autochthons. They are in love with earth and its seasonal rhythms, its recurring transience. Even Dante was, in Auerbach's phrase, a *Dichter der irdischen Welt*. Poets have never quite forgotten the gods and the sanctities of earth, but it was not until the Christian shadow withdrew and science's claim to account for reality came, very recently, to seem implausible, that they could take these things with full seriousness again. It is only in our time that a poet can say, as Pound has so often done, "I assert that the Gods exist. . . . Without gods, no culture. Without gods, something is lacking."[22] It was in the prison camp at Pisa that Pound found eyes to look out on a nature once again brilliant with divinity.

The poets of the Christian centuries can speak more truly than they know, bear involuntary witness to a sacred they cannot fully account for. They give us hints and traces. If we want more, we must go further afield. Herrick's Aurora that throws her fresh-quilted colors through the air is charming poetry; but Dawn that, rose-fingered, bursts into radiance twenty times in the *Odyssey* is something else, "an event, an epiphany of a goddess."[23] Herrick's unshorn god, Apollo, is a decorative little piece of classic learning, Ovid's *deus intonsus* (*Tristia* 3.1.60). But behind this literary godling, Roman or English, stands Pindar's ἀκερσεκόμας Φοῖβος , and when Pindar speaks in his first *Isthmian* ode of

> dancing unshorn Apollo in sea-washed Khios,

this is not just poetry, for the poetry is dancing the god into presence.

Our classroom response to the poets, in other words, seems to point a way to the old pieties and even to a sacred universe. What if we tried to take our response *outside* the classroom? The academy frowns on such a step since it violates the orthodox notion of literature as existing within a distanced aesthetic realm to which we accord not belief but aesthetic assent. Yet even in the academy the problem of belief crops up, and students have to be taught not to raise it. In their naivety they want, if they are at all earnest, to bring their own sense of life to the books they read. Should they read the *Cantos*, they are often worried by the question that worried Eliot, "What does Mr. P. believe?" Does he, that is, believe in his gods and so forth, or are they just part of the poem? Take a passage like this (from Canto 74), one of several where Pound speaks of a statue of Aphrodite set facing the sea:

> each one in his god's name
> as by Terracina rose from the sea Zephyr behind her

> and from her manner of walking
> as had Anchises
> till the shrine be again white with marble
> till the stone eyes look again seaward
> The wind is part of the process
> The rain is part of the process.

Opening with the verse from the Book of Micah which became important to Pound in the Pisan camp, the passage quickly reveals itself as one of the poem's many epiphanies. The goddess is coming out of the sea. This is not just poetry; men have really seen her appear. Botticelli saw her in the fifteenth century in reborn Italy, with Zephyr speeding her ashore, and recorded his vision in *The Birth of Venus.* An archaic Greek poet saw her and in the Homeric hymn told how she lay with Anchises and conceived Aeneas, the founder of the city whose name also spells AMOR. The twentieth-century American poet had guessed at something like this many times (mysteriously, at the end of Canto 23: "and saw then, as of waves taking form, / As the sea, hard, a glitter of crystal, / And the waves rising but formed, holding their form. / No light reaching through them"). Now, to eyes purged by suffering and with no books to fall back on, the goddess reveals herself more fully.

Her ascent begins a movement ("till the shrine be...") that leads to and is completed by the embodying of the divine presence in a stone image. This does not take place in present, actual time, for the poet uses the subjunctive; it is something still to come. Then, in the two identically cadenced lines of the final couplet, the capitals marking a new gravity of tone, movement gives way to repose, becoming to being ("The wind is... The rain is..."), and we are granted a vision of the whole, of the process or *Tao,* in which wind and rain and earth and sea and air are drawn into unity around the benignant form of the goddess.

To the reader at all learned in the *Cantos,* Pound's allusions and fluid ellipses present no problem. The passage is entirely lucid and surely very beautiful. But Pound intends more than this. He has a design upon us, his poem is meant to bring about a redirection of the will. He says, in unambiguous prose: "I wd. set up the statue of Aphrodite again over Terracina.... To replace the marble goddess on her pedestal...is worth more than any metaphysical argument."[24] Why is this so important to him?

22

Because, answers Donald Davie, the statue or the raising of the statue expresses "man's ceremonious waiting upon the elemental energies of air and water."[25] Very good! but of course this is just literary criticism and is not meant to be taken outside the poem or outside the classroom. Pound, however, would say that putting up the statue is an important act in itself, quite apart from any function it may have in his poem. The statue is the visible sign of the divine as revealed to the instructed eye of love and only when "grove hath its altar," as we read in the great 90th Canto, and stone takes form in the air can man celebrate his kinship with the living earth.

Pound's poem, like much good poetry before the Romantic period, is meant, in Dewey's words, "to breed a disposition toward the world and take overt effect." The *Cantos* is a didactic poem, which is the main reason why criticism has had such difficulty in accepting it. Didactic poetry claims to be telling the truth, truth that we are required to believe (or reject as untruth) and act upon. Aesthetic consciousness has no place for such work, nor has scholarship, though it knows about didactic poetry and can mimic the appropriate response. Aestheticism and scholarship between them have created ways of reading—in a diluted form they are practiced in the mass classroom where the future citizen consumer is uselessly exposed to the Great Books—which have led a good many people to wonder if the study of literature should not be dropped. If we think it has to be kept, we need to come up with better reasons for thinking so. Literature matters, more now than ever before, because it bears witness to something no longer found anywhere else, to what Pound calls "a lost kind of experience," the letter that has silently fallen out of a line of type; because it points, with an evidence we cannot altogether deny, to something that is missing, a gap or hole at the center of things. Literature matters because, housing the living past as nothing else (except language) can, it remembers and keeps reminding us, at a time when everything else tells us to forget and be content with what we have, that we are living without something that humankind has always had. Literature matters because it teaches us to resist society's insistence that its reality holds the sum of all things possible. But it can do none of these things unless we devise stronger ways of reading. Reading that makes greater demands on the texts, and allows the texts to make greater demands on us. We need a new form of literacy.

23

*   *   *   *

We should now be in a better position to understand the sense in which literature bears witness to kinds of experience that are missing here. And I think we may go further and claim that literature provides not simply experience but *knowledge*.[26] At a terrible moment in *King Lear*, Edgar says:

> I would not take this from report—it is.

This is how we respond to great literature. Though it can please beyond all pleasing, we turn to it not for aesthetic pleasure but for its power of ontological disclosure. The text says what is. In the academy, because of the way it approaches the texts and because it stands too close to the surrounding society, literature does nothing of the sort. It can speak, and grant its own kind of knowledge, only in enclaves resolute enough to resist society's pressures. A minority knowledge, then. Let me here borrow a term from the sociologist Peter Berger and call those searching for this knowledge a *cognitive minority*:

> By a cognitive minority, I mean a group of people whose view of the world differs significantly from the one generally taken for granted in their society. Put differently, a cognitive minority is a group formed around a body of "deviant knowledge."[27]

Knowledge here denotes the body of socially acquired beliefs, values and skills that tell me about the nature of my world and how to live in it and that build the construct I accept as reality. The deviant knowledge around which Berger's cognitive minority is formed does not merely propose a different view of reality; it builds a different reality. In my terms, it is the knowledge *of* a different reality. The members of the group have turned away from their old reality and (with very great difficulty) entered a new one. They have turned about or in other words been converted, and it is in the phenomenon of religious conversion that this reality switch occurs most strikingly. It is worth remembering that conversion is originally not a Christian but a classical concept. Plato uses it in speaking of a philosophical education which turns the soul away from the world of appearance to the world of true being (*Republic*, 518). The turn required by our texts is different but no less radical. Open a Greek book at random—or better, quote from memory:

$$\text{ἰὼ γᾶ βοῦνι, πάνδικον σέβας.}$$

Women in a play of Aeschylus (*Supplices*, 776) are calling on their ancestral land for help. They say, according to a standard translation, "O land of hills, land of our righteous veneration." To translate these words involves, first, trans-lating ourselves into the world from which they speak, and then finding some ground within our world where they can come to speech again. But is there any such ground here? The word *sebas*, the lexicon says, means "the object of reverential awe, holiness, majesty," and *dikē*, the root of the adjective *pandikos*, before and beyond the sense of right or justice means everything from "the way things are" to "the order of the universe." So what the women may be saying is that their dwelling place is, itself, an awe or holiness in which the laws of heaven and earth and all the sanctioned ways of things are ingathered. This is what lies *ursprünglich*, originatingly, behind George Eliot's "kinship for the face of earth," a kinship that was vanishing as she wrote. By Pound's time the great labor of retrieval had begun, and in the lines from Canto 74 and in many other passages of the poem ("man, earth: two halves of the tally," Canto 82), the sense of kinship is far stronger, even though Pound was exiled from his native place. The way to the old is through the new; somewhere in between we lost the way.

It is well to be clear how much a turn of this sort involves. As I read the Greek words (mediated by Pound's English words) and seek to enter the world they speak from, I feel the abrupt, bracing shock of alienation from everything my society accepts as reality. What speaks there has no place here. I know that I must hold onto this sense of alienation and cherish it, for it may mean that I am passing beyond the reach of culture into a region where its writ does not run. It is the greatest gift the texts can now give. At the same time it would be foolish not to recognize that it may be a dangerous gift. In the eyes of the intellectual spokesmen of the mass reality, this lost experience is at best nonsense, a childish nature mysticism. Or it is part of some conservative agrarian movement, probably with fascist overtones. Perhaps it is becoming clear why I called my center a center of resistance. No society, however supposedly permissive, for very long tolerates within its borders people openly hostile to it. And the official intellectual community that stands guard over society's ideas, while very liberal toward any thinking that accepts its house rules, becomes decidedly illiberal when those rules are seriously questioned. There may in other words be some element of hazard in belonging to a cognitive minority.

Or is this unduly alarmist? Though we may think our studies very subversive, it hardly seems likely that anyone else will do so. Perhaps this points to something wrong with the program. Considering the claims I have made, is it not much too passive? All that is proposed is to read. . . . An intense receptivity, it may be, but one that finds no external expression, neither leading to nor completed by any form of action.

In reading, I attend to what is missing. What is present has no power over me—I simply shut it out? No, what is present is very powerful indeed. The indignity of our social reality was what first sent me, with a new urgency, to my studies, looking for some alternative to the life I lead. *There,* in the texts, I found something that is missing *here.* Does the fact of its absence mean that there is no relation between here and there, between the world of the texts and the world around me? Not at all. The something I found in the texts is not simply missing here; it is being actively, continually, violated. My response to this violation, now that I know *what* is being violated, is the link between the two worlds. Call it my sense of outrage. This word comes from Old French *ultrage* and Latin *ultra* and means originally a "passing beyond bounds," the dictionary says, later "a violent injury or wrong." The sense of outrage is my response to what violently, boundlessly, injures and wrongs. The English form of the word suggests too something that "rages" and bursts "out" when I am confronted by violence or violation, something so immediate and instinctive that I may hope it is the violated thing itself that is addressing me before it has become the object of a socially conditioned reflexive consciousness. Something too naked to be argued with cries out and for a moment my whole being says No.

This No was not learned from my texts. They came afterward and taught me what speaks in this No.

What provokes outrage? Every day human beings are wronging their own kind and certainly there is cause for outrage here.

26

This wrong is however recognized, even if it is not always righted. It has been worked up into an elaborate construction; a special organ, my social or political conscience, has been provided for it. This is all to the good, and yet the naked sense of outrage speaks less strongly when it has approved forms within which to speak. It is better to look elsewhere. Perhaps, anyway, humankind is receiving too much attention now. Watch a line of trees being cut down to make room for one more stretch of highway; drive on that highway past the dead animals killed by people going nowhere in particular at high speeds; return to the place where I was born and look for the hillside where I played as a child, feeling then some unspoken kinship with it as though it were alive to my hands and feet (the fragile minor of what Aeschylus's women felt for their ancestral land); search for this hill and find that it has been bulldozed off the face of the earth to make room for another "development"; even accept, in lieu of bread, cellophaned pulp that feels and tastes like cotton wool. Experiences of this sort arouse the sense of outrage in a very pure form because the things that produce it are thought either to be trivial or, unfortunately, necessary. For a moment, outrage floods my whole being, but then with a sigh I let it go.

I need do so no more. My sense of outrage is no less immediate but it is no longer untutored. There is a two-way movement between my outrage and my reading; they fuel and ignite each other. The outrage I experience every day tells me *that* something is being violated; my texts tell me *what* is being violated. From such seeds, planted by my society, nurtured by my texts, a reverence for natural forms can slowly grow and by extension for those ancient makings of man's hands which are filled with his sense of the holy.

On my way, my learning way, the poets go with me and prevent me everywhere. The first impulse, to turn about and head in a different direction, comes from me. The poets give me nothing I do not potentially have, but they awaken unused possibilities in me and teach me new needs, teach me a new way of looking at things, train my groping responses and provide a support around which they can grow. I find in the poets in a thousand places, places I had not specially marked or not understood (or thought beautiful without asking the region from which that beauty came), a grammar of natural piety and even hints for the appropriate devotional exercises.

27

The poets go with me, but I cannot go as far as they go. As far as the modern masters I may hope to go, for they inhabit the same ravaged earth that I inhabit. But not nearly so far as Pindar or Sophocles, or Homer, the source of things. Respect for natural forms I can hope to learn. But reverence? Reverence for the sacred body of earth has played no official part in high Western culture for centuries, nor did it ever belong to the Christian scheme of things, though the Catholic church inherited and marginally preserved some of the pieties of our older religion. When the sacred has been so deeply profaned, it does not quickly reveal itself again.

The most I can hope for is the sense, and then falteringly the knowledge, that where once was an overwhelming presence there is now only an absence. "Only," and yet this absence is not simply a blank nothing. It bears witness to presence. A presence that *once was* and therefore *can be again*, though we do not know when. The task, so far as I can understand it, is to keep close to this absence, this hole at the center of things. "Gottes Fehl hilft," Hölderlin said. The absence of the god or the gods is my form, my only form, of their presence.

Out of dark, thou, Father Helios, leadest.

*   *   *   *

No, it couldn't happen on the campus. The university is not a serious house. Even so, that might still be the place to start from. You have to start somewhere.

28

II

WEAVING WITH POINTS OF GOLD :
PINDAR'S SIXTH OLYMPIAN

Weaving with points of gold,
gold-yellow, saffron...

Pound, Canto 5

"Two of his sublimest poems are on mule-races," Gilbert Murray once remarked, adding, predictably on this view, "Few people care for Pindar now." But *Olympian* 6 is not really "on" a mule-race, even if the victory it celebrates was won in such a race, for Pindar ignores the actual contest. Nor is "sublime" quite the word. It is enough to say that this is one of his most beautiful poems. The language, which is unusually simple, seems still to reflect the joy of its distant occasion; the much discussed problem of the unity of the Pindaric ode does not arise to plague us, for *Olympian* 6 is transparently unified; and for once the function of the myth, itself enchantingly told, is perfectly clear. The victor's family, the Iamidai, held the hereditary post of prophet or seer at the altar of Zeus at Olympia and the myth narrates how Apollo first granted this gift to Iamos, the founder of the clan.

Despite this impression of lucidity, *Olympian* 6 proves to be elaborately made. Pindar himself, in an image from weaving, calls it *poikilos,* a word that can be used of inlaid work or tapestry and this provides a way of seeing the poem: bands or spirals of vivid color laid side by side in some intricate design. There is artifice too in the telling of the myth and in the conduct of the poem as a whole, a pattern of repetitions, with image and incident anticipating or echoing each other, which led Gilbert Norwood to speak of "a governing idea of duality."[1] Yet none of this teases the mind; *Olympian* 6 is one of those works where the artist seems to have solved all his problems in advance. At the same time the ode does not yield itself readily. It offers its glowing surface, its subtle archaic patterning, and that is all. With such a poem there can be no "method" of interpretation, no violence of scientific rigor; what is called for is a lively submission. The task is not to explicate, as we used to say, to force the tightly folded petals apart, but simply to find a way *in*, to learn a way of moving freely inside the verbal space until part relates to part and the shape of the whole is revealed.

Pindar begins with an architectural image: "Lift the portico on golden columns, as though we were building a marvelous house." The face, the facade, of a new work, he goes on, must be *tēlauges;* it must shine and be seen from afar. The final lines look forward to the victor's journey across a sea lit with gold. Is it this gold-faced house that shines on his wondering gaze, so that—in Pindar's circular manner—the poem ends where it begins? Nothing compels the speculation or forbids it.

The house is said to be "marvelous," *thaēton.* Since the gold portico is figuratively the prelude and the house it fronts the poem itself, Pindar is presumably doing no more than promise his client a fine performance. Or should we remember that the verb from which this adjective derives means to gaze at in wonder and is later used of the mind's contemplation? A similar image in an earlier poem, *Pythian* 6, suggests that this building is a treasury in which the victor's triumph is to be stored up and preserved. The purpose of every epinician ode is to give the moment of victory a longer life, even an immortal life. The Games began, we may reasonably suppose, as funeral celebrations for Heroes and although by Pindar's day the most important of them were performed in honor of the gods and hence their origins may have been largely forgotten, it seems likely that serious-minded people sensed in these brave spectacles of young life stretched to the full an attempt to confront the mystery of death. So it is that grave and final thoughts find their proper way into poems that praise the happiness of athletic success. For all the sweetness of victory, the games must have brought home

30

to Pindar the bitter paradox that haunted the Greek mind for so
long: that in an immortal universe man alone is mortal through
and through, and that the acts by which he measures his greatness and seeks to transcend his mortality are in themselves the
least durable of things.[2]

But there is no bitterness here and in a grandly playful way
Pindar goes on to imagine a man worthy to stand in this House
of Praise, a man who would truly deserve epinician triumph by
meeting three conditions, each in itself difficult enough, taken
together all but beyond human reach:

> If *someone* were to win first prize at Olympia
> and served at God's prophetic altar there   5
> and were founding father of a famous town like Syracuse—[3]

There couldn't be such a man but if there *were*, "how could he
escape [*phugoi*] an ode, if his townsfolk were the kind not to
grudge him his due of delectable song?" As though the victor
were the reluctant target of praise and the praising poem a mis-
sile, as indeed it sometimes is in Pindar. It is not clear, nor does it
matter, where these townsfolk belong. We learn later that the
victor had two cities, Syracuse and Stymphalos in Arkadia (this
is one of the many doublets that prompted Norwood's remark
about duality), and the text strongly suggests that the ode was
performed in both places.

With great emphasis (and an assumed air of surprise?) Pindar
now announces that there *is* such a man and declares, still not
looking the victor quite in the face:

> Let the son of Sostratos know   8
> this sandal fits his blessed foot.

> ἴστω γὰρ ἐν τούτῳ πεδίλῳ δαιμόνιον πόδ' ἔχων
> Σωστράτου υἱός.

The colloquial phrase ("If the shoe fits," we still say) is lifted by
the high word *daimonios*, heaven-sent, and means, a scholion
tells us, that the praise conditionally proffered in the first strophe
fits (*prosērmostai*) the victor perfectly, "as a shoe fits the foot"
(Drachmann, 14 c.). The effect, we guess, is still playful—guess,
because we attend these ceremonies at best as learned bumpkins,

31

not knowing how to look or when to clap. Certainly we are not expected to laugh, any more than we laugh when *Figaro* is playing; but there must be a great gaiety in the air. The victor is coming into focus. Starting as faceless Someone, he has quickly acquired a father and a name—Hagesias—so that he can be addressed and praised. To praise him, Pindar draws on an episode from the war of the Seven against Thebes. No smiling now:

> Hagesias! for you the praise is apt
> that he who led the Seven once spoke
> from truthful lips for the prophet Amphiaraos
> when earth snatched him and his shining horses down.
> After the bodies on the seven pyres had burnt to nothing   15
> he said in Thebes: "I mourn for the eye of my army,
> a good prophet and a good hand with a spear."
>   And this word suits
> the man from Syracuse, lord of our festal rite.

But for the final lines, one would take this to be the beginning of the myth. It is in fact a proto- or miniature myth,[4] introduced, we may guess, for the sake of a single line (17) which, with one word changed, would make a hexameter and probably comes from a lost epic, the *Thebais.* An existing verse of heroic poetry, then, fits the present occasion and the present victor, for Hagesias too was a prophet and skilled in that mimicry of warfare, athletic contest. Just as the poem begins, it may be, by describing the place its final lines will point to as the goal (so that, though full of movement, it doesn't to our thinking "get anywhere"—the end is already present): in the same way, we may feel that Hagesias's triumph hardly amounts to much since it is merely the repetition of something that has occurred before in heroic legend. It does no more than re-present the past.

This relating of contemporary event or person to some thing or one in the past is found in many archaic cultures and is at the heart of epinician poetry. Thus in *Beowulf,* immediately after the hero has defeated Grendel, his act is glorified in a poem that relates it to an act already performed. The singer begins to praise Beowulf, then we are at once told (874 ff.):

> he uttered everything
> he had heard men say of the valor of Sigemund.

The valor not of Beowulf but of the old Norse hero Sigemund, whose war against a dragon and giants the singer goes on to relate, with no further mention of Beowulf. Beowulf's performance, to be seen in its true light and thus truly praised, must be joined to the appropriate heroic archetype, a point that Mircea Eliade insists on in his studies of archaic thought: "Any human act whatever acquires effectiveness to the extent to which it exactly *repeats* an act performed at the beginning of time by a god, a hero, or an ancestor." Again, the contemporary act "is given an articulation and an interpretation that conforms with the atemporal model of the heroic myth."[5] Atemporal: for such a view takes an act out of linear, historical time and sets it in relation to the archetypes or *arkhai* which alone have true being. In so doing it saves the act from what Hannah Arendt calls the frailty or futility of human affairs. And the doer of such an act is, if not thereby himself made immortal, then freed from the full burden of mortality. This does much to explain the air of magnanimous joy which bathes the victory odes. It also explains why something is *missing* there, an absence that makes many readers find Pindar, finally, unsatisfying. There is no place in such a view for tragedy. What he offers at his highest is "festal sublimity, a thing much rarer than tragic sublimity."[6] Rarer, and today perhaps more valuable, for although we can no longer create genuine tragedy, our literature is obsessed with the theme of solitary suffering. This archaic master might help us to learn a way back to a poetry of celebration which is not exclusively anthropocentric.

We may see this relation to the archetypes as repetition or, with Norwood, as duality; Pindar, in the present poem, speaks of things that *fit* each other. This notion is first planted in the homely image of the shoe, a domestic fit followed in the brief Theban myth by a heroic fit. The utterance in praise of Amphiaraos is said to be *hetoimos* for Hagesias. "Apt," I translated; a scholiast's gloss is *harmodios*, fitting (18 d). It is possible too that Pindar found the same idea in Amphiaraos's name. Like other Greek poets he believed in the significance of proper names, in *Isthmian* 6.53 deriving Aias from *aietos*, eagle, and later in this poem Iamos from *ia*, violets. In Amphiaraos he may have heard *amphi-arariskein* (the compound happens not to be recorded), to fit around. There was no call to devise new terms of praise for

Hagesias; words spoken in legendary times fit him like a well-made shoe. This is a guess, yet we find a good deal of "fitting" in the diction and thought of this poem. It may be worth glancing forward to a curious expression that has not, I think, been fully understood. Pindar says to the chorus master who is to conduct the performance of the ode: "You are a true messenger, a *skutala* of the Muses." The word refers to a method of communication whereby a message written on a strip of leather and wound round a stick could not, once detached from it, be read unless it was wound round another stick of precisely the same dimensions. The words then do not simply mean "You are a dispatch-bearer of the Muses" or the like. They have a more exact significance. The chorus master is a true messenger because he is a staff of just the right size; the poem *fits* (round) him perfectly.

Another feature of this introductory myth needs to be noted, one that does not seem consonant with its joyful occasion. It is about defeat, and death. Visually the dominant image is the glare of the corpse fires. Amphiaraos, however, though mourned as dead, did not die. What we are told is that earth seized him and took him down, *kata gai' emarpsen,* a verb regularly used of men carried off by divine agency. (Compare, for example, Sophocles, *Oedipus Coloneus,* 1681.) He is in fact one of those heroes discussed by Rohde in his chapter on "Subterranean Translation" who were taken down still alive to the world below where they continued to live, sending up their prophetic intelligence to mankind. We have, then, something that looks like a death but is really a *descent* into the earth. The horses swallowed up with him were shining, Pindar says. The poem asks us, I believe we shall find, and the Greek allows us, to suppose that they were white.[7]

The first triad identifies and praises the victor, directly and by means of the brief Theban myth, and ends with a vibrant affirmation of the poet's commitment to his theme (19-21). Now, as the second triad opens, it is time for the myth proper to begin, and to introduce it Pindar turns to the driver of the victorious mule team:

> Quick, Phintis, yoke your strong mules!
> We must set out on a clear road
> and come to this man's stock.

34

Who better can lead the way
than your team who took the garland at Olympia?
Fling wide the gates of song for them!
I must reach Pitana in good time today
by Eurotas ford—

Farnell sensibly wondered about the poetic logic whereby the
mules are said to know the way.[8] The quick answer is that they
know the way because they won the race. It is victory itself that
opens up a path for the poet, a path that is now "clear" or un-
obstructed (*katharos*). For the brief while that the light of victory shines, the passage between living and dead, between the
ephemeral present and the timeless archetypes, is open. It is
hardly too much to say that the whole epinician art, as Pindar
understood it, depends on this openness.[9]

The victor has been celebrated, provisionally. The poet must
now set out on a journey and, leaving the immediate so to say
raw fact of victory behind him take a road that leads *pros
andrōn kai genos*, "to the very race of the men" (of this family).
It is a journey into another dimension of being, into myth, yet
the poet describes himself as traveling across earth, for the myth
has a geographical location. He must go to Arkadia, where the
victor's family came from, and before that to Pitana in Sparta,
where the clan was founded. Pindar's geography is however unlike ours, for when he reaches his destination he comes not to a
place but a person. Pitana *which* is situated by the Eurotas turns
into Pitana *who* at the beginning of things lay with a god. Look
at the transformation, the familiar turn on the relative pronoun:

πρὸς Πιτάναν δὲ παρ᾿ Εὐρώτα πόρον δεῖ
σάμερον ἐλθεῖν ἐν ὥρᾳ·

ἅ τοι Ποσειδάωνι μειχθεῖσα Κρονίῳ λέγεται
παῖδα ἰόπλοκον Εὐάδναν τεκέμεν.

I must reach Pitana in good time today
by Eurotas ford—

who, men tell, lay with Poseidon
and bore him a daughter, Euadna violet hair.   30

A familiar device, yes, but nothing in Pindar is really familiar. What sort of landscape is it where a town turns into a girl? We may call her an "eponymous nymph" but that doesn't take us very far since no one knows what ontological status to attribute to such a personage. It may be that our critical signposts serve mainly to disguise the radical strangeness of Pindar's world. It is best to move naively there.

The poet, however, moves with supreme confidence and, apparently, utter seriousness in these fluid aboriginal regions where human and divine can come together in love. What happens next? Pitana tries to conceal her pregnancy ("she hid her virgin labor in the folds of her dress") and when the child—Euadna violet hair—is born, sends her to Arkadia, into the safekeeping of the king who lives by the Alpheos. (The river rises in the Arkadian hills and flows past Olympia where the poem is heading.)

> Euadna grew up there, and her first taste
> of the sweetness of love was in Apollo's arms.   35

But my version is at this point more inadequate than usual:

> ἔνθα τραφεῖσ' ὑπ' Ἀπόλλωνι γλυκείας
> πρῶτον ἔψαυσ' Ἀφροδίτας.

It is not easy to guess at the height of felicity proposed by these words: "She touched sweet[?] Aphrodite in Apollo's arms." Nothing has been lost more completely than the full religious sense of these divine amours, so called. A point of contention already in Greek antiquity (for Xenophanes who objected to the poets' tales of adulterous gods, for Euripides with his bitter account of Apollo's rape of Kreousa), they were as time passed to be allegorized and denounced and moralized and relished at whatever unworthy levels. ("Then might you see the gods in sundry shapes, / Committing heady riots, incests, rapes.") The mystery of the sacred marriage, for that is what these encounters are in origin, would seem today to have gone beyond recall. And yet this too, like other ancient things, has returned, fragmentarily, in the poetry of our time, in Yeats and, with a deeper sense of what is involved, in Pound.[10] For Pindar, certainly, beyond all other Greek poets, they were gracious infusions of

36

divine strength and beauty, and it was a mark of how greatly the line of the Iamidai was favored that not one god but two took part in their begetting, Poseidon first and then Apollo.

Like the victor Hagesias who belonged to two cities, Syracuse and Arkadian Stymphalos, Iamos was descended from two gods, and this pattern of repetition or duality is underlined, as everyone has noticed, by the curious parallelism between Pitana's story and that of her daughter. With child by Poseidon, Pitana hid her pregnancy; Euadna, with child by Apollo, tried to do so too:

> All through her term she hid the child
> God had given her. The king was not deceived.

He went off angrily to Delphi to inquire who the father might be; she went off to the woods to bear her child. Farnell, no doubt with Wilamowitz in mind,[11] remarked that Pindar's "account of the birth has nothing of the style of folklore, but much that suggests an epic original" (I.32). Nothing of the style, certainly, which is elevated, though the language is supple and tender. Yet surely there is more than a suggestion of folklore or fairy tale in the scene itself, an effect enhanced by the lilting movement of these lyrical dactyls. We mark, too, the precious coloring:

> ἁ δὲ φοινικόκροκον ζώναν καταθηκαμένα
> κάλπιδά τ᾽ ἀργυρέαν λόχμας ὑπὸ κυανέας
> τίκτε θεόφρονα κοῦρον. τᾷ μὲν ὁ χρυσοκόμας
> πραΰμητίν τ᾽ Ἐλείθυιαν παρέστασέν τε Μοίρας·

> And Euadna loosed her crimson yellow belt
> and putting down her silver jug   40
> lay there under the bluedark of the bushes
> to bear her divining child.
>   Apollo Goldhair sent
> the birth goddess to stand beside her gently minded
> and the Destinies.

The word *phoinikokrokos* is usually taken to mean "of purple woof" (*LSJ*) or simply "crimson" (Slater, *Lexicon*), but I suppose[12] that Pindar saw two colors here, crimson or purple (*phoinix*) and yellow (*krokos*). This play of contrasting colors, light and dark—the silver jug, the bluedark of the bushes, the divine

37

gold of Apollo's hair—presses increasingly on our attention as the poem proceeds, and if at this point we take the effect to be merely pictorial, it comes to seem a controlling element in the design. Before long we will find these contrasting colors blended and harmonized in the flower, colored like his mother's hair, from which Iamos takes his name.

The fairy-tale atmosphere, still carried by the same stately diction, is felt even more strongly in the next scene. The language has the fluidity that marks Pindar's writing at its best. Boundaries are dissolving; something is to be revealed:

> ἦλθεν δ' ὑπὸ σπλάγχνων ὑπ' ὠδῖνός τ' ἐρατᾶς "Ιαμος
> ἐς φάος αὐτίκα. τὸν μὲν κνιζομένα
> λεῖπε χαμαί· δύο δὲ γλαυκῶπες αὐτὸν
> δαιμόνων βουλαῖσιν ἐθρέψαντο δράκοντες ἀμεμφεῖ
> ἰῷ μελισσᾶν καδόμενοι.

From the glad pain at her womb Iamos came
straight into the light. And sick at heart
she left him there, on the ground.   45
                                But glint-eyed two
great snakes by god's device fed him
with the innocent venom of bees. They cared for him!

Divinely engendered and protected, the birth is itself miraculous. The gods move swiftly to their ends and the children they father come swiftly and painlessly into the light. (So in *Nemean* 1.35 ff. the infant Herakles comes "straight," *autika*, into "the marvelous brightness.") The birth is followed at once by the miracle of the snakes' tendance. Mysterious, often sacred, creatures from the dark earth, they feed the child with the golden liquid made by creatures of the air. Honey grants inspiration and prophecy and also, perhaps we should remember, the gift of poetic speech.[13] And because of its association with nectar, it can hold out the hope of immortality. There is further, in the kenning that calls honey the innocent venom of bees, an untranslatable play on words, since venom, *ios*, is close to *ion*, violet.[14] Again, then, we notice the contrasting colors, light and dark. And another element of design may be starting to claim attention. Early on in the poem we had a dramatic descent, as Amphiaraos went down into the earth. The present passage suggests a two-way movement, up and down. Honey normally comes to us from bees, creatures of the *above;* here it is brought by snakes, from the *below.*

In the meantime the king returns from Delphi with two pieces of information which confirm the promises implicit in the previous scene. The child, who is Apollo's son, will be a surpassing prophet; and "his race will never die." He asks where the child is, but no one in the house can tell him. "No," Pindar goes on,

> for he lay hidden in the reeds, in the tangled briars,
> violets   yellow and purple blaze   55
> drenching his delicate skin. So his mother declared
> that he should be called for all time
>
> *Iamos,* immortal name.

ἀλλ᾽ ἐν

> κέκρυπτο γὰρ σχοίνῳ βατιᾷ τ᾽ ἐν ἀπειρίτῳ,
> ἴων ξανθαῖσι καὶ παμπορφύροις ἀ-
>   κτῖσι βεβρεγμένος ἁβρὸν
> σῶμα· τὸ καὶ κατεφάμιξεν καλεῖσθαί
>   νιν χρόνῳ σύμπαντι μάτηρ

> τοῦτ᾽ ὄνυμ᾽ ἀθάνατον.

Literally "this immortal name," the last three words are emphasized by their position at the beginning of the epode. We mark the precious coloring again and, once again, the contrast of light and dark. The vision is very delicately and yet very intensely seen. The flowers do not simply glow but blaze: the word Pindar uses of their rays, *aktines,* can be used of lightning or the rays of the sun. And this blazing light is then said to *drench* the body of the Divine Child. We may call this synesthesia (citing parallel passages), but the term is dubious since it assumes a disjunction or compartmentalization of the senses from which poets like Pindar and Aeschylus seem not to have suffered. Whatever term should be used, the effect is to enforce what we are coming to see as a consistent pattern of imagery. The drenching light that shoots from these purple and yellow flowers recalls the golden liquid the snakes dropped into Iamos's mouth, the "venom" that we knew meant honey but also suggested the word violets. Found lying amid violets, *ia,* the child must naturally be called by the "immortal name" of Ia-mos. The light that irradiates him

so clearly marks him as something more than mortal that we un-
hesitatingly accept that Iamos is indeed an immortal name, without, I think, at this stage knowing exactly *why*.

Whatever the reason, the next episode shows that Iamos has a
right to his name. He is now a grown boy—or to put it in the
poem's terms, "he plucked the flower of Heba, golden-crowned"
(gold shone at his birth and at his coming of age)—and he goes
down to the river Alpheos where his mother was sent as a baby
and invokes the two deities who founded his line. Duality once
again:

> he went down to the Alpheos
> and wading in midstream, cried to the lord Poseidon
> his ancestor, and to his father the Archer
> who watches over Delos, island grounded by gods.
> He asked for the honor that falls to the people's shepherd   60
> at night, under open sky.
> Spoke clear in answer
> his father's voice, searching him out: Arise!
> my son, and follow
> the track of my words to a place where men will gather.

The passage has the power and immediacy of all Pindar's epiphanies, recalling the moment in *Olympian* 1 when Pelops goes
down alone at night to the gray sea and cries to Poseidon who at
once reveals himself, or the scene in *Nemean* 10 where Polydeukes, standing beside his mortally wounded brother, calls on
Zeus who comes to him and declares, "You are my son." This is
superb religious poetry but it is religious in a special, some
would say a limited, sense, certainly a very un-Hebraic sense.
Pindar's heroes and to a lesser degree their contemporary descen-
dants stand open to the *numen praesens*, not indeed familiarly
but directly. Man's powers are far inferior to those of the gods
and yet we come from a single mother, Earth, and "we resemble
them in some way, in greatness of mind or bodily aspect"
(*Nemean* 6). Just as there is no tragedy in Pindar's poetry, so
there is no *mysterium tremendum*. A world that to our eyes[15]
looks so unfallen, so unseparated, denies us certain satisfactions.

Apollo does not in fact appear here. Iamos is vouchsafed only
the sound of his voice which, by a strong hysteron proteron that
some have contrived to find difficult, "answered and sought him
out" as he stood there beneath the open sky. The epithet applied

to the divine voice, *artiepēs*, is said to mean "clear-speaking" (Slater) and I so translated it. One may wonder, though, if the sense is not rather that the god's word (*epos*) was *artion*: that is, it fitted the occasion.[16] It met his son's need and came pat to his prayer. As I argued earlier on, the pattern of duality or repetition which is so strong in this poem can also be expressed in terms of two things that fit each other.

So off they go together, Iamos and the divine voice. If we could witness a performance of the ode, with music and dance disposing the words in lively space, we would no doubt be made to see the way the central triads, 2, 3, and 4, all begin with a movement from one place or condition to another. The second triad sets out from the raw fact of victory, as I put it, victory proclaimed but not yet realized in song, and begins the poem's first journey into myth where the origins of victory must be sought. Get the mules ready, Pindar said, "that I may come [*hikōmai*] to the source of this man's race," and after they have passed through the gates of song, "I must come [*elthein*] to Pitana today." The third triad starts with the same verb *ēlthen*: Iamos "came," with Apollo's help, into the light of day. And so too in this fourth triad, "they came" (*hikonto*), on the second of the poem's main journeys, from the world of myth to Olympia where the Iamidai will set up their altar and Hagesias win his victory. Performance might have set all this before our eyes. Since we have only the words, it may help us to see the poem's emerging shape if we put the two journeys side by side:

Phintis and the poet, from the here and now of Hagesias's Olympian victory, travel into the family myth, touching down first at Pitana in Sparta and then on to Arkadia. Iamos, the family's founder, goes in the myth from Arkadia to Olympia, where Phintis will win the victory for Hagesias.

Or put it in this still more circular form:

Phintis, to compete in the race, took the mule team to Olympia and must go, in the myth, to Arkadia...from where Iamos will set out for Olympia...where Phintis will win the victory (...which will send him to Arkadia, from where...)

Circularity, in one form or another, is common in Pindar but here it seems unusually pronounced. We have not yet asked what it means, if indeed it "means" anything and is not simply a habit of mind or trick of style. Again, we can accept that the victor's performance is modeled on the acts of his ancestors, but we still have to account for the very strongly accented pattern of repetition or duality here. What relation, if any, all this may have to the play of contrasting colors, or the movements of descent and ascent: this again we have not attempted to inquire. The charm of *Olympian* 6 is that its difficulties—"difficulties" only if one stands back from it critically—do not tease the mind. If we are content simply to submit to this poem, we seem to move through a serene and satisfying landscape that may have its enigmatic features but in no sense requires explaining.

With Apollo's promise of the family's gift of prophecy, lines 65-70 (*two* kinds of prophecy, in fact), the myth is over and Pindar can announce, with proper solemnity:

> Very famous since then in Hellas   71
> the race of Iamos.

This would be an appropriate place for a regular epinician element, the list of contests in which the victor and his family triumphed on previous occasions. The Iamidai seem, however, to have been better prophets than athletes, so Pindar simply describes the kind of victory that (unnamed) Iamids are in the habit of winning. Poetically, this has its advantages. Though he handles it with great dexterity, the bristling list of names and places must have been the most obdurate feature of the genre. An imaginary victory can more easily be made to play its part in the poem's unfolding pattern:

> Setting high store
> by great performance they walk
> on a brilliant path. Their every act
> proves this. Rancorous censure hangs
> on them beyond all others
> who drive in first on the twelfth lap   75
> as awesome Joy sheds winning
> fame and beauty on them.

With the arrival at historical Olympia we have emerged from the myth and moved into the known world where men compete in the games and face the ordinary hazards of mortal life. Yet the light of the myth still shines as we watch the members of this privileged race walking on the brilliant path that leads to its culmination in Hagesias's victory. "Rancorous censure" (*mōmos phthoneontōn*) is not of course a hint at his shaky political status; that would be wholly out of place here. It is simply, as Bundy has taught us to see, an encomiastic device: achievement of this sort is bound to make people jealous.[17] The description of "awesome Joy" (*aidoia Kharis*) "shedding" (*potistaxēi*) beauty on the winner may be purely conventional,[18] but it is a mistake to suppose that because a word is sometimes conventional it must always be so. This is moreover a dubious way to approach a great poet working in a genre that is still rich and vital. It is wiser to say that a familiar epinician motif serves here to develop the imagery used of the infant Iamos earlier on. The snakes brought him honey; the violets drenched him in their blazing light. And now fructifying Kharis sheds on this Iamid victor fame and beauty and the shine of immortal life.

So far, the poem's course has been, for Pindar, unusually straightforward. He now seems to pause and, as though summing up what has gone before, to gather strength for some important new assertion—or a move in a new direction:

> If it is true, Hagesias, that your mother's people
> living by the foothills of Kullana
>
> have in their piety always prayed and all ways
> sacrificed to Hermes, herald of the gods,
> marshal of the games and ordered contests,
> who honors the brave people of Arkadia: 80
> then it is he, O son of Sostratos,
> with his deep-chested father who keeps your luck so good!

One might paraphrase:

> If you are truly from Arkadia—as you are!—and worship Hermes (as you surely do)—if, that is, you spring from the rich Arkadian origins I have been describing: then heaven favors you indeed!

The apodosis is more handsome and emphatic than my paraphrase suggests (κεῖνος, ὦ παῖ Σωστράτου, / σὺν βαρυγδούπῳ πατρὶ κραίνει σέθεν εὐτυχίαν), but it doesn't all seem quite to answer, or satisfy, the long ranging protasis. Something more is needed, or coming, and it comes at us dramatically, bursting out in excited asyndeton:

δόξαν ἔχω τιν᾽ ἐπὶ γλώσσᾳ λιγυρᾶς ἀκόνας,
ἅ μ᾽ ἐθέλοντα προσέρπει καλλιρόαισι πνοαῖς.

These difficult lines seem to say that the poet has on his tongue a thought or idea (*doxa*) that is (like) a whetstone. That is, it drives him to praise Hagesias in exact, honed words (neither short of the mark nor beyond it) uttered in the high, clear tone that the Greek ear found pleasing. Though he receives this thought willingly, it comes over him in power (*proserpei*),[19] accompanied by the liquid breath of (flute?) song. The passage is difficult—and was found so no less by ancient than by modern critics—because Pindar is trying to say something for which there were no words in fifth-century Greece and for which there are no adequate words today. He is talking about the way the elements of a poem come together in a poet's mind, a process of creative surrender (*ethelonta*) to something that takes forcible possession of him, a process in which the thing to be expressed and the means of expressing it are inextricably fused. The thought Pindar has to utter is itself the disciplined impulse to speech (*akonas*—"it sharpens me like a whetstone" to praise Hagesias, a scholiast glosses, 140a) and also the kind, even the tone (*liguras*), of speech in which it will be uttered. This incipient thought/speech-act which is "on (the tip of) his tongue" is then at once translated into its own poetico-musical realization as he hears the liquid breath of the flutes that will accompany the performance of the completed ode.

The evident excitement of these lines—and the reason that Pindar has been driven to look in at the nature of the poetic process—is that an essential element of the poem has been given him, a missing piece he did not even know was missing. Suddenly the pattern stands clear, and exultantly he reveals his new thought, once again in asyndeton:

ματρομάτωρ ἐμὰ Στυμφαλίς, εὐανθὴς Μετώπα,

E' πλάξιππον ἃ Θήβαν ἔτικτεν, τᾶς ἐρατεινὸν ὕδωρ
πίομαι, ἀνδράσιν αἰχματαῖσι πλέκων
ποικίλον ὕμνον.

Yes! there
she flowered, my mother's mother, Metopa,

5   whose child was Theba: her horses crowd the streets,
      hers are the lovely streams I drink   85
      as I weave for fighting men
      these threads to patterned song.

This is the only place in the poem where the movement does
not come to a stop with the end of the triad but runs over into
the next one. What the effect would have been, in performance,
of the comma that stands in our text after Metopa we can only
guess. Perhaps the dancers, instead of returning to their original
positions and beginning a new movement, would have carried
straight on, driven forward by the high poetic emotion that we
still feel in the words: the excitement that has carried them across
from Arkadia to Thebes where the poet, in his ecstasy, is drinking[20] the visionary water that the Muses made to spring up and
is, at this moment, composing the poem that is being enacted
before us.

Pindar has been tracing the victor's origin, without (the dramatic fiction of the poem is) knowing that he was also tracing his
own. He has tracked Hagesias down to his sources in Arkadia
and now suddenly realizes that he too has his sources there, for
Thebes—or rather Theba, another "eponymous nymph"—was
the daughter of Metopa, the tutelary of a body of water near
Stymphalos, one of the two cities Hagesias came from. Now we
understand why the apodosis of the long conditional sentence
just before did not seem quite satisfying. In the light of the discovery the poet has made we see that it should have gone like
this:

If you, Hagesias, are from Arkadia: *then we are kin.*

Pindar can speak with new authority, for he has learned from
the myth he fashioned with such loving care that prophet-victor
and poet are one. In the poem's terms, they fit each other, just as
the story of Amphiaraos (and still more that of Iamos) fitted
Hagesias.

We know better now than to take a passage of this sort as rep-
resenting Pindar's personal interest in his own background, an
autobiographical intrusion we can forgive because we are glad to

know more about him. He is not, as a poet was to put it in a far more private age, recording "in verse the origin . . . of his own powers." Rather, in showing that Hagesias's family came from the region where his own city had its legendary beginnings, he is showing how perfectly qualified he is to praise him. This said, and it still needs to be said firmly, given Pindar's not quite defunct reputation for splendid irrelevance, we are free to grant that *Olympian* 6 is in an important sense about the nature of poetry and to that extent is a personal poem or one that includes personal elements.[21] We should use our new understanding of the strict epinician form to enrich Pindar's odes, not impoverish them. There is often, in the best poetry, an element of the gratuitous: more is given than could ever be expected. Pindar very amply fulfills his commission, praising Hagesias as Olympian victor, as prophet, and as the inheritor of a proud family tradition. Yet he saw himself as a prophet too, the *prophatas* or spokesman of the Muses (*Paian* 6.6), and the search for Hagesias's origins could not but touch him closely. Most of all, he must have found in the myth that told how Iamos came by his immortal name a confirmation of his own profound belief in poetry's immortalizing power, on which the whole epinician art depended.

The poem, then, by a curiously subtle fiction, is at this point dramatizing the circumstances of its own composition. It has now firmly taken shape in the poet's mind; he has nearly all the "threads" he needs and can look forward to the challenge of performance. This new thrust is expressed in words that suggest the now familiar figure of a journey. Just as, near the beginning, he told the mule driver Phintis to take him into the family myth— that is, into the material from which the poem was to be formed. So here he turns to his chorus master, Aineias, and seems to send *him* on his travels, on the first limb of the poem's final journey:

> Up Aineias, rouse your friends.
> First a song for the Maiden Hera,[22] then let me know
> if we, by words told true, escape their ancient taunt,
> *Boiotian pig!* You carry the tale straight.   90
> Fitted to your muse-measure my song takes shape,
> blends and resounds in the bowl that your hands lift.

Aineias (about whom we know nothing, despite Wilamowitz's researches)[23] may well be the local chorus master at Stymphalos

46

in Arkadia, in which event Pindar is doing no more than urge him to do a good job. The passage is however written in such a way as to suggest that the *poem's* journey, from the place where it was composed to the two places where it is to be performed, is a journey undertaken by *Aineias*. The opening of the fifth triad shows us Pindar himself at Thebes; with the reference to the Maiden Hera the scene shifts to Stymphalos where the poem is to be given first and then, at the start of the antistrophe, to Hagesias's other city, Syracuse. At all events the long journey that began as Phintis and the poet took the road into myth is nearly over. The poem has emerged from its rich sources, Spartan, Arkadian, Theban, and will soon stand in the hard light of performance.

The temptation to take "Boiotian pig" in a personal or auto-biographical sense should (once again) be resisted. As a man Pindar may have resented Boiotia's reputation for provincial boorishness, but he is speaking here as a poet, an epinician poet whose credentials must be perfectly in order if his client is to be perfectly praised. We are expected to recall an earlier moment in the poem. In the first strophe, as he imagined his triply qualified victor, Pindar asked in an odd phrase how such a man could escape (*phugoi*) songs of praise. He now turns the expression about and asks how his Boiotian poet can escape (*pheugomen*) insult. Target of earned applause, target of unearned taunt: who could doubt that a poet who *fits* his client so well is fully qualified to praise him? It is a very neat stroke and we are surely meant to take pleasure in its accomplishment. Even more so as Pindar proceeds to show just how undeserved the taunt is, rolling out two gorgeous choral phrases which I shirked in my translation:

ἠϋκόμων σκυτάλα Μοισᾶν, γλυκὺς κρα-
τὴρ ἀγαφθέγκτων ἀοιδᾶν

"*Skutala* [the cipher-stick round which the message fits] of the Muses whose hair is splendor, lovely mixing-bowl of resounding songs" (91). Boiotian pig, indeed!

Finally, the second limb of the journey, to Syracuse. Pindar begins with some words about Hieron, the high and mighty ruler of the city. Politically tactful, no doubt— and complimentary to Hagesias—thus to associate him with so important a personage. And poetically required:

I have told you to remember Syracuse,
Quail-Island too,
where Hieron rules, so clear in his office.
His mind matches each occasion, he observes the rites
of Demeter ruddy-footed   95
and Persephone of the White Horses
and Zeus the power of Aitna.

"His mind matches each occasion" is in Greek *artia mēdomenos*,
literally "devising fit things." The notion of fitting has no special
thematic force here; and yet at this late stage of the poem, when
everything is coming together, it is appropriate enough. More
important are Hieron's religious observances. The trinity of
deities here balances the reference to Hera's Arkadian cult just
before, but it is the two goddesses, whose hierophant Hieron
was said to be (Scholia, 160d), who interest us. Each goddess is
provided with her stately epithet:

$$\phi οινικόπεζαν$$
$$ἀμφέπει \ Δάματρα \ λευκίππου \ τε \ θυγατρὸς \ ἐορτάν,$$

Demeter *phoinikopeza*, ruddy-footed: Persephone *leukippos*, of
the white horses. Whatever the significance of the first of these
epithets, a vexed question I propose to put off for the present,
there is no doubt of their effect together. They recall and, in their
deliberate juxtaposition, enforce the poem's series of color contrasts, light and dark: Euadna's violet hair, her purple and yellow belt, the silver jug she set down beneath the dark bushes, the
golden liquid brought by creatures from the (dark) earth, the
yellow and purple rays of the violets which drenched Iamos's
body and, perhaps, the "beauty" that Kharis shed on the victor.

And there is another recall or repetition here. Persephone is
leukippos, a scholiast explains, because "after the rape which she
suffered at Plouton's hands she was found by her mother and
brought up (*anēkhthai*) to her father Zeus on Olympos in a
chariot drawn by white horses" (160 c).[24] Her ascent, at this
point near the end of the poem, echoes and as it were answers
the descent near the beginning when Amphiaraos was taken
down into the earth by his shining (white...) horses. The two
movements complement, and fit, each other; they are two parts
of a single movement. And since Persephone's ascent must bring

to mind Demeter's grief at her descent, these lines, while contributing to the poem's color contrasts, play an equally important part in the other main element of its design: not only light and dark, but up and down.

The poet's business is almost done. The festal note begins to sound and allows a transition from Hieron to Hagesias, the true focus of attention, and at the same time points toward the conclusion of the final journey:

> The soft call
> of the lyre knows Hieron, and the dancing.
> May time to come not trouble
> his joy. Let him in heart's courtesy
> receive Hagesias and his rite of triumph
>
> when it travels home from home, leaving
> that walled city in Arkadia, mother   100
> of a land where sheep graze.

Everything is reassuringly familiar. There is no room for originality here; the genre is in full control. We expect a prayer for prosperity, Hieron's and of course Hagesias's. Expect, at this high reach of happiness, a reminder of vicissitude,[25] and the next sentence goes on to provide an exquisitely conventional hint that fair weather can always turn foul:

> In a stormy night
> best let down two anchors
> from your fast ship's side.

The two anchors embody, in almost emblematic form, the poem's abiding concern with duality, expressed yet once more in a prayer for the victor's two homes. ("And may God in his love / make them happy and famous, / Arkadia, Syracuse.") Appropriate gear for someone about to set out on a sea journey, they call forth the poem's final prayer for Hagesias as he sails for Syracuse:

> δέσποτα ποντόμεδ ων, εὐθὺν δὲ πλόον καμάτων
> ἐκτὸς ἐόντα δίδοι, χρυσαλακάτοιο πόσις
> Ἀμφιτρίτας, ἐμῶν δ' ὕμνων ἄεξ' εὐτερπὲς ἄνθος.

> And you, Sea's lord, Poseidon,
> with your Amphitrita, grave at her gold spindle,

> Grant them a quick sailing and no mishap.
> Ripen my songs of joy, make them flower.   105

Poseidon is invoked because it was he who lay with Pitana in love and founded the house of Iamos; and because it is he who must grant safe passage across this sea lit with gold[26]—a passage, I suggested, to the golden house of the opening lines. To our thinking, this is to put it the wrong way round. The voyage across a sea always changeable and sometimes dangerous ought to come first and the poem end with the house of praise where achievement is stored up safely forever. But Pindar's thinking is circular and images of permanence and impermanence meet as the serpent grasps its tail. Poseidon is invoked, finally, not only as the sea's lord but as *posis das*, Husband of Earth, as *phutalmios*, He who makes plants grow. May he foster the poet's song of joy for a victor whose family was named after a flower. Stripped of its imagery, the meaning of the last line, Heyne charmingly suggested, is simply *Fac ut hymnus meus placeat*. Which would let the poem close like a Shakespearian comedy:

> But that's all one, our play is done,
> And we'll strive to please you every day.

C   *I liked best the part where Iamos lay in the flowers.*

B   *Or the way they did Metopa. How was it . . . ? "Yes! there she flowered, my mother's mother, Metopa." They hung on her name for a moment and you thought they were going back, but instead they whirled straight on.*

C   *They danced old Amphiaraos going down splendidly.*

B   *Saving his presence. He did me a good turn the time I went to Knopia to ask him about buying that piece of meadow.*

A   *The song was ful of movement, people going to and fro. By the end you felt it had really arrived somewhere, though in fact it was only starting on another journey.*

C   *The journey to the gold house they began with.*

A   *I thought so. Anyway, there was a gold picture at each end. The golden sea—Poseidon was going to gentle it but the sea's tricky all the same—and the beautiful gold house. They held the poem, like the clasp of two arms.*

50

B   *We don't have houses like that here. Perhaps it's in Syracuse. That's a grand town, they say.*

A   *I don't think the house was anywhere. It was just a place to . . . put Hagesias's victory, though it wasn't ready to go there yet.*

B   *He'd won, hadn't he?*

A   *Oh, he won all right, and winning's a great thing, but it doesn't last unless—Let's leave that for now and go back to the two gold pictures at either end. Inside, you had Amphiaraos going down—*

C   *With his white horses! You could see him.*

A   *Shining white horses, yes. And at the other end Persephone and her white horses, coming up: descent, ascent. But that still leaves such a lot in between!*

B   *You went to the rehearsals. I haven't got it all clear in my head right now.*

A   *After Amphiaraos, the poet went into the family history, in the mule cart—through "gates of song."*

B   *Are those gates here?*

A   *I think it's more a matter of* what *they are. They were something he had to go through, to leave behind, before he could start on his journey.*

B   *South to Sparta first, then over here to our land.*

C   *Yes, but he was going to the blessed ancestors, so he must have been going down, into the earth. That's where they live. To lady Pitana and lord Poseidon. I didn't know about that. Then to Euadna and lord Apollo.*

B   *Things repeated themselves a bit here.*

A   *They were meant to, don't you think? The whole poem went in twos. Hagesias has two homes, two gods founded his race, Apollo gave the Iamidai two kinds of prophecy, there were two anchors at the end.*

B   *Yes. Why was all this?*

A   *I don't know but I expect we should keep it in mind. And then Iamos was born—*

C   *Those scenes with the bright colors!*

A   *He grew up and waded into the river and called on his gods—two gods, Poseidon and Apollo—and lord Apollo told him to go on a journey. Another journey.*

B   *To Olympia. That's where the family have their altar. Hagesias won the prize there.*

A   *Where did you reckon they were in this part of the song?*

B   *Going to Olympia, I just told you.*

A   *A real place. You've been there, maybe. Where had they come from?*

B   *From here, Arkadia. I don't understand....*

C   *They'd come up from the story, you mean? First, they went down to the ancestors. The story didn't exactly happen down there, I suppose. Perhaps it just happens in your head.*

A   *No, not just in your head. It really happens—out there somewhere. But for the story to happen, the poet had to go down first and that led him in the end to Olympia, here on our earth. He came up, you could say. This part is not quite so clear, but I think I see the pattern. At either end, the two gold pictures. Then, inside, Amphiaraos's descent and Persephone's ascent. And inside that again, another descent and ascent. The journey down to the fathers and up into the world. The song went back and forward. Or round and round....*

C   *You mean, it went from Olympia, where Hagesias had his victory, to Arkadia where—*

A   *Iamos was born and later went to Olympia where...*

B   *All right! You want me to say, Where Hagesias had his victory. I still don't see why it had to go like this.*

C   *I don't see why we keep talking about it. I had it all clear in my mind till you started asking questions.*

A   *It will come clear again, and stay clear much longer. Why did it happen like this, though? Why all this to-and froing and up-and-downing?*

B   *They always have these stories in victory poems.*

C   *I see! When someone wins a great race, he shines, he seems to be on fire. You've seen how it is. He shines so brightly that he lights up all the men who bred him, right down to the Founder himself. He'd be nothing if it weren't for the sap they send up into his veins.*

B   *But it's the victor who—*

C   *Of course he does, but they give him his crown, don't they? Not that he doesn't have to sweat for it himself.*

B   *But then all the same it's not the victor who wins. That can't be right.*

A   *The victory he wins was won a long time ago; and he*

wins it today. He repeats, renews, the act they performed at the beginning of things.

C   That was why the song kept repeating itself?

A   One of the reasons. The victor's light goes down to the ancestors: who send the light of victory up to him. Up and down, round and round.

B   I don't remember Hagesias shining.

A   But you remember how Iamos came to Olympia where Apollo promised that his family would always be prophets. Then there was some praise and then a bit of victory, not Hagesias's, mule teams don't make much of a show. Just victors, Iamids, winning. Remember how it went?

> who drive in first on the twelfth lap
> as awesome Joy sheds winning
> fame and beauty on them.

Joy—he means Kharis—sheds—

C   Sheds beauty like honey! Like the snakes dropping honey on Iamos's lips. When that happens to a man he'll never die. Not altogether.

A   A victory song always says this in one way or another. It has to. Why do we have the games if it isn't to bring the shine of immortality down on us for a little?

C   I'd like to be Hagesias.

B   Some Iamid you'd make!

A   It's so much slower to think a song than dance it. Aineias must have thought it before he could dance it, though. Pindar too. We haven't thought very far yet. We didn't do too badly with the end parts, the clasping arms that held the poem together. But there's a lot in between. There were three scenes I really remember. First Euadna going off to the woods to bear her child. Then the snakes came and fed him with honey. And then you saw Iamos lying in the flowers. Three scenes, right in the middle of the poem, all about Iamos and all beautifully colored. Two kinds of color, light and dark. There's no need to talk about it. We can see it all in our minds.

C   You're forgetting the gold.

A   The divine color. That was part of it, a very important

53

	part. One of the light colors was honey. That's golden.
B	*It made Iamos a prophet.*
C	*And made him immortal. And as I said, the beauty which Kharis shed on the victor was really honey. Kharis who makes things grow—*
A	*Kharis who makes flowers grow. Iamos was a kind of flower; his name said so. Flowers grow from the earth and rise into the light and shine there a while, then go back into the earth.*
C	*Like the snakes who brought the honey up.*
B	*We've all got to die.*
A	*We all die. Even Hagesias will fall back into the earth.*
B	*Like Amphiaraos.*
C	*But he didn't die.*
A	*Dark is a sad color, the death color. Thanatos wears black in the plays. The first thing they really made you see (after the gold house) was death: the funeral pyres for the heroes who fell at Thebes. That's what the song had to . . . overcome—even if Amphiaraos didn't really die.*
B	*They mourned for him as though he did.*
C	*He didn't really die, so the horses that took him down were white. Is that it? Like the ones that brought Persephone up.*
A	*The light colors are for joy and growth and life, even immortal life. Light and dark, life and death. In our eyes they stand against each other but the song brought them together. The rays of the violets were purple and yellow. They gave Iamos his name—*
C	*And made him immortal. Remember how they danced the new movement just after that:*

this: immortal: name!

They fairly stamped the words out.

B	*I didn't understand why that made Iamos immortal, all the same.*
A	*Not at the time, no, though perhaps you guessed. But later, when the two goddesses—*
C	*That was much later. There was Olympia and the victory and then the most exciting part of all, when they danced on past Metopa's name and came to Thebes where the*

54

poet was drinking the holy water. Why was it so exciting,
do you think?

B   Pindar made it that way. Poets like the limelight too.

A   I think it was exciting because everything suddenly came
clear—and came together. Remember how the song kept
on saying the same thing in different ways? It kept finding
that things that look separate or opposite really belong
together and fit into each other. The praise at the beginning fitted Hagesias like a shoe; so did old Amphiaraos.
Well, this was the fit that made it all happen—victor and
poet made a perfect pair. They grew from the same roots.
I think he meant that . . . victory and poetry both do the
same thing. They make a man live on after he's dead. But
only if they work together. What's a shoe without a foot
inside it?

B   Did the poet really think of all this?

A   Hard to tell what they have in mind sometimes. They're
makers, you see, not thinkers. It's for us to think about
what they make. Wise poets need wise listeners.

B   Let's get on with it. It was just after this that your friend
Aineias got his cue. I guess he enjoyed that bit. The song
was done here first, of course, at Stymphalos.

A   But the part about Syracuse was even better, didn't you
think?

B   Rich folks always get the best cut.

A   Syracuse gave the poet the two goddesses. I'd say he knew
he had to get them in somewhere and it was a stroke of
luck, King Hieron being their priest and a friend of Hagesias too. So it wasn't just for Hieron that he made it so
grand:

> he observes the rites
> of Demeter ruddy-footed
> and Persephone of the White Horses.

Those are the horses that bring her up to us every year, in
the spring. That's what the Hymn says:

In spring when Earth puts out her multitudinous sweetly
scented blossom of flowers, up from the glooming mirk
you will rise again, a marvel to gods and to men who die.[27]

55

*It made you think of Amphiaraos going down, earlier on.
And it brought back the three scenes with the contrasting
colors. First there were the violets blazing purple and yellow, but it was only when the goddesses danced that you
saw dark and light belonged together, like up and down.*

C   *I understood the white horses, but why did Demeter have
ruddy feet?*

B   *Poets like those big adjectives. Never pay much attention
to them myself. Aineias says there's another song where
Pindar gives Hekate red feet. That doesn't make much
sense, that I can see.*[28]

A   *But does it prove anything about the word here, when it
goes so closely with another word that does make sense?*

B   *He's thinking of the statues, then. They often paint the
goddesses' feet red.*[29]

A   *You mean he just copied a statue? What a funny idea.
Why should a poet do that? He can see lady Demeter just
as well as the man who makes statues. He sees the same
thing and puts it in his own way, in words and dance.*

C   *Perhaps it's because of the color of the fields in autumn.*[30]

B   *Our fields aren't red in autumn.*

C   *Maybe over in Thebes . . .*

A   *Poets' pictures are not like that. They make pictures of
the inner look of things, not the everyday look you and I
see. When they are very good perhaps they see things
almost in the way the blessed gods do. Persephone's
horses aren't called white because spring is white. White
is the color for something. For joy and growth and happiness.*

C   *And so he gives Demeter a dark color and calls her ruddy-
footed because in autumn the year is getting ready to go
into the dark when everything dies down?*

A   *Down, up—remember how they danced this bit? In a
round, holding hands. One half circle of sad-faced people, the other half smiling. Then they circled about and
the smiling ones grew sad and the sad one started smiling.
You see it every year as the seasons go round.*

C   *Then the goddesses were dancing . . .*

A   *That's it! They were dancing immortal life. Dark is for
down and death. All the dark colors said that Hagesias
must die, like us. But the light colors . . . Remember when*

Iamos was born. Apollo Goldhair stood there watching and the snakes dropped honey into his mouth. He couldn't die after that.

C   Lucky Hagesias!

B   If I won in the games I'd want a song about winning, not dying.

A   Winning is a great thing but it doesn't last unless you get a poet who understands what winning really means. Not just the look on a man's face when he comes in first or the crowds and the music back home. That's over in a flash. The poet has to take this quick shining thing down to the blessed ones who made it and find out how it really happened. He has to build it into shape, and then when it's ready he brings it up and—

C   And puts it in the gold house, forever.

A   That is one way of saying it, the victory way. It was specially for Hagesias, though it was for the rest of us too. We all feel an immortal twinge when one of our men wins the crown. But there was another way of saying it. The song went in twos. This one was more like nature's way—when the violets blazed on Iamos and the goddesses danced their round and down came up and up went down and dark and light shone in a single color. That was for all of us, though it was only the victory that made it happen.

C   And then the lyre began playing and they did the victory dance—just a few steps to let you know, and there were prayers and gods and everything came together. I felt so happy. I wish I was Hagesias all the same. . . .

B   I wish I could remember it all the way you two seem to do.

A   Look, Aineias is going to Syracuse next week. Why don't we pay our way and go with him? Then we can see the song round again.

APPENDIX
Root, Tree, Flower: A Pindaric Path of Thought

We are told several times that dead ancestors have a share in the victory celebration: for example, *Olympians* 14.20 ff. and 8.77

ff. or *Nemean* 4, which is in part built around the conceit that the dead compose epinician poetry themselves (more clearly if we follow the manuscripts at line 90 and read *aeisetai*). This relation is presented in a way we find stranger at *Pythian* 5.98 ff., where the dead kings of Libya "hear somehow with their enearthed minds (*khthoniai phreni*) great achievement watered with the soft dew of song outpoured," a joy (*kharin*) they share with their victorious descendant. Discussing this passage, R. W. B. Burton speaks of "the fantasy of the dead kings listening...to the hymns in praise of their posterity" (*Pindar's Pythian Odes* [Oxford, 1962], 144). Fantasy for Pindar, or merely for us? There is reason to think that for Pindar this was not fantasy at all but part of the reality from which he wrote, and while we cannot simply enter Pindar's reality, there is no justification for setting him in, and judging him by, our own. There is a whole network of images or rather, perhaps, a whole buried structure of thought which criticism must uncover if it is to achieve more than the formal understanding of the victory ode at which we are now aiming. Pindar's master image is that of a tree—the continuing life of the city—whose roots are the buried heroes and their foundational acts, its leaves and flowers the city's sons and their achievements. Thus Zeus plants (*phuteusai*) Aiakos in the nymph Aigina (*Nemean* 7.84), heroes are planted by the gods (*Nemean* 5.7), and the eponymous heroine Libya has the root of cities (*asteōn rhizan*) planted in her (*Pythian* 4.14 ff.). These roots, normally hidden or only dimly sensed, are made visible by victorious achievement (*areta*). Looking at a young victor, Pindar can see that he has the seed root (*spermatos rhizan*) of his ancestors in him (*Olympian* 2.46), and Achilles, himself an ancestral hero, doing great things at Troy, reveals or shows forth (*prophainen*) Aigina and his root (*Isthmian* 8.61); that is, his acts open a path to the origins. At *Nemean* 11.37 ff. "the ancient *aretai* send up (*ampherontai*) the strength of men in alternate generations." (Cf. the similar image at *Nemean* 6.8 ff., and also at *Pythian* 4.64 ff.: "Even now, as when spring puts forth her reddest blossoms, in the eighth generation Arkesilas flowers," *thallei*.) Victors are blossoms on the city tree and, thanks to their *aretai*, she bursts into flower, *thalēsen* (*Olympian* 9.16, *Nemean* 10.41 f.). A family, the city in miniature, may also blossom with achievement (*Isthmian* 4.4), and victory itself grows and breaks into new flower (*Nemean* 9.48 f.).

In the passage from *Pythian* 5.98 ff., *areta* is said to be watered by the dew of song. The song that victory calls forth—that it thirsts for, *Nemean* 3.6 ff.—waters the roots and ensures that the tree will continue to bear its heroic blossom, a favorite theme I discussed briefly in "Three Preludes for Pindar" (*Arion*, n.s., 2/2, [1975], 188 f.). Some noble lines in *Nemean* 8.40 ff. speak of *areta* as a tree that is fed by the dew (of songs of praise) and shoots up into the liquid air. *Olympian* 7 offers the greatest of these images, perhaps the greatest in Pindar, the island of Rhodes growing like a rose from the primal sea into the arms of the Sun.

A number of these images appear to be common property of the genre. Bacchylides also speaks of *areta* growing like a tree (fr. 56). What is striking in Pindar is their pervasiveness and consistency. Perhaps we should see them not simply as poetic stylization, let alone as one more epinician convention, but rather as part of what I called a structure or path of thought. It may also be, though this needs to be considered carefully, that much that we take to be metaphorical or "poetic" may for Pindar be very nearly literal,[31] for his poetry is grounded in the archaic sense of the unity of being, a unity that embraces living and dead and sees man's single life as part of the whole life of nature. We would have little hope of understanding something so remote from our culture were it not that this archaic vision has emerged, spontaneously and as though in answer to a need that is beginning to be felt, in modern poetry. "Man, earth: two halves of the tally," wrote Pound who by some great reach of the mind learned to see the city as Pindar saw it, growing like a tree:

> The roots go down to the river's edge
> and the hidden city moves upward
> white ivory under the bark.
> (Canto 83)

Or more simply, in a pun, near the end of Canto 82: "Let the herbs rise in April abundant." In the *Cantos* this vision is inevitably fragmentary and tentative. In Pindar it is fully developed and it is this that gives the *Odes*, carried inertly by the tradition for so long, their great importance in our time. Reading Pindar today, guessing out to the reality behind and around the words, can be a first step toward retrieving (to turn some words of Plato in a way he might not have liked) an old knowledge that belongs to us.

BIOGRAPHICAL NOTE

I quote from C. M. Bowra's edition of the *Odes* (*Pindari Carmina*, 2d ed. [Oxford, 1947]) except at lines 82-83, where I follow Bruno Snell (*Pindari Carmina* [Leipzig, 1971]). The only other references that need be given here are A. B. Drachmann, *Scholia Vetera in Pindari Carmina* (Leipzig, 1903), I, and William J. Slater, *Lexicon to Pindar* (Berlin, 1969).

III

DEIANEIRA'S DARK CUPBOARD:
A QUESTION FROM SOPHOCLES

Near the end of Sophocles' *Trakhiniai*, Herakles, preparing to die, tells his son Hyllos that he must marry Iole, the young girl who, as Hyllos sees it, is responsible for the death of both his parents. How could anyone do such a thing, Hyllos asks, unless he were mad? What he actually says is: *Unless he were suffering from a sickness brought about by avenging spirits.* The words have no special thematic significance here; they are simply a strong way of expressing the boy's dismay at his father's command. The question is: How are we to approach a work from a culture where such a "sickness" can be taken for granted? It seems to suppose a reality so remote from our own that we are likely to misunderstand the forms that even central, universal kinds of experience take there. If so, what hope is there of entering imaginatively into a Greek play? Are we not forced to remain within the confines of a strict historicism? That might indeed be the best course, were it possible. The attempt to see the text with no interposition of our own interests is however not possible. Even the objective study of antiquity is controlled by directives from the life of the student, all the more powerful for being unacknowledged.

We must accept the play's distance and recognize its presence. For a text is not some unchangeable object stuck in the past nor is it, in the usual sense, timeless; it is temporal in nature and has its being in recurrence, never quite the same, never entirely different. The *Trakhiniai* that is here now, carried here by a tradition in which we too stand, has something to say to us. To find out

61

what, we put a question to it, a question derived from our provisional sense of what is said there and from our own experience. This does not mean imposing modern interests on an ancient work. On the contrary, it means risking them, for we find that the play takes over the assumptions we bring to it and challenges them. The questioner discovers that he is being questioned. In this interplay, text and interpreter come together on a common ground where past and present fuse.

The question I want to put to the *Trakhiniai* is about man's relation to nature. An empty phrase, it may seem, one that the mind glides over without taking hold intellectually. The phrase still looks empty even if we try to fill it out with whatever lies behind the immediacies of the environmental crisis, whatever makes this more than a problem for an improved technology to overcome. Perhaps the question of man's relation to nature will take on more substance and become more questionable if we face it not in today's eroded terms but in those of fifth-century Athens, where a good deal of thought was given to the process whereby man had emerged from what Euripides called "a confused, beastly existence"[1] and become civilized—a very rapid advance that brought its inevitable tensions. Sophocles' play shows the great culture hero Herakles[2] and his wife Deianeira both destroyed by the forces that he, and in a subtler way she, had to overcome in order to create and maintain the human artifice. Or almost destroyed. Herakles at least is able to turn defeat into a kind of triumph. It is however a very painful, bitter triumph, won at heavy cost. It is this cost I want to ask about.

In what language am I to put my question? The *Trakhiniai* does not consist of a series of propositions that can be interrogated. It would not even be accurate to say that the play makes a statement that the poet has embodied in a myth or symbolic image. Rather, Sophocles experienced the matter of his play in this form, a form that cannot be translated into conceptual terms without destroying its integrity. And yet we have the sense that the *Trakhiniai* is saying something. Paul Ricoeur may point a way out of this impasse. The symbol or myth, he says, gives rise to thought: "The symbol gives; but what it gives is occasion for thought, something to think about."[3] I shall attempt, then, to listen to this play speaking its own mythic or symbolic language and then try to think about it and question it. If my question is misconceived, the play can be trusted to dismiss it.

1

The *Trakhiniai* starts with a speech by Deianeira. It is not a pro-
logue, in Euripides' manner; she is talking to her ayah. "There is
an old saying," she begins, "that you cannot really tell [*ekma-
thois*] whether a person's life is good or bad until he is dead."
While it is still being lived, life has no pattern, no meaning. This
can be detected only when a life has reached its conclusion, and
then only by someone else. But Deianeira is not willing to accept
this and boldly lifts her fate out of the realm of uncertainty by
proclaiming that she already knows (*exoida*) the pattern of her
life. It is a sorrowful one. The first trial came when, still a girl,
she was sought in marriage by no less a being than the river
Akheloos, patriarch of the whole Hellenic freshwater creation.
He appeared to her in three forms: as a bull, as a coiled, shimmering (*aiolos*) snake, and as a composite creature, bull-head on
human trunk, spring water running from his beard. Did this
seem odd to a Greek, we wonder. Certainly it is hard to imagine
Antigone or Electra faced with such a lover. And certainly Deianeira recoiled from him in terror: "I prayed that I might die
before coming near his bed!" The oddity (for us at least) is
heightened by the fact that this old fertility daimon, this amal-
gam of elemental powers, should be associated with the thoughtful, fully humanized figure of Deianeira. It looks as though
Sophocles is bringing together, in a kind of modal clash, two different orders of being.

Deliverance came in the person of Herakles, "the famous son
of Zeus and Alkmene." He fought and overcame the river daimon, thanks to Zeus: "Zeus the arbiter of strife brought the conflict to a happy end, if it was happy," words that may take on a
deeper meaning when we come to think about the play as a
whole. Deianeira goes on to describe their married life, which
has been a difficult one. "Night follows night, each bringing a
fresh trouble to replace the trouble it dispelled." Oh yes, she
says, we have had children, "but he sees no more of them than a
farmer sees a distant plot of land, at seedtime and harvest." The
ancient image of woman as ploughed field represents, culturally,
a stage forward from the kind of union promised by her first
suitor who harks back to an earlier age of the world, but this picture of woman caught up in the ceaseless, uncaring round of
nature does not readily consort with our sense of Deianeira as

someone self-reflective enough to stand back from the immediacy of life and concerned to chart her own individual course. In her mouth it may even carry a hint of violation.[4]

She now introduces an important theme, that of time. In nature there is no time, merely recurrence. Time begins only when man breaks off from nature and sets out on his linear path, introducing into the seasonal regularity of the natural world a new instability and uncertainty. Herakles has been away fifteen months, she says (he is across the water in Euboia, making war on the king Eurytos). When he went off on this last exploit, she tells their son Hyllos who has just come in, he declared that it would end either in his death or, if he survived, that he would live from then on in pease. Later we hear about another unit of time, twelve years. It is a curious feature of this play that its action, set in motion by the timeless power of Aphrodite working in part through creatures of the prehuman world, should be laid out on a very precise temporal grid.

Hyllos leaves in search of his father as the chorus of young unmarried women of Trakhis step forward and begin their first song:

ὃν αἰόλα νὺξ ἐναριζομένα
τίκτει κατευνάζει τε φλογιζόμενον,
Ἅλιον, Ἅλιον αἰτῶ...

You, born of shimmering Night as she is stripped and slain, You that she puts to bed in flame, Sun! Sun! I call on you, O flashing in the brilliance of light: Where is Herakles, by the sea straits or leaning against the pillars of the two continents? Tell us, excelling eye.[5]

Such magnificence would be wasteful unless something essential was being said. At one level, we guess, the opening lines are a means of relating the two main characters who govern their separate parts of the play and, like night and day, never appear together. We will find that both imagery and action do a good deal to associate Herakles with light, Deianeira with aspects of night. Like night and day they directly or indirectly destroy each other, and Deianeira's device for winning back Herakles' love will literally put him to bed in flame. Not that there is any neat equivalence; Deianeira's reflective intelligence suggests light rather than darkness. What I am arguing for is a powerful symbolism that is in part expressed through the two leading characters. In part. For these lines surely point beyond any particular human relation to some cosmic, eternal principle of complementarity through strife, the war or rhythm of polar opposites bound in a unity they cannot transcend without wrenching the frame of things.[6]

The chorus now turns to Deianeira and their language connects her sorrowful life at home with the initial appeal to the sun. Night puts the sun to rest (*kateunazei*) but brings no relief to Deianeira who cannot put to rest (*eunazein*) her longing for Herakles.[7] It is well to recognize here the motif of night sounded in her opening speech, night as the time of woman's anxiety, but not at the cost of obscuring what is uppermost, the real human suffering and desire that speak through the dense weave of the syntax. Deianeira is not, as she has been too often portrayed, a distressed matron; she is a passionate woman still very much in love with her husband.

The song next picks up and develops the question to which her opening words were addressed, the question of uncertainty or vicissitude, first in terms of the sea, then of the stars:

As waves driven by south wind or north come and go, so life's troubled stormy sea now whirls Herakles off course[?], now lifts him up.

This picture of pure inconstancy is at once corrected: "Yet always some god is there lest he fall, guarding him from death." And then the two positions are brought together in a statement that combines vicissitude and pattern: "Zeus grants no man a life free from pain. Sorrow and joy circle round to all in turn, like the whirling paths of the Bear." There is a promise of order here but one that brings only a limited comfort. For, as Jacqueline de Romilly points out, "If the stars' movement is in itself cyclical and regular, seen from the point of view of man it means change and nothing else. The star is now here, now there, and later here again.... The world can be orderly, and yet provide the experience of perpetual loss and modification." The final lines, as though to test our fragile sense of pattern to the utmost, present conflicting states in bewildering alternation. Nothing remains stable, neither shimmering (*aiolos*) night nor misfortune nor riches. "Suddenly all that is gone and it is another's turn to rejoice—then lose his joy." The passage means to be reassuring: since she has known sorrow, a time of happiness should be coming round. But to Deianeira, who would rather know that her lot is a hard one than face uncertainty, this is scarcely enough. They end with words of ambiguous comfort which may prove to be true but will do nothing to help her: "Who has ever seen Zeus careless of his children?" (Exceptional mortals like Herakles, that is, whom Zeus literally fathered, not mankind in general.)

Whitman called his chapter on the *Trakhiniai* "Late Learning" and saw the play's theme as the tragic insufficiency of man's knowledge.[8] My own stress is different. What I see, in both Deianeira's and Herakles' conduct, is man's attempt to master, through intelligence and purposeful, heroic action, the purposeless flux of existence as it appears in the natural world to which they are both exposed. A plant or an animal, we assume, does not suffer from vicissitude. Secure in its seasonal rhythms, the Akheloos world—what Pavese in a convenient term calls the *selvaggio*—looks for no further pattern. To man, separated from nature by the fact of being man, nature's ceaseless come-and-go can seem intolerable, a threat to his very being. He may, like Jocasta in the *Oedipus Tyrannus*, erect inconstancy into a principle and say: "There is no foresight; we must live at random." He may do as Oedipus does and as Deianeira to some extent finally does, impose his own meaning on things and take responsibility for his life, even if this means putting an end to it. Or he may search for the meaning that the gods have written darkly into things. What he can no longer be is "natural"; yet this is what Deianeira now bravely attempts. Better mere seasonal ebb and flow than the inconstancy just proposed in the ode. Speaking to the leader of the chorus she says: You are young and inexperienced; may you never know what I suffer:

> Youth grows in its own sheltered places. The [sun] god's heat does not trouble it, nor rainstorm nor buffeting winds. But joyfully, untroubled, it lifts up its life until . . .[9]

The image is a great constant in our poetry (Catullus's *Ut flos in saeptis*, Ariosto's *La verginella è simile alla rosa*), but here it has a special poignance because a woman is speaking, a woman conscious that she is growing older (hence her husband's prolonged absences?) and facing the universal pain of aging. Kamerbeek

66

finds "more restrained bitterness in Deianeira's words than most translations...show," but it is restrained, by the grave formality of the verse and perhaps by a certain stiffness or distance in the language. (Is her use of the neuter participle, *to neazon*, "youth" instead of "a young girl," rather mannered?)[10] In part at least the play is concerned with man's relation to nature, and Deianeira, the field "ploughed" by Herakles on his infrequent returns home, before that the terrified object of Akheloos's suit —the bull's stabbing thrust, the river's fecundating deluge—is seeking refuge from the uncertainty of things by trying to see woman's life, her own life, as part of nature: nature in its most comforting aspect. In youth, our life is almost at one with the elements that nourish it, free from the trials of the adult world (from the sun's heat, as she puts it, a beautiful woman thinking of what has so tried her and will try her again, the heat of male sexuality) and to that extent "divine." As commentators notice, her lines echo the description of Olympus at *Odyssey* 6.43 ff. Then all too soon the young life is expelled from paradise and passes into the separateness and pain of maturity. So she continues, and once more we hear the theme of woman's night: "Until she is called not maiden but wife and gets her share of the troubles that come at night, worrying about husband or children."

Deianeira then turns again to the theme of time, closely related in this play to prophecy or prediction. When Herakles set out on his last campaign, he took the unusual step of leaving her precise instructions about the division of his patrimony, should he fail to return. Fixing a date in advance (*khronon protaxas*), he said that the decisive moment would come in fifteen months' time. According to a prophecy given by Zeus's oracle at Dodona,[11] when this period elapses he is either to die or live henceforth free from trouble. The period has now been completed and Deianeira is watching the clock. Kamerbeek comments on "her extraordinary preoccupation with Time." Yes, and perhaps we should observe too that her speech juxtaposes two sorts of time: the cyclical time or properly timelessness of natural process in which biologically we are all involved, and human time, cut into fixed periods, which imposes a pattern on process and provides us with a measure to live by. This measured human time, we also note, is given to man by Zeus, Zeus who helped Herakles to deliver her from Akheloos.

A messenger bursts in. Herakles is on his way home in triumph from Euboia. "O Zeus, lord of Oita's unshorn meadow," Deianeira exclaims, "you have granted us joy, though late in time." As she speaks, she turns to the huge mass that looms above the imagined scene of the action and dominates it. At the summit of Mount Oita, more than 7,000 feet above sea level, was a sacred place dedicated to Zeus. Such places were left uncultivated, the scholiast notes; cattle could not graze there.

After a brief song celebrating what Deianeira calls "the light of this news that has risen beyond my hope" ("la clarté qui jaillit d'une telle nouvelle," Mazon—the motif of light or sun again),[12] Herakles' herald Likhas arrives with a troop of captive women and provides a long and, as it turns out, misleading account of what his master has been doing for the last fifteen months, "this immeasurable stretch of days he has been away," as Deianeira puts it (246-247). He spent "the larger part of it" in Lydia, Likhas says, enslaved to the barbarian woman Omphale, a punishment from Zeus for having treacherously killed the son of his host Eurytos. Then Likhas delimits the period more closely: Herakles spent a year in Lydia, after which he took his revenge on Eurytos and sacked his city, killing the men and sending the women home as captives. Deianeira responds joyfully but her joy is soon clouded by pity as she looks at the women. One girl arouses her particular sympathy, on the characteristic grounds that "she alone understands what has happened to her" (*hosoiper kai phronein oiden monē*, 313).[13]

It is not long before she gets the true account. The real reason for Herakles' campaign against Eurytos is that he conceived a violent passion for his daughter Iole—the girl who is standing silently on stage—and Eurytos refused to hand her over. "It was Eros alone of the gods who beguiled him into this feat of arms. ...He is burning with desire for the girl" (354-355, 368). Deianeira now turns on Likhas and again looking up at the great mountain demands, "in the name of Zeus whose lightning flashes across the high places of Oita," that he give her the true story. "You will be speaking to a woman who understands human life," she says, "and knows that it is not in our nature always to delight in the same things. To take up arms against Love: that is foolishness. Love rules even the gods as he wishes, and certainly I am in his power. Why not another woman too? I would be mad indeed to blame my husband for having fallen sick in this way. Or blame the girl, partner in nothing that shames them or wrongs me.... He has had many women before now, and not one of them has ever heard a word of reproach from me" (438-448, 460-462).

It is too magnanimous, of course. Faced with a situation that strikes at her control, she is forced in a perfectly honorable sense to act, to set her feelings in the best light, so that she can be a little proud of herself. What she is trying for is that absolute *sōphrosunē* Theseus exhibits in the *Oedipus Coloneus* when he says, the great king speaking to the old beggar man: "How should I reject you? I know that I am a man and that my hold on tomorrow is no stronger than yours." Deianeira doesn't reach this height; in her situation, how could she? All the same, it is a mistake to question her sincerity and ask if she "really means" what she says. She is trying to confront the great powers of life and death in the way men have always done at times of high civilization: through a noble submission to necessity.[14]

As her death scene will show, Deianeira belongs to Sophocles' heroic breed of men and women who prefer to die rather than compromise the estimate they set on themselves. (See her words at 721-722 and compare, e.g., *Ajax* 479-480 or *Electra* 988-989.) At the same time she is wiser, in the Greek sense, than Sophocles' other heroes usually are, and we should take seriously the words Likhas addresses to her—"Lady, I see that you who are mortal think mortal thoughts and are not stupid" (472-473)—words that are so blank in English and in Greek carry so much power. Theseus, in the great utterance I quoted just now, is thinking mortal thoughts. "Stupid," in the present passage, *agnōmōn*, is used in the way *amathēs* sometimes is, not of "ignorance of facts or theories, but ignorance of how to behave,"[15] and beyond that, of the very nature of things. This essential knowledge or wisdom Deianeira possesses, and in its light she is trying to do something very remarkable. She is trying to allow for the full elemental power of Eros while maintaining a standard of civilized behavior. She is attempting to fit a great natural power into the delicately adjusted human institution of marriage.

And she makes another revealing remark, though its implications may have been misconceived by critics like Whitman. She asks Likhas to tell her frankly about Herakles' relation to the girl. "Don't think to upset me. Not to know would be far worse. What is terrible about knowledge?" (457-459). Her words have sometimes been distorted by being taken as though they occurred in the *Oedipus Tyrannus*. The thrust here is different. Deianeira's conviction that it is better to know, even to know the worst, accords with her opening words where she lifted her fate from the realm of uncertainty by proclaiming her knowledge of what it was to be. Her concern with knowledge is related to her preoccupation with time: both are ways of mastering the mere flux of existence by imposing a human pattern on it. Others recognize this drive in her. The chorus in the first song was reading her a lesson in vicissitude, the baffling here-and-there of things. The ayah's last words over her dead body assert the folly of counting on tomorrow. But Deianeira, as committed in her way to the creation and maintenance of the human artifice as her husband, demands order, pattern, an intelligible structure. Through her encounter first with Akheloos and then with centaur Nessos she has seen the dark reverse of these things and hates and fears them, what from her achieved human perspective appears as the senseless violence of the merely natural, what I am calling the *selvaggio*.

Finally she turns her attention to Iole and says movingly: "I do not reproach the girl, even if Herakles is melted deep in love with her. [Or, the Greek may say, even if she is melted deep in love with Herakles. Or perhaps Deianeira has not made up her mind who is in love with who?] I pitied her the first time I saw her, since her beauty has ruined her life" (462-465). This echoes her words at the start of the play, describing her feelings as she watched the struggle between Herakles and Akheloos, "terrified to think that my beauty might bring me only pain" (25). She has in fact much in common with Iole. Both have been or are loved by Herakles and both (perhaps) love him; he won both through a desperate conflict. They are two successive aspects of woman: maiden (*parthenos*) and wife or adult (*gunē*). Hence the chorus in the ode that follows, a celebration of the universal power of Aphrodite, fluidly enters into her thoughts and leaving the present crisis returns to the time when Herakles fought for *her*.

It is a very brilliant composition. The barnyard tussle of these two lust-maddened creatures fighting for their female, elemental Akheloos and scarcely less primary Herakles, is submitted to an intense stylization. When the *selvaggio* really breaks into the human fabric, as it does in the next scene, its irruption is not distanced in this lyrical way. All that need concern us here is that, whereas in Deianeira's initial account of their struggle Herakles appeared as her deliverer and the arbiter was Zeus, here the two suitors seem more or less on a par; both do battle *hiemenoi lekheōn*, eager for her bed. And this time the arbiter is Aphrodite.

Whatever else the ode may be doing, it brings Aphrodite to the fore, revealing her as a major (not, I shall argue, the dominant) power in the play. After this demonstration of her authority, Deianeira's protestations look pretty unconvincing, and when she steps forward again we see that her mind has moved some way. Her "reasonable" attitude to Iole, she has decided, was a mere fiction. She knows she cannot tolerate the girl's presence in her house, for (in Mazon's version) "ce n'est plus une jeune fille, c'est une vraie femme." The word she uses of her, *ezeugmenēn*, yoked, is quite complex—this is a civilized woman speaking—and picks up her earlier lines about the sheltered places of youth. There she pictured the young life as blessed in its freedom from the constraints of adult life, that is, in Greek, from the yoke of necessity. Now Iole has had to put on the yoke and Deianeira's use of the word shows that she can't help pitying her. But Iole has not only been driven from the blessed garden; she has been driven into Deianeira's house, into—she becomes almost gross as she contemplates the situation her "good faithful" husband has prepared for her—into her bed:

> Here we are, the pair of us, under the same blanket waiting for him to take us in his arms. (539-540)

"In themselves, Herakles' many passions are no cause of anger to Deianeira," Kamerbeek remarks; "she feels herself threatened in her position as housewife." No! Even today there is a curious reluctance to credit her with strong sexual feelings and allow that she is still in love with Herakles and, a few lines later (she moves rapidly between a variety of emotions in this scene), furiously jealous of Iole:

> What I am afraid of is that people say Herakles is my husband and . . . this girl's lover.

It is in the light of this fear that she returns to the plant imagery she used earlier on:

> I see the flower of youth here coming to full blossom, there fading. One flower men's eyes love to pluck; from the other they turn away.[16]

71

"The diction is bold, and somewhat careless," Jebb says. "She expresses her meaning in almost general terms," Kamerbeek says. Yes, but surely we should ask why. If Deianeira generalizes or fails to say what she really means, it is because she desperately needs to keep the situation at arm's length. She is facing the supreme crisis of her life; not only her marriage is at stake but her cherished picture of herself, her pride. In the passage about the garden of youth she tried to see human and plant life in terms of each other, the human fitting harmoniously into the contours of the natural. But now, thanks to Herakles' sexual brutality, she is exposed to the full force of the "goddess" whose tidal current sweeps irresistibly through the whole realm of *phusis*, and the same imagery tells a different story. She now feels the natural as a violation of the human. Iole's life is ripening, hers is withering on the stalk: so Herakles "picks" Iole and rejects her. Perfectly natural. Humanly quite intolerable. Even less tolerable is the thought just behind her words that she and Iole do not really have a separate human existence but are simply aspects of woman in her biological role. She has gone too far in the principle of individuation to accept this picture of herself as a fading flower, a field that must die into fall and winter. Yet this is the only role that nature will allow her.

What follows is perhaps the most difficult moment in the play, one where our limited ability to catch the tone of Greek dramatic verse—in anything approaching the way we can hope to catch Shakespeare's—is crippling. Protesting that it would not be right for a rational, sensible woman (*gunaika noun ekhousan*) to be angry with Herakles, Deianeira describes the steps she has taken to recover his love. The verse, suddenly very remote and solemn, registers (surely) a sharp shift of tone:

> ἦν μοι παλαιὸν δῶρον ἀρχαίου ποτὲ
> θηρός...

"For a long time I have kept a gift that an ancient beast once gave me" (555-556). The adjective *arkhaios* does not refer to the age of the beast, the centaur Nessos. Rather, as Campbell well notes, "The Centaur is thought of as an old-world creature belonging to a state of things that is passing away." This "gift," breaking into the action of the play (a formalized domestic drama rich in psychological nuances, it must seem at this stage), has come to her from the alien, chaotic world she has set her face against. She goes on to describe how when she left home with Herakles just after their marriage they came to a river and being for some reason unable to carry her across himself, Herakles entrusted her to Nessos who acted as ferryman. On the way over he tried to rape her, a more brutal version of the assault from the *selvaggio* embodied in Akheloos's courtship, if Jebb's interpretation of the name Nessos is correct: "The name symbolises the *roar* of the angry torrent: the Sanskrit is *nad*, loud sound, whence *nadá-s*, 'bellower' (bull), or river: *nad-í*, flood . . ." (note on 557 f.) Once again Herakles, "the son of Zeus," came to her rescue, as earlier, with Zeus's aid, he had saved her from Akheloos, sending through the creature's chest a poisoned arrow that had been dipped in the blood of the Lernaean Hydra. As he died, the Centaur told her that if she collected the blood "clotted round the arrow at the point where the monstrous Hydra tinged it with black gall," she would have a love charm strong enough to win back Herakles' affections, should he turn to another woman.

Deianeira has kept the love charm carefully and now proposes to use it. Our immediate question is: Do "sensible women" keep jars of clotted blood stored away for years in cupboards? Or perhaps we should ask if Athenian women did so. The latter is the kind of question to which scholarship can return its answer,[17] but it is doubtful how far information about Athenian attitudes to love magic can help, for the *Trakhiniai* is hardly a "slice of life"; what matters is how Sophocles uses this device. The text should be able to tell us. It suggests that the chorus leader, though not unduly enthusiastic about Deianeira's scheme, does not actively dissuade her (588-589). It shows that Deianeira herself, as a civilized, moral woman, realizes that she is doing wrong (582 ff., 596-597). But what we really want to know— how she *feels* about using the charm—the text declines to tell us. H. A. Mason remarks of the passage starting with the line I quoted: It "read[s] to me as if Deianeira had shut off consciousness. She has no attitude towards herself, to the actions she relates, or to those who are listening."[18] Hence, perhaps, the remote, epic color of her language here: *shaggy-chested* Nessos, the *deep-flowing* river, and the description of the Centaur's mode of conveyance ("he carried me across in his arms, neither rowing with oars nor using ship's sails") which, as Mason remarks, sounds rather like Housman's celebrated parody. Does she speak in this stiff, stilted way because she wants to detach herself from the whole business?

If she shuts off consciousness here, it is not only because she knows or guesses that she is doing wrong but because her action represents a defeat of the civilized claims she has made for herself and others have made for her. She who responded with so fine a temper to the news of Herakles' liaison is proposing, now that the crisis has come, to put their marriage to rights with the aid of this horrible brew. It is a piece of primitive magic coming from the *selvaggio* and belongs, we are insistently told, to the dark. The congealed blood must not be seen by "the sun's light or sacred precinct [with its altar fire] or flame of the hearth" (606-607). It has been "hidden in a bronze urn" (556) since Nessos told her to keep it "in a secret place away from fire and never touched by the sun's hot ray" (685-686). After she rubbed it into the robe she intends to send to Herakles, she laid the robe away in a chest "out of the sun's light" (691). To the two different forms the night motif has so far taken—cosmic night which puts the sun to bed in flame, the human night of woman's anxiety— we must add this third form, the evil night or dark from which the Centaur's gift will emerge to strike at man's world. Understood not in terms of the play's symbolism but psychologically we may take the charm's association with darkness to mean that Deianeira is entering upon a course of action that must not be brought into the full light of consciousness.

It will help my subsequent argument to quote at this point some words from E. R. Dodds about the Athenian retreat from rationalism during the Peloponnesian War: "Under the stresses that it generated, people began to slip back from the too difficult achievement of the Periclean Age; cracks appeared in the fabric, and disagreeably primitive things poked up here and there through the cracks."[19]

The forces Deianeira has released quickly show their true nature. After a joyful song bidding Herakles return home quickly, she describes in horrified detail how she took a tuft of wool to smear the mixture onto his robe and then threw the wool away, into the full light of the sun:

> As it grew warm it dissolved and powdered away to nothing like the dust you see when a saw is eating wood. It lay there like that, disinte-

grating. And from the spot where the wool had been, clots of foam bubbled up, the way the juice of Dionysos just pressed from the blue grapes foams when it is poured on the ground. (697-704)

The violence of the charm's action is conveyed by the image, noted admiringly by the scholiast, of the saw eating word. ("In a sense the saw is eating the wood when it throws off that fine dust.")[20] The foam (*aphroi*) that bubbles up shows that Aphrodite is at work here, but what we see here is not simply a demonstration of the power of "love," for Dionysos is present too ("not only the liquid fire in the grape, but the sap thrusting in a young tree, the blood pounding in the veins of a young animal, all the mysterious and uncontrollable tides that ebb and flow in the life of nature".[21] What has lain concealed in the charm is raw undifferentiated *phusis*.

The task of culture, Freud says, is to protect man against nature. He uses its powers to create the human artifice, which then serves to shield him from the full force of those powers. He yokes Eros or Aphrodite into the institution of marriage and by another act of transcendence gentles Dionysos into the gracious solace of wine. But the liquid we have just seen foaming on the ground is like must, the raw juice of Dionysos before the art of fermentation has done its work and turned it into wine. This dreadful potency, the gift from the Centaur and more distantly from the monstrous water creature, the Hydra, has been let loose in man's world by Deianeira, the most humanly developed character in the play but also the most exposed to the *selvaggio*. The forces that both Herakles and Deianeira in their different ways have struggled to subdue are striking back.

So terrible is the love charm's action on inanimate matter that we hardly need the speech describing its effect on Herakles. Greek dramatic convention nonetheless required a full account and Sophocles makes a virtue of necessity by putting the speech into the mouth of Hyllos, letting the son tell his mother how she has destroyed his father. The first chorus sang of night and day eternally consuming each other, polar opposites bound in a unity they cannot transcend. Through the persons of Deianeira and Herakles, she associated with aspects of night, he with light and sun, the play is to show how this great bond was broken. The disjunction of the two characters which the structure insists on—never appearing together, bringing about each other's death at a distance—points to a far larger disjunction, one that will open up a rift in man's experience of the world.

So Hyllos tells how Herakles stood on a high place in Euboia, to sacrifice twelve perfect bulls to his father Zeus as a thank offering for the success of his campaign against Eurytos. We should see him, as Deianeira earlier imagined him, brilliantly lit, standing in the full splendor of appearance, *phaneros emphanōs statheis* (608), "debout, en pleine lumière" (Mazon).[22] Likhas duly turns up with the cloak. Joyfully Herakles puts it on and the dark power hidden in the charm emerges, and strikes. Before long the cloak is fastened agonizingly to his flesh, "then, like some deadly poisonous viper, it begins to devour him" (770-771). In his torment he grabs Likhas and hurls him to his death in the sea and the crowd silently watches the grotesque spectacle of the great hero now twisting convulsively on the ground, now leaping in the air, howling with pain and cursing his wife. Glaring "through the altar smoke that shrouds him" (794), he catches sight of his son and summons up the strength to order him to take his tortured body out of men's sight. Hyllos obeys and puts Herakles on board ship, to make the last journey home. The story over, Hyllos turns savagely on his mother who leaves the stage without a word in self-defense. This is the last we see of Deianeira.

The great ode that follows searches for the hidden meaning of this dreadful scene. It begins by setting Herakles' agony within a temporal scheme. Earlier in the play we heard of a period of fifteen months after which he would either die or live in peace. Here the period covered by the prediction (a fuller version of the same oracle or another one, it is idle to inquire) is extended to twelve years:

> How suddenly it has come upon us, the prophetic word spoken of old by divine foreknowledge, that when the twelfth plough time had come and gone with its full tally of months, it would put an end to the toils laid upon the very son of Zeus.

All has truly come to pass, for Herakles is dying and the dead toil no longer. This oracle, like all the oracles in the play, comes from Zeus, as we are told later (1165 ff.). There may be a shred of comfort here. Herakles' terrible and seemingly senseless death brought about by a mere error of judgment on his wife's part

76

may be part of the divine intent. Though he may chastise them with his wrath, Zeus is not careless of his children. And yet, as the antistrophe tells us, a passage almost Aeschylean in the primitive terror it conveys, the agents of Herakles' death belong to the *selvaggio*, the bestial, prehuman world that Herakles has with the gods' aid been subduing. There seems to be a conflict here which we must look to the play to resolve:

εἰ γάρ σφε Κενταύρου φονίᾳ νεφέλᾳ
χρίει δολοποιὸς ἀνάγκα
πλευρά, προστακέντος ἰοῦ,
ὃν τέκετο θάνατος, ἔτρεφε δ' αἰόλος δράκων,
πῶς ὅδ' ἂν ἀέλιον ἕτερον ἢ τὰ νῦν ἴδοι,
δεινοτάτῳ μὲν ὕδρας προστετακὼς
φάσματι.

For if compulsion that works through guile is smearing [stinging?] his body with the Centaur's deadly cloud as the poison melts into him, the poison begotten by death and bred by the shimmering serpent, how shall he look upon tomorrow's light, melted into the dreadful phantom of the Hydra?

Whatever the full force of *dolopoios ananka*, the immediate sense, as Kamerbeek says, is that "Herakles' ineluctable fate has been contrived by the Centaur's fraud." "Deadly cloud" is a puzzling expression which some commentators have understood as a net. But nets play no real part in the imagery of this play, even though Herakles, using a fairly obvious figure, later calls the robe "a net woven by the Furies" (1051-1052). F. J. H. Letters has a cleverer explanation: "The metaphor would strike a Greek ear as especially apt . . . because the Centaur, begotten by Ixion on the cloud he mistook for Hera, is a cloud nature from his very beginning."[23] This allows for a rich interpretation. The Centaur belongs to the shapeless or misshapen world that Olympus has condemned and Herakles spent his life subduing. The cloud is deadly or bloody because Herakles killed the Centaur ("an old-world creature belonging to a state of things that is passed away") which is now striking back at him. We may also, if we wish, reflect that clouds obscure the light of day and recall, as Jebb did, the phrase at 794 about the smoky flame that enveloped Herakles.

The race of Centaurs in whom bestial and human were combined and at odds ("that mongrel horde that live aloof and march on horses' hooves, insolent, lawless, huge in strength," as Herakles later calls them, 1095-1096) had been to some extent softened by Greek art and poetry. The Hydra is another matter. Bred by a pair of snakish horrors, Ekhidna (Viper) and the storm monster Typhoeus who was blasted by Zeus, part of a brood that included the many-headed hell-hound Kerberos and the fire-breathing Khimaira, the Hydra belongs to a far earlier world which, from the humanized perspective of this play, is one of pure terror. The creature is described as an *aiolos drakōn*, a shimmering serpent. The phrase was first applied to that other visitant from the *selvaggio*, Akheloos (11-12), and in the ode that followed the adjective was twice used of night, night that puts the sun to bed in flame. Admittedly Greek poets do sometimes repeat words with no purpose that we can discover, but this striking fourfold repetition suggests a conscious intention. *Aiolos*, a word that conveys both attraction and repulsion,[24] is applied in this play both to the *selvaggio* and to night. Like the love charm, the Hydra belongs to a world that is seen as distant and also dark, and this dark past, though supposedly defeated, has now returned and not merely assaulted its conqueror but in some horrid sense entered into him and become part of him. The verb *prostēkomai*, occurring twice in this passage, is said to mean "stick fast, cling to" (*LSJ*, following a reductive gloss by the scholiast).[25] Jebb accordingly says that the poison "cleaves" to Herakles' side, that he is "close-locked" in the monster's deadly grip; and Mazon, translating not Sophocles' Greek but the scholiast's, writes: "l'Ombre de l'Hydre...collée à lui." There is however no doubt that the simple form of this verb means, in the passive, "be dissolved, melt away," and that another compound, *entēkō*, used earlier of Herakles' love for Iole (or vice versa, 563), means in the passive "to be poured in while molten, to sink deep into" (Kamerbeek; *colliquefactum inhaerere alicui*, Hermann glosses). Hence it seems likely that *prostēkomai* conveys something stranger than the commentators recognize, perhaps because their usual method of interpreting a word (how is it used elsewhere?) breaks down when the poet is subjecting language to such pressure and even passing beyond what we think of as the boundaries of Greek experience. Deianeira's rash act has opened up the human world to an incursion from without or below, to what in the next strophe is called (the meaning of the words is disputed) "things that come from an alien will through a fatal encounter." We are witnessing an invasion of human substance by ghostly, incorporeal enemies—the Centaur's *cloud,* the Hydra's *phantom*—in a kind of transubstantiation. To quote Letters again: "The Hydra's poison in the Centaur's gore is in fact a commingling of two natures. . . . Herakles is smeared with, is adhering to, is *dissolving into* the composite phantom of snake and centaur consuming him" (my italics).[26] Perhaps the best commentary comes from a poet whose culture allowed him to draw on the full resources of the grotesque, the man-snake permutations in Dante's *Inferno:*

> Ellera abbarbicata mai non fue
>   ad alber sì, come l'orribil fiera
>   per l'altrui membra avviticchiò le sue.
> Poi s'appiccar, come di calda cera
>   fossero stati, e mischiar lor colore,
>   né l'un né l'altro già parea quel ch'era.[27]

The ode now turns to Deianeira and then to Iole, the innocent occasion of these horrors, and ends:

> It is Aphrodite, working in silence, who stands revealed as the author [praktōr] of these things.

This may seem to offer a quick route home to an easy reading of the play. All these troubles have come about through "love" which, as we know, the Greeks regarded as a grave calamity. An easy reading but an impoverishing one, though of course less so if we keep in mind that behind the humanized though still terrible goddess of love stands the naked power that dissolved the tuft of wool into froth and is now burning its way through Herakles' flesh. However, if Aphrodite is said to be the author of these ills, the author (*praktōr*) of Herakles' enslavement to Omphale was said to be Zeus (251 ff., 275 ff.). It was Zeus who at the beginning helped him to overcome Akheloos, and the last line of the play tells us that "nothing is here that is not Zeus." Are there two authors of Herakles' fate, now one operating, now the other? If so, are they working together or in conflict: This conflict, if it is one, must be left to the play to resolve, like the conflict between Zeus and the *selvaggio* which I found at the beginning of the ode.

Deianeira has killed herself. A brief song at once announces Herakles' death agony and his ravaged body is carried onstage. The two are never brought face to face. The critics have been puzzled by the way the play seems to split into two parts—the first and longer part dominated by Deianeira, the second by Herakles—and have felt constrained to decide which of the two characters the play is "really" about. "Deianeira is indeed beautiful, but she is incidental," one writes; "the subject of the play is the death of the great hero."[28] Another falls so deeply in love with Deianeira that he has little time for a "fantastically gross Herakles, interested solely in himself," and reads his death scene as "a planned cruelty in order [*sic*] that Deianeira . . . may still be alone, and unloved."[29] But surely Aristotle tells us that tragedy is the representation of an action and that what matters is the structure of its constituent parts, "since tragedy represents not men and women [for their own sake] but an action and a life" (*Poetics* 1450a 15-17). What proportion of a play's action is carried by this or that character is up to the dramatist. It is the total structure that counts and the structure of the *Trakhiniai* is flawless, the Deianeira action and the Herakles action dovetailed so cunningly into each other that one can only wonder at the critical debate.

Sophocles nonetheless faced a difficult problem here. His theme is rift, a decisive parting of the ways. Between Deianeira and Herakles there is to be, in human terms, no reconciliation, and equally little reconciliation in the symbolic conflict between night and day which they embody. One side is defeated (I shall argue), the other triumphs. On the other hand the play's structure must exhibit the formal unity required of any successful work. Sophocles preserves continuity by keeping before us the thematic interests that have governed the play so far. He can do so because Deianeira and Herakles are both, in their different ways, threatened by the *selvaggio*; both are concerned with the maintenance of the human artifice. Deianeira has, so to say, done all she can; we are now to see Herakles take over his wife's unfinished business and advance it. All the same there was a real danger that with Deianeira's death the play would break in two. Sophocles holds it together very cunningly.

It has been observed[30] that whereas Herakles complains that he dies cravenly like a woman (1071, 1075), Deianeira dies heroically, not on the rope (the way women normally kill themselves in tragedy) but by the sword. The chorus leader asks: "Did a woman's hand do so great a deed?" (898), that is, a deed one would expect from a man, and the old ayah who was with her mistress in the opening scene of the play describes the manner of her death, bringing vividly before our eyes the resolution and energy with which she acted. Herakles, by contrast, is shown as a broken, impotent wreck. And yet there are a number of touches that serve to relate the way they face their deaths, slight enough in themselves and yet sufficient to carry the play across this tricky bridge passage. Herakles roars or bellows in his agony (*brukhōmenon*, 805), a word Homer uses of the death cry of wounded men; the same verb is used of Deianeira as she prostrates herself before the household altars (*brukhato*, 904); Herakles then describes himself as crying (*bebrukha*, 1072) like a girl. Earlier he tells Hyllos to carry him to a place where no one can see his death pains (*entauth' hopou me mē tis opsetai brotōn*, 800); Deianeira, preparing to die, hides herself in a place where no one can see her (*krupsas' heautēn entha mē tis eisidoi*, 903). Since a single actor played both parts, these details could in performance carry more emphasis than they do in the bare text.

But we have not quite finished with Deianeira; her last note is still to sound. She ends as she began, attempting to take control of her fate. She does so this time not through an assertion of knowledge but tries rather by a great act of daring (*mega tolmēma*, scholiast on 898) to arrest the chaos into which her life has fallen. We are tempted to give her the lines Cleopatra speaks at the start of the scene leading to her triumphant suicide:

> and it is great
> To do that thing that ends all other deeds;
> Which shackles accidents and bolts up change.
> (*Antony and Cleopatra*, 5.2.4-6)

The last words the ayah speaks over Deianeira, however, far from bolting up change, seem to hand her back to the realm of vicissitude and thus sound like an ironic refutation of her initial claim:

> To reckon on two or more days to come is foolishness. There's no tomorrow until you've got through today safely. (943-946)

In a banal way, this is true enough. Deianeira did not know what most concerned her to know: that before the day was out she would kill both her husband and herself. Messengers' speeches, which this in effect is, do of course often end with trite gnomic tags, but it looks as though something is being said here. Deianeira, as I read her, is a person who feels the need for pattern and order. *Diablement affligée par des monstres*, tried sorely by her impossible husband, she persisted in seeing herself as a "reasonable" woman who understands the way of things. Then Herakles went too far and to put matters to rights she dropped her own best standards and turned to the enemy for help. Swiftly her world collapsed. Through her death she has in a measure retrieved herself, and yet her heroic suicide is only a provisional solution—*could* only be, if the play is not to split in two. As it is, the issue is still open, the forces that led to her death are still triumphant. Witness Herakles' tortured body now before us. Moreover, though she has wrested a kind of triumph from defeat, she has not done so through the qualities she most prized in herself, her reflective intelligence and "wisdom," but simply through a last act of bravery.

Gazing at his father's agony, Hyllos cries in one of Sophocles' great brief phrases, *emmemonen phrēn*, "my heart is wild." What he finds unbearable is to see him "destroyed by a blind disaster," as Herakles himself later puts it (*tuphlēs hup' atēs ekpeporthēmai talas*, 1104),[31] to stand by and watch suffering that is not merely passive but seems quite meaningless. Certainly Herakles finds no meaning in it, no sense that he has done anything to deserve his torment. Not all critics have agreed with him. Kitto, for instance, asks us to see him as a justly stricken sinner. Recalling how, after he was punished by Zeus for murdering Eurytos's son, Herakles proceeds to take it out on Eurytos by sacking his city and then thanks Zeus for helping him, Kitto writes: "Zeus directly punished Herakles for an act of treacherous violence; will he then accept thankoffering for the destruction of a city, an act of vengeance for the punishment which Zeus himself had inflicted? 'The gods, too, have no liking for hybris' [280]: the destruction of Oikhalia looks very much like hybris."[32] Yes, and this looks very much like the scenario for a play by Aeschylus. Sophocles' gods usually deal less directly with men and, though they may doubtless be just, they are so remote and mysterious that we cannot easily predicate our value words of them. Moreover, if Sophocles had wanted us to see Herakles' sufferings as a punishment for sin, he would surely have said more about this aspect of the matter. It is true, as we have noticed, that Herakles calls the poisoned robe "a net woven by the Furies," but in context this sounds more like a grand way of bringing out the enormity of Deianeira's crime than of confessing his own. It is also true that the chorus says that Iole has bred "a dread Erinus for the house" (893-895), but there is no mention of Herakles and the point may be simply, "What a disaster the girl has brought on us!" If the stress really falls on crime and its punishment, something more weighty would surely be required. The most serious objection to this view of the play, however, is the way Herakles is presented at the end. The quivering wreck that has just been carried onstage is transformed into a figure of sovereign authority.

So while we need not deny that Herakles has offended and been duly punished, we find little in the text to encourage us to see him as a stricken (and since he shows no consciousness of his crime, deluded) sinner. Rather than ask whether his torments are deserved we should notice the form in which he experiences them. Hyllos described how the robe clung to him like a deadly viper and devoured him (just as the saw ate its way through wood). Almost Herakles' first words are "Again it bites me, the foul thing" (987).[33] A few lines later "It has seized me, it comes on again" (1010), and at 1026 it "jumps" on him. He imagines that a savage beast is burrowing into his body: "It has devoured my inmost flesh, it is lodged in my lungs and drains the passages dry, it has drunk my living blood" (1053-1056). This is the closest Herakles comes to the chorus's more dreadful vision (which we should bring to our experience of this scene) of a commingling of substance, the horror of dissolution into some anterior state. In his lucid moments, whenever the agony lets go, his thoughts return to his old campaigns and the creatures he killed. He is fighting them again—and *losing*. He is being driven back, as in a different way Deianeira was driven back, into the monster-haunted world he thought he had overcome. Three times, with steadily increasing strength and detail, he evokes his former triumphs (1046-1047, 1058-1061, 1090-1100, where the contests are with wild beasts, we notice, more than with lawless men), the *mission civilisatrice* that made him the best of men. And yet, the evidence is before our eyes, the monstrous world has won. He is sustained by nothing except a furious power of will and his hatred for Deianeira.

The turning point comes only when he can make sense of his sufferings. Hyllos manages to tell him the truth about Deianeira (1122 ff.), how she did what she did in order to recover his love and killed herself when she knew how hideously she had failed. He is simply not interested. But then Hyllos describes the means she employed (1141-1142):

Νέσσος πάλαι Κένταυρος ἐξέπεισέ νιν
τοιῷδε φίλτρῳ τὸν σὸν ἐκμῆναι πόθον.

The centaur Nessos long ago persuaded her to use such a charm to madden your heart with desire.

This "adamantine sentence" (Kamerbeek) recalls Deianeira's solemn tone at 555 when she spoke of the Centaur's gift. That line marked the beginning of her defeat, her descent into the world of the *selvaggio*. These two lines lead to Herakles' recovery and ascent. *Iou, iou dustēne*, he cries, Sophocles' signature for the moment when the pattern of a fate is revealed. There is anguish here, certainly; any lingering hope he may have had of surviving is dispelled. But there is something more important: knowledge. "Now I know (*phronō dē*) the pass I have come to," he declares, and from this time on he never falters. What is happening, he understands, is happening according to predictions long ago given him by his father Zeus. He asserts his recovered authority by summoning his family to hear his last testament. They are not at Trakhis and Hyllos must stand in their stead. Then he reveals what it is he knows, and the full heroic utterance which was intermittently heard before, only to be drowned in howls of pain, now sounds strong and clear (1159-1173):

Long ago my Father revealed to me that I should die by the hand of
none that draws the breath of life but by one that has passed into the
house of Hades. Here is my killer then, as the divine voice foretold,
the savage Centaur who, dead, has killed me living. And I'll reveal
new oracles concordant with the voice of old prediction, oracles I set
down within the sacred wood of the Selloi, those mountaineers whose
bed is on the earth. I had them from my father's oak tree with its
thousand voices, telling me that at this present living time the toils
laid on me would end. Live happily henceforth, I thought they said,
when all they meant was death. No trouble touches the dead.[34]

One has only to listen to the steady, majestic movement of these
lines, the voice perfectly under control and yet suggesting huge
reserves of power, to know once and for all that there is no
scanting of Herakles in this play and that this is no picture of a
deluded sinner. We are not asked to like him, only to recognize
him as a very great man.

What allows him to speak with such grandeur? It is in part
that he has reached one of the high places of tragedy, the
moment of lucidity after the agony and just before the end when
the hero knows that despite everything he is still himself. (Compare the recovered pride of utterance in Othello's speech beginning "Soft you! a word or two before you go.") In the terms of
this play, his new confidence comes from the fact that he can
now see his death as ordained by Zeus; Nessos was no more than
the means foretold by his father. Zeus who helped him in the
struggle with Akheloos has come to his aid, with the gift of
knowledge, in this far grimmer struggle with Centaur and Hydra
and the great natural power of Aphrodite which struck at him
through his own wife and his own disorderly passions. For a
while it looked as though Aphrodite was indeed the arbiter of his
fate, but neither she nor the *selvaggio* has any power over him
now that Zeus has shown his hand.

It is knowledge that saves him—knowledge granted by divine
prediction which allows man to steer a course through time and
discern there not simply random succession but pattern and
meaning. He is taking up his wife's themes and taking them further than she could. Deianeira knew of only one oracle, the one
governing the fifteen-month span, and that only at second hand.
Herakles knows of the twelve-year prediction (the one he calls
"new," that is, more recent) and also of the oracle telling him the
agency through which he would meet his death. On the grid of

these three oracles (or two, one revealed in two parts?) he can
plot the pattern of his fate. Where before there was only the cruelty of chance and obscene, meaningless suffering, there is now
full clarity. To be sure, he possessed all the necessary knowledge
before, but only at this point do the pieces click into place. Deianeira used a love charm she got from Nessos . . . dead Nessos
whom Herakles himself killed . . . Herakles destined to die at the
hands of no living creature . . . to die at this present living time,
the time predicted twelve years ago and now upon him.

So it is in something like triumph that he turns to Hyllos and
cries, in the words that Pound has made perhaps the best known
in Sophocles:

> Come at it that way, my boy, what
> SPLENDOUR,
>   IT ALL COHERES.

> ταῦτ᾽ οὖν ἐπειδὴ λαμπρὰ συμβαίνει, τέκνον.

Jebb finds no more here than "since these oracles are clearly finding their fulfilment"; Mazon, "puisque ces oracles se réalisent
clairement aujourd'hui." But *lampros* is a strong word in Greek[35]
and here at least Pound's instinct was right, even if he over-
translates.[36] Herakles has been associated with light from the
beginning. The first ode set his actions beneath the sun's brilliance and called on that excelling eye to declare his where-
abouts. Deianeira, hearing of his promised return, spoke of a
brightness risen, sunlike, beyond her hope. We saw him standing in the full splendor of appearance on the high place in
Euboia. Then disaster struck as Deianeira brought the charm out
of her dark cupboard and Herakles' light was dimmed by the
Centaur's deadly cloud. Now he is moving out of the dark into
his native element, and the play will end by setting him on the
pyre on the summit of Oita sacred to Zeus, all uncertainty burnt
away in the absolute clarity of fire. Perhaps we are starting to
see why there can be no reconciliation with Deianeira, whatever
the cost to our sympathies. It is not just Herakles' bloody-mind-
edness. It is because she has been associated with or carried the
motif of night. Through the symbolic conflict of night and day
the tragedy is pointing to an event more momentous than we can

yet realize, one that will permanently disrupt or even cancel the great rhythm announced in the opening chorus.

Masterminding his own death in every detail, Herakles now gives his last instructions to Hyllos, binding him by the solemn principle of *peitharkhein patri* (1178), obedience to the authority of the father. He can act with such sovereign assurance in these final moments because he knows that he is following this principle himself. "Swear by the head of Zeus who begot me." "I swear, Zeus be my witness." "You know the high place of Oita where Zeus rules?" You must take me there, Herakles goes on, his eyes turning to the huge mass which Deianeira had twice invoked, and heaping up branches of deep-rooted oak and tough wild olive (the first tree sacred to Zeus, the second brought to Greece by Herakles to crown Olympian victors), with the bright flare of a pine torch,

> set   fire.
>
> καὶ πευκίνης λαβόντα λαμπάδος σέλας
> πρῆσαι.

Anxious to obey his father so far as he can, Hyllos is made to refuse to do this: so that in a last act of mastery Herakles, still alive, can set fire to himself.

And one more task, still harder, Hyllos must perform: he is to marry Iole. Needless to say, Herakles is not thoughtfully providing for his latest mistress's future. With the absolute single-mindedness that characterizes the Sophoclean hero, he is thinking of himself: he must suffer no taint. For Iole to know another man, even after his death, would be infidelity to him. Hyllos alone can take her, since the son's seed is the same as the father's.[37]

Herakles' final words are addressed to himself, to his own harsh spirit (ō *psukhē sklēra*), bidding it grant him

> a curb of steel for lips set hard as stone. No more cries. Joyfully you
> will do what has been laid upon you to do.[38]

I follow the sense of Jebb's interpretation. Kamerbeek objects on the grounds that "this introduces a note of joyousness . . . entirely inconsistent with Herakles' mood and indeed with the tone of the whole scene." Taking *hōs* not with *teleousa* but with *epikharton* he would translate: "Performing an unwilling deed as a thing to rejoice at," that is, to rejoice at "only in so far as death . . . will release him from his sufferings." I wonder. For a man of Herakles' kind, as for the Christian martyr, physical pain in itself simply does not matter in comparison with the meaning of the act he performs, the victory it brings. So long as the assault on Herakles' body seemed a mere senseless indignity, then the pain was really intolerable. But now he knows that everything is happening in accordance with the will of Zeus, and in that knowledge Herakles is himself again, greater indeed than ever before. Poor Deianeira, in the solitude of her bedroom, bravely did what she could to rise above defeat. Herakles, apparently defeated by the same powers, has far greater resources at his command. He will go out in a blaze of splendor before all men's eyes, lifted on high.

Perhaps we have let ourselves be misled by Hyllos's famous closing words about "the great cruelty of the gods, who beget sons and are called fathers and yet can look upon these sufferings." What is to come, he declares, no man can tell: "As for what is happening now, it is sorrowful for us, shameful for them, and harshest of all for the man who now endures this ruinous fate." If we go on and give the last four lines to Hyllos and let him proclaim that

Nothing is here that is not Zeus

then it is indeed difficult not to read the conclusion as a Hardy-esque cry against the cruelty of heaven. A stronger manuscript tradition, however, assigns these lines not to Hyllos but to the chorus, and this makes enormously better sense. The chorus then corrects Hyllos's outburst and allows us to take it not as the play's "message" or as Sophocles indulging in a bit of subversive theology, but as a dramatic utterance, the plain man's baffled response to these mysterious events. For that is what Hyllos is: a commonplace, decent human being who, by a familiar Sophoclean juxtaposition (compare Ismene:Antigone, Khrysothemis: Electra), is set off against a heroic absolutist. When Hyllos learns that his mother used the love charm quite innocently ("She went wrong, with the best intentions," 1136), he sensibly forgives her.

Herakles will not hear a word in her defense and responds to her suicide by regretting that she has deprived him of the chance of tearing her to pieces (1133, 1066-1069). Hyllos quite fails to understand the source of Herakles' confidence or the meaning of his two demands and can even suppose that he regards self-cre-mation as a novel form of therapy. ("How can I heal your body by setting it on fire?" the poor boy asks, 1210.) Where Herakles can see his coming death as an act of grim but glorious transcen-dence, Hyllos sees only incomprehensible disaster. He is not stu-pid or weak, just ordinary, and his presence is indispensable: it is through his plain view of things that we make out the full, outra-geous proportions of Herakles, Sophocles' most extreme study in heroic intransigence.

If my reading of this scene, though heterodox, proves at all convincing, the question then arises as to why Sophocles sup-pressed any clear allusion to the familiar account of Herakles' end: the thundercloud that enveloped his pyre and conveyed him to Olympos, there to enjoy a blissful immortality. This would have put it beyond doubt that he did indeed die glori-ously, at one with the will of the father. The simplest answer is that this is not the sort of play Sophocles had in mind. The dark grandeur of the conclusion would have been ruined if Herakles knew himself to be going to his reward. It may also be that Sophocles realized he could have it both ways. The story of the apotheosis was well enough established to let him count on its coloring his audience's response, even if, for good dramatic rea-sons, he made no mention of it. To take a parallel nearer home, no powerful play about Joan of Arc, whatever its religious omis-sions, could deter an audience of French Catholics from seeing her death as a glorious one.

My own preference is to avoid speaking of Sophocles' un-known and unknowable intentions and to ask rather what the play is saying: what it said then, what it says now. Approached as I have approached it, in the light of a question about man's relation to nature, the *Trakhiniai* shows Nature, subdued to make room for culture, striking back and destroying—or nearly destroying—her conqueror. ("Striking back" is metaphor, of course, suggested by the play's mythic or symbolic speech. How far, today, we can translate this metaphor into our conceptual terms remains to be seen. Perhaps we can only guess at what is said here.) Thanks to Zeus, however, who in his mysterious way approves man's endeavor, the play ends with a triumph: man's triumph over the forces external and internal which oppose his *mission civilisatrice*. The triumph is however painful and somber, won at very great cost. It is not I think clear why it should be so painful, since the things Herakles fights against are hateful to gods and men. The other feature of the play which has been found puzzling is the strict separation of its two main actions, emphasized by Heracles' total and quite inhuman rejection of Deianeira. Whatever Sophocles' conscious and perhaps limited intentions, the material he is using here—material of great cultural significance taking shape in the mind of a master poet at a decisive moment in Western history—is asking a question that still engages us today: a question about the cost of civilization. In the next section I shall look further at the dimensions of that question in Sophocles' own time, and in the final section, at the form it takes as the play comes to understanding today.

2

"The indisputable fact remains," Victor Ehrenberg says robustly, "that Attic tragedy was written under the impact of, and is therefore our chief witness for, the spiritual life of fifth-century Athens."[39] I take him to be right. What then does this fable about Herakles and Deianeira tell us about the inner life of the time? It is best to look first at Deianeira and her part of the play. With her, Sophocles could do more or less as he wanted,[40] and she is generally felt to be one of his most original, deeply felt creations. Her character has been carefully studied by the critics; less attention has been paid to the situations into which Sophocles puts her. We would be surprised if a papyrus turned up in which Antigone, on her way to tell Creon about the unwritten laws, had to fight off an amorous satyr, and yet that is just the sort of thing Deianeira has to contend with. By exposing this refined and surely intelligent woman to the primitive, the *selvaggio*, Sophocles sets up what I call a modal clash, a confrontation between two different orders of being which runs through the play. Like her husband, Deianeira has to cope with nature in the raw and she does so in two ways. Sometimes, as in the two passages presenting woman's life in terms of plant imagery, she tries to see herself as part of the natural world, but she fails, finding that this violates her humanity. More often she is shown struggling to overcome or transcend nature; she attempts to fit elemental Eros into the human institution of marriage and searches for an intelligible structure in the flux of existence. There is nonetheless that jar of clotted blood which this sensible woman turns to when her crisis comes.

It is not too fanciful to catch here a reflection of something that often startles us in the life of fifth-century Greece and may well have disconcerted an intelligent Athenian. Imagine such a person, familiar with the speculations of Anaxagoras, believing that pure, unalloyed mind rules the universe, enjoying discussions about the difference between conventional and natural morality and whether the gods exist in reality (*phusis*) or simply by convention (*nomos*). Imagine such a person on his travels in Greece—at Phokis, for instance, watching a blood offering being made to a Hero, the greasy liquid poured through a hole in the grave mound.[41] Did he frown at this unreclaimed patch of *Urdummheit?* Or smile—what else can you expect in the sticks? Back at Athens, though, in the headquarters of intelligence, he could have found much in usage and ritual which struck him as hardly less ridiculous. Much too, so rapid was the pace of the Enlightenment, in his own mind. Plutarch records that in his last illness Pericles "showed a friend who had come to visit him a charm which the women had hung round his neck, so much as to say that he was in a very bad way to submit to such foolishness."[42] No wonder, then, that Deianeira, faced with her husband's "illness," should give way to a similar foolishness. Move still closer, into the mind of Sophocles himself, and consider the curious story, threadbare though it has become, of his entertaining the sacred snake of Asklepios. "Nothing better illustrates the polarization of the Greek mind at this period," Dodds remarks, "than the fact that the generation which paid such honor to this medical reptile saw also the publication of some of the most austerely scientific of the Hippocratic treatises."[43] I have already quoted the passage where Dodds speaks of the way cracks appeared in the fabric of Periclean rationalism under the stress of the Peloponnesian War, allowing "disagreeably primitive things" to poke up. The date of the *Trakhiniai* is of course quite uncertain, but even if it was written a decade or more before the outbreak of the war, we can surely allow Sophocles some measure of foresight.

Set off against the delicate figure of Deianeira, Herakles, the great benefactor whose death will plunge Greece into mourning (1113-1114), may seem a mere brute. One way of understanding his exploits, Kirk has recently suggested, is in terms of the polarity between nature and culture.[44] As the *Trakhiniai* shows very clearly, the culture hero who destroyed wild beasts and lawless men and made the human artifice possible failed singularly to subdue the bestial and lawless sides of himself. The figure of Herakles speaks, on the one hand, to the strong contemporary interest in the growth of civilization, the process whereby man raised himself from "a confused, beastly existence" to his present plateau. On the other, he bears witness to the survival of the primitive violence that resists civilization and makes its maintenance precarious. As to Deianeira, we feel that she is threatened by external forces (though of course she herself decides to use the Centaur's gift). Herakles embodies those forces in himself. The ode that describes his battle with Akheloos shows him hardly less elemental than the creature he vanquished. And, as we saw, it was his sexual "naturalism" that drove Deianeira to reach into her dark cupboard.

The *Trakhiniai*, as I read it, shows something that we would not expect from a poet of fifth-century Athens still in the first flush of its successful advance, something that only today are we coming to experience: nature striking back at its conqueror. Since this is far from the usual reading of the play, it will be as well at this point to recall the famous ode from the *Antigone* which shows that Sophocles thought to some purpose about the course of civilization. Πολλὰ τὰ δεινά, it begins. Many things are *deinos* (terrible, strange, wonderful, even awe-inspiring), but nothing is more *deinos* than man. Two passages from fifth-century poetry, one by Aeschylus, the other by Sophocles himself, define what these *deinos* things are. They are the fearful creatures of the early earth and sea and also "the dread elemental powers of nature": the seasons, the succession of night and day, the winds and sea.[45] But man, so ingenious and resourceful (*periphradēs, pantoporos*), subdues both nature and its creatures to his will, then goes triumphantly forward to his characteristic achievements, teaching himself to speak and to think, learning the arts of city life, architecture, and medicine.

Guthrie remarks of this ode that it makes "no mention of higher beings: 'man with his skills' . . . is the most dread and wonderful thing in the world."[46] Yet the next ode ("Blessed are they whose life has not tasted of evil") abruptly reverses the perspective. Here the poet solemnly proclaims that no mortal transgression (*huperbasia*) can limit the ageless power of Zeus, and that not simply transgression but greatness itself may bring down the divine displeasure: "Nothing great comes into the life of man without disaster" (*ektos atas*), and the same two words are repeated at the end of the ode. The full meaning of this dark saying can be determined only from within the play, but it can hardly be doubted that it sets a large question mark against the praise of man's achievement in the preceding ode.

There too, in fact, there are clear signs that his project is not without its hazards. Sophocles calls man *deinos* because of what he does, of what he dares. The ode begins with two forms of activity that may be less harmless than they look, navigation and agriculture. That earthborn, earthbound man should take ship and venture across the alien sea: this, for early thought, was often seen as a kind of trespass.[47] And what is agriculture, seemingly the most peaceful of pursuits, but the imposition of man's will on earth? "Earth, first and eldest of the gods, immortal, tireless," Sophocles calls her, and yet year after year man wears away at her and vexes her (*apotruetai*)[48] as he drives his plough to and fro. In building the human artifice man violates, must violate, an original repose that was there before he came and will outlast him.

How should we relate this statement to the *Trakhiniai?* Even if, as some believe, Herakles is there shown as a sinner justly punished by Zeus, he is certainly not being punished for subduing nature to man's purposes. His cultural labors are glorious, whatever may be thought of his *vie amoureuse*. It is commonly said that we should not ask of a poet the intellectual consistency required of a philosopher. The poet may reveal different aspects of a question without troubling to reconcile them. Or Sophocles may have changed his mind about the advance of civilization, at one time taking the progressive view, at another the conservative[49] (whichever play came first). Or perhaps there really are two aspects of this question, both of which have to be taken into account, even if they seem incompatible.

A remarkable passage from Hannah Arendt may help to clarify the issue. Man's individual life, she writes,

> is distinguished from all other things by the rectilinear course of its movement, which, so to speak, cuts through the circular movements

93

of biological life. This is mortality: to move along a rectilinear line in a universe where everything, if it moves at all, moves in a cyclical order. Whenever men pursue their purposes, forcing the free-flowing wind into their sails, crossing the ever-rolling waves, they cut across a movement which is purposeless and turning within itself. When Sophocles (in the famous chorus of *Antigone*) says that there is nothing more awe-inspiring than man, he goes on to exemplify this by evoking purposeful human activities which do violence to nature because they disturb what, in the absence of mortals, would be the eternal quiet of being-forever that rests and swings within itself.[50]

What makes man awe-inspiring, in Sophocles' view, and at the same time makes his cultural enterprise border perilously on transgression, is that in imposing his will on nature he is setting his own powers against or above that which is greater than himself. Sophocles inherited much of the thinking of the archaic age and his relation to the Enlightenment was ambiguous at the least. Even if his characters sometimes act as though they stand at the center of the stage, the poet knows that this is not so, and when we read in the *Antigone* ode of man irrupting violently into the world of divine *phusis* we should hear behind it the older view of his relation to nature, as expressed for instance in the lines of Simonides to the person who boasted that a funerary monument would last as long as

> ever-flowing rivers and the spring's flowers, the Sun's flame and flame of the golden Moon and the eddying sea.[51]

"All [mortal] things are weaker than the gods" (that is, the immortal powers of nature), Simonides declares, and the poem ends contemptuously: "The person who thought that was a fool." And yet in his old age, when the Persian Wars had brought a new sense of heroism into the world, Simonides celebrated the "everlasting glory" of those who fell at Thermopylae, curiously enough using the same adjective (*aenaon*) he had used of the divine rivers.[52] The tension was beginning to be felt. It is present far more strongly in Sophocles in whom we find two opposing positions held with equal or almost equal energy. There is the sense of human greatness, of the absolute will that is driven to outreach the limits set to man's action. The end of the *Oedipus Coloneus* suggests that with part of his mind Sophocles believed that this stretched, heroic will reaches most deeply into the meaning of life. At the same time he is profoundly aware of finitude, of man's helplessness before the overarching power of the divine.

This is the primary source of the tragic in Sophocles, the source of the warnings against the dangers of transcendence which are often addressed to his heroes. It is twice said of Ajax that he "does not think like a man" (761, 777); his thoughts are too high for mere mortality. Antigone compares her fate to that of Niobe, and when the chorus warns her, "But she was a god and born of gods; we are mortal and mortal-born," she cries out fiercely that she is being "mocked" by its trite reminders of finitude. So the chorus tells her: "You have gone to the furthest reach of daring and struck against the high altar of Justice" (853-856). Perhaps a hint of a similar attitude appears at the start of the *Oedipus Tyrannus*, when the high priest, confronted by the king's towering pride, speaks of him as "not equal to the gods but the first of men" (31-34).[53]

The Herakles of the *Trakhiniai* unquestionably belongs to this heroic company, and though he is not presented with the kind of crisis that faces Antigone or Oedipus he is at least as much of an absolutist. And yet no one reminds him of man's finitude. Given the stress on his paternity he might well have been shown raging against the fact that he, the son of Zeus, should be so humiliatingly brought low. And the chorus might tell him that he is mortal and born to suffer, but it does nothing of the sort. Moreover, in this somber picture of the great conqueror destroyed by the forces he himself subdued, there is no suggestion that man's heroic enterprise is a kind of transgression. This is hardly to be expected, it may be said, considering the sort of creatures he subdued. The nature that Herakles had to overcome was not the immortal *phusis* of Simonides' lines or the elemental powers of the *Antigone* ode. It was nature in its bestial aspect, the Centaur's deadly cloud, the monstrous phantom of the Hydra, the lawless, chaotic world that the gods also hate. This is an answer of a sort, yet it hardly seems satisfactory to speak of one nature that man must reverence, another that he has to overcome, or to say that his greatest achievement may also be a grave violation, depending on which nature is involved. One has only to put it in these crude terms to see that the question is not to be silenced with a quick answer. It is in fact not to be answered at all; it must be reached, lived, into more deeply, so that its full dimensions may appear. For Sophocles has brought us up against a very large question indeed, a question about the cost of civilization and man's mode of being in the world. Since this is not simply a Greek question but one that faces man everywhere as soon as he sets out on his cultural enterprise, it may be best at this point to seek a fresh perspective by looking at the way similar themes were treated in other cultures.

Beowulf, a heroic poem whose author may have known something of Virgil, is distant enough from the *Trakhiniai* and yet not so far out of cultural range that a comparison of some aspects of the two works is unfruitful. They have more in common than the fact that in both the hero is a monster-killer and that the monster, Grendel, is a spirit of darkness while the hero is "consistently associated with light."[54] The first action in *Beowulf* is the building of the great hall Heorot, an outpost of human joy, conviviality, and ordered ceremony set in a world more somber than any known to the Greeks. No sooner is the hall built than we are told (86-90):

> But the outcast spirit haunting darkness
> Began to suffer bitter sorrow
> When day after day he heard the happiness
> Of the hall resounding: the harp ringing,
> Sweet minstrelsinging . . .[55]

Heorot rises and flourishes. The outcast spirit Grendel attacks. There seems almost to be a causal relation between the two events, as though the building, the very existence, of the glad lit human place inevitably arouses the anger of the dark spirit. There was just a hint of this curious relation in the *Trakhiniai* where Deianeira, as the most fully humanized character in the play, should have been the most immune from *selvaggio* and yet was the most exposed to it. The point is made far more emphatically in *Beowulf*, for the poet speaks from a world where the human artifice was still fairly weak and the *selvaggio* very strong. More important though than these material factors is the cast of the poet's thought. He is full of the old, brave sense, so crucial to the northern concept of heroism, of the frailty of every settlement, human or divine, and the strength of what threatens it. In "The Deluding of Gylfi" the great Snorri Sturluson tells how, after the gods had established Mithgarth (middle earth) and Valhalla, "a builder...offered to make them a stronghold so excellent that it would be safe and secure against cliff giants and frost ogres, even if they got inside Mithgarth."[56] Today a roaming giant or frost ogre, on the last day Ragnarök when the wolf Fenrir will break loose and the Mithgarth Serpent rise from the ocean.

The thinking behind Scandinavian mythology is dualist and holds that the forces of chaos are at least as strong as those of creation and will in the end overwhelm them. For the Christianized *Beowulf* poet there can of course be no question of God's defeat, yet he sees in Grendel a threat not only to man's order but to God's. The first event we hear of in the newly built hall, the minstrel's song, is the song of creation and it is this that provokes Grendel's attack. Heorot, the human structure, is an analogue for God's greater structure.[57] Both are exposed to the destructive power, the power not simply of chaos but of evil. Grendel is the descendent of Cain and hence a damned soul, "mankind's enemy" (164). He is also *Godes andsaca* (786), God's adversary (111 ff.):

> Progenitor he [Cain] was of the miscreations,
> Kobolds and gogmagogs, lemurs and zombies
> And the brood of titans that battled with God
> Ages long; for which he rewarded them.[58]

A Greek parallel to this could be found, though it would mean going well behind Sophocles' play, either to the story of the great sinner Ixion who tried to violate Hera and was fobbed off with a cloud on which he begot the misshapen race of Centaurs, or to the *Theogony* for an account of the Hydra's monstrous kin. This old demonology somewhere in the background of the play explains why in the end Zeus must forgive Herakles, despite his sins. He has been warring against the lawless pre-Olympian world which the gods hate. But it is in the background. The *Beowulf* poet makes the point much more strongly, bestowing on his hero's mission the highest sanction he knows: far more directly than Herakles, in ridding the world of monsters Beowulf is seen to be doing God's business.

To the question, then, that we set out from—How can the creation of the human artifice be at once man's greatest achievement and a kind of violation?—the Anglo-Saxon poem replies in

effect that no violation is involved. What threatens man's creation threatens God's and must be destroyed at all costs. Yes, a
Greek might say, but this solves the problem by removing the
very thing that makes it problematic, the lingering sense of transgression. To which the *Beowulf* poet objects that the Greeks, in
their more fortunate southern world, never saw the enemy full
face. "Take the very inadequate account your poet gives of
Grendel's Mediterranean cousin Polyphemos. Certainly the
Cyclops puts Odysseus and his men in great physical danger, but
there is no sense that he threatens the whole sum of things. Why,
the poet even makes a case for him! Think of the way Odysseus
begins his story: 'We came next to the land of the Cyclops, arrogant lawless beings who, trusting in the immortal gods, neither
plant nor plough but all things come up for them unsown and
unploughed.' Lawless brutes who . . . trust in the gods and live as
men did in the age of gold. What sort of halfhearted stuff is
this?" "Homer is like God," the Greek replies, "there is no telling
what he has in mind."

The Anglo-Saxon poet has a point. Grendel's actual on-
slaughts are bad enough, and make Polyphemos look very small
beer, but far worse is the persistent sense that the monster—
aefengrom, as he is unforgettably called, evening-angry (2074)—
is the visible shape of darkness and the unknown, of all that
challenges man's tenure and must destroy or be destroyed.
Sophocles shows how the love charm belongs to the dark and
emerges from it to strike at man's world. But there is nothing in
the *Trakhiniai* to match the description of Hrothgar, the builder
of Heorot, retiring to bed after a joyful evening with his warriors, in the full knowledge that (646 ff.)

                                  the truce
In that monster's war on the great hall lasted
From the time when their eyes first saw the sunlight
Till lowering night and the forms of the gloomy
Vaults came gliding over man and world
Black beneath the clouds.

Let alone the description of the mere where Beowulf goes to do
battle with Grendel's dam (1357 ff.), perhaps the finest statement
in literature of the "other," the irreducibly alien and *unheimlich.*
And the irreducibly evil? Certainly the *Beowulf* poet thought

so. We may however offer a different explanation and admire here a fine if unconscious sense of strategy. At his more modest reaches, man can live companionably on the earth, taking only what he needs, but for the full realization of the cultural project, as the West at least has understood it, nature must be dominated and subjected to his will. To detach himself from the matrix to which he had always belonged and turn his hand against that which he had always held sacred must have been a task of enormous psychic difficulty, perhaps the hardest man has ever had to perform. It would have been easier for him, however, if he contrived to face nature as the enemy, seeing it only in the most hostile, hateful form. He could then forgive himself for his great act of transgression and regard conquest as a duty, to his fellow men and to God.

Beowulf, then, may throw light on the apparent difference in attitude between the *Trakhiniai* and the *Antigone* ode. It answers the question that Sophocles put to us by means of a powerful dualism. This is valuable and warns us against taking the *selvaggio's* attack on the human artifice as no more than an unfortunate setback which man must surmount. The dualism proposed by the poem—the (good) creative act inevitably brings the destructive principle into play—is, however, too simple, too black and white, though it has served man's purposes well. It silences the question's questioning power and allows man to go ahead with further acts of conquest, freed from the burden of guilt. *Beowulf*, as we have seen, contains a brief creation poem. To retrieve the question and set it in a new light, I now turn to a full-scale creation poem that culturally is closer to the Greek world, the Babylonian *Enuma Elish*.[59] As all works of its kind must, it shows the Grendel aspect of what has to be overcome. But it shows something else, a different face of the enemy.

The *Enuma Elish* begins with the watery chaos when nothing existed save Tiamat, the primal saltwater ocean (or perhaps the serpent deity lodged there), and her husband Apsu, the sweet waters. Somehow this ancient couple give birth to a new, turbulent race of deities:

> The divine brothers banded together,
> They disturbed Tiamat as they surged back and forth,
> Yea, they troubled the mood of Tiamat
> By their hilarity in the Abode of Heaven.[60]

In his distress Apsu cries to Tiamat:

> Their ways are verily loathsome unto me.
> By day I find no relief, nor repose by night.
> I will destroy, I will wreck their ways,
> That quiet may be restored. Let us have rest!

The young gods band together to resist and Apsu is killed. Tiamat, resolving to avenge her husband, calls on a formidable personage named Mother Hubur who assembles all the terrors of the world to defend the old order. The description of her savage battalion is given no less than four times (first at I.132 ff.):

> Mother Hubur, she who fashions all things,
> Added matchless weapons, bore monster-serpents,
> Sharp of tooth, unsparing of fang.
> With venom for blood she has filled their bodies.
> Roaring dragons she has clothed with terror,
> Has crowned them with haloes, making them like gods,
> So that he who beholds them shall perish abjectly....
> She set up the Viper, the Dragon, and the Sphinx,
> The Great-Lion, the Mad-Dog, and the Scorpion-Man,
> Mighty lion-demons, the Dragon-Fly, the Centaur.

The new gods are at first dumbfounded, but then they find a champion in Marduk who comes to their aid and, claiming supreme authority in return for his services, goes off to do battle with Tiamat. They meet in a heroic combat (IV.94-95). Tiamat is killed, and splitting her in two like a shellfish Marduk forms the sky from one half, the earth from the other, and then creates the rest of the universe, including—rather as an afterthought, it seems—man, whose task is to do the gods' dirty work and leave them at their ease.

The *Enuma Elish* fully honors the heroic energy of the creative act, even if it transposes it to the divine level, unwilling to credit man with such powers. It faces the swarming horror of what must be overcome before the work of creation can begin. In these respects it is close enough to our own energetic tradition. Where the Near Eastern poem goes outside our range is that it allows us to contemplate, if only briefly, the other face of chaos, of what from Marduk's point of view appears as chaos. It is striking, to our Western minds, that the poem does not start with the dragon world of Mother Hubur or with the abrupt assertion of Genesis ("In the beginning God created the heaven and the earth"), but with a vision of original will-less peace. This is something that does not find expression in Greek literature, for with most of its mind Greece believed, with Aristotle, that the end of life is a *praxis*, not a *poiotēs*, "une certaine manière d'agir, non une manière d'être."[61] It is outside the main Western tradition, though we find traces of it here and there, very beautifully in the wondering awe of the question that Milton's Adam puts to the divine historian Raphael:

> what cause
> Mov'd the Creator in his holy Rest
> Through all Eternity so late to build
> In Chaos . . .
> 　　　　(*Paradise Lost*, 7.90 ff.)

But Milton has in effect already given his answer, the Western answer, to this question in Uriel's great vision of Creation in Book 3.708 ff.:

> I saw when at his Word the formless Mass,
> This world's material mould, came to a heap:
> Confusion heard his voice, and wild uproar
> Stood rul'd, stood vast infinitude confin'd;
> Till at his second bidding darkness fled,
> Light shone, and order from disorder sprung.

This is our authentic voice, the imperial will that imposes the stamp of its order on whatever lies to hand. Almost everything we are and have done is grounded in this attitude, today as in the past. It seems impossible to get away from it.

The *Enuma Elish*, speaking from a world far less confident of man's powers, allows us to see at least a glimpse of a different attitude. In *Beowulf* what opposes the hero's mission is a horror of great darkness which must be destroyed if man is to survive. Sophocles, though in the *Trakhiniai* he shows the ugly aspect of the forces that oppose the hero, is aware that this is not the whole story. Man's drive to mastery is awe-inspiring, yes, although, or because, what he must master is Earth, eldest of the gods, or in Hannah Arendt's words, "the eternal quiet of being-forever that rests or swings within itself." The opening of the *Enuma Elish* affords a precious glimpse of this original repose and, what is more, suggests that it was the turbulence of the new creative gods that transformed the ancient peace of the primal pair into bristling aggression. The text of *Beowulf* gives me no warrant whatever for guessing that a kind of strategy, a concealed human purpose, was at work in the depiction of Grendel's world. The more philosophic Babylonian poem holds open the possibility that it is Marduk who first creates the chaos he must overcome.

Behind the hostile, chaotic forces that oppose man's project, then, may lie something utterly unlike them: original repose, a repose that man must violate, to be man. He cannot gently break loose from and turn his hand against nature. To realize his own mode of being he is forced to violate a power greater than himself. This is what Sophocles is saying in the *Antigone* ode, Arendt suggests. He evokes "purposeful human activities which do violence to nature because they disturb what, in the absence of mortals, would be the eternal quiet of being-forever."

How should we understand this? Without question, Apsu's call for the restoration of quiet speaks to something very deep in us, especially at a time like the present when the tranquillity of being is lost in the convulsive need always to be doing. And yet Apsu's may still be the voice of the enemy. Can we be sure that a proper contempt for today's gross parody of man's cultural project does not conceal a hostility toward the real thing? Freud has taught us, in one of his great lessons, how ambiguous our attitude to civilization is. We cannot help half hating it for the burdens it imposes, forcing us to renounce and even to violate something we hold dear, our strong impenitent animality. At the same time we must and do love it and must fight for its survival, since it is the greatest thing we have made. Freud's explanation, his account of the contested ground on which the polis rises, is familiar. He puts it powerfully in *Beyond the Pleasure Principle:* "What appears in a minority of human individuals as an untiring impulsion towards further perfection can easily be understood as a result of the instinctual repression upon which is based all that is most precious in human civilization."[62] This impulsion, Freud believed, is not only not universal; it is not even an original element in our composition. He could find no "innate instinct towards perfection at work in human beings." On the contrary (I

102

quote from his summary in *Civilization and Its Discontents*), he found that "besides the instinct to preserve living substance and to join it into ever larger units, there must exist another, contrary instinct seeking to dissolve those units and to bring them back to their primaeval, inorganic state."[63] For my purposes it is worth quoting the fuller statement from Freud's earlier work:

> The attributes of life were at some time evoked in inanimate matter by the action of forces of whose nature we can form no conception. It may perhaps have been a process similar in type to that which later caused the development of consciousness in a particular stratum of living matter. The tension which then arose in what had hitherto been an inanimate substance endeavoured to cancel itself out. In this way the first instinct came into being: the instinct to return to the inanimate state.[64]

This instinct Freud called, perhaps too dramatically, the death instinct. Working in opposition to the creative or life instinct, it is ceaselessly trying to restore an earlier state of things and return to the quiescence of the inorganic world. We have come upon a dualist view again, but a more fertile one than the black and white dualism proposed by *Beowulf*.

Whatever the status of Freud's hypothesis in contemporary psychological thought, its essential truth I take to be confirmed by the fact that it can be embodied in a great poem. (Its essential truth, I will be understood to mean, to our inner world. But what if myth is not or not only a picture of the human psyche? What if the sense of violation which civilization seems to involve has been transferred from its original object on to ourselves?) If we look at the *Enuma Elish* in this light, not in sequential narrative terms but as the representation of certain permanent states, we see in Marduk the drive to join life into larger units, to create civilization, while the primal pair Apsu and Tiamat oppose his project and seek to preserve or restore an original repose. Less directly but very powerfully Freud's hypothesis also illuminates puzzling aspects of the *Trakhiniai*. It helps to explain why, if the play ends in a triumph, it is so painful and bitter: because Herakles is defeating not simply an external enemy but something deep in himself and in the nature of things. It also helps with particular passages, notably the difficult lines in the ode describing Herakles' torments. He is said to be "melting" into the dread phantom of the Hydra (the *aiolos*—shimmering—serpent, a word conveying both attraction and repulsion). As I put it, a kind of transubstantiation is taking place. Not only are the substances of the dead Hydra and Centaur passing into his substance: *he is passing into theirs,* dissolving or returning to an earlier, bestial form of life. The dense words *dolopoios ananka,* the compulsion that works through guile, now take on a precise meaning. The poison that is destroying him is a compulsion in the strictest sense, a drive inherent in all organic life. It works through guile because, on the narrative level, it was the Centaur's deception of Deianeira which first set it in motion and, further, because it is silently active in man, treacherously opposing his conscious, higher purposes and seeking to bring them to naught.

We must be on our guard, then, against Apsu's appeal. Equally (I think Freud the great dualist would allow) we should never shut our ears to it, if only because it cannot be silenced and will return to haunt us in one form or another: the longer and more thoroughly it is silenced, the uglier the form. The West, during its creative periods, has nonetheless sided with Marduk and his project of dominion, "the enlarging of the bounds of human empire," in Bacon's fateful words, "to the effecting of all things possible." The driving thrust of the will has taken care that quiet should not be restored and if possible should not even be allowed to break out. It was said of the Athenians just before the Peloponnesian War that "they are by nature incapable of living tranquilly [*ekhein hēsukhian*] themselves or of allowing anyone else to do so" (Thucydides 1.70), and it is in Athens in the fifth century B.C., the central period of what has recently been called the Greek breakthrough, that the outlines of this new ambition are first clearly discerned. The term "breakthrough" is applied in a recent issue of *Daedalus*[65] to the momentous movements that occurred at roughly the same time (the first seven or eight centuries before Christ) in different parts of the world: the rise of classical Judaism in Israel, Zoroastrianism in Persia, the Upanishads in India, Confucianism and Taoism in China, and in Greece the evolution from Homer and Hesiod to pre-Socratic and classical philosophy. A breakthrough, very roughly, is the successful response to a "breakdown," a period when the traditional way, the way things have "always" been, fails and the traditional values are questioned and found wanting. The response may take many different forms but to succeed it must transcend the limiting horizons the society previously accepted as given and reach to a new more universal vision, a "message" that can be exported and speak to men over a wide area.

The aspect of the Greek, or Athenian, breakthrough I am concerned with (one that the contributors to *Daedalus* apparently thought not worth their attention) finds expression in the well-known fifth-century debate. On one side is *polupragmosune*—the need always to be doing; in its darker form *pleonexia*, Nietzsche's *Haben- und Mehrhabenwollen*. On the other side stands *apragmosune*[66] which, from the activist's point of view, is idleness or lack of public spirit; seen positively, it is related to the virtue of *hesukhia*, tranquillity. What gives this debate its power is that it brings into sharpest focus the paradox that had always lain, sometimes dormant, in the traditional Greek view of man. He is a limited creature whose nature drives him beyond limit, a mortal who aspires to immortality. He is haunted by dreams of transcendence, by the temptation—at once his greatest glory and the high road to ruin—to pass beyond the human condition (to think more than mortal thoughts, Greek says). The *polupragmōn*, at his noblest, lifted on the wings of his ambition, soars into these forbidden regions. The *apragmōn* or man of *hesukhia*, at his noblest, knowing that all that rises must fall, moves proudly within the given space of his mortality.

The locus classicus for this debate is the *Birds* of Aristophanes. The play has been so admirably discussed, from what I take to be the correct position, by William Arrowsmith[67] that I need do no more than recall the conclusion where a runaway Athenian, having traveled to the kingdom of the birds in search of the *apragmosune* he cannot find at home and discovered instead his own inveterate *polupragmosune*, takes over their kingdom and from there blockades the gods into submission. He finally marries Basileia ("Miss Universe") and, assuming the powers of Zeus, is hailed as "the greatest of the gods." Only in high visionary farce could the truth be told so bluntly, but the end of the *Trakhiniai*, as I read it, points darkly in the same direction, even if here, for reasons already discussed, there is no question of transcending mortal limit. Here it is Zeus, standing closer to earth than usual, who lends his authority to a great assertion of human will and power. Herakles has defeated the monsters twice, first in physical combat and then, a harder struggle, in his own tormented flesh. He has utterly rejected Deianeira, in human terms an expression of his harsh, heroic spirit, symbolically an annulment of the great polar rhythm of night and day proclaimed in the opening chorus. The tranquillity of being that spares and lets be and shelters has been defeated by passionate doing and the thrust of the will to conquest. Now, alone on Mount Oita, the place of transcendence, his mission confirmed, Herakles gives himself to the fire that will take him, tradition held, to the Father. And our most absolute tragedian sets his teeth and looks, heaven knows how far, down the road that Western man was triumphantly to take.

Similar ambitions were being voiced in the restricted sphere of political action. The war seemed to be going badly for Athens in the summer of 430 B.C. and Pericles, in the second of the two speeches Thucydides gives him, felt the need to remind his fellow citizens how strong they were. "You think it is only over your allies that your rule extends," he told them. "No. Of the two parts of the world which lie open to [man's] use, the land and the sea, you are the absolute masters of one"; he goes on to speak of Athens's naval supremacy (2.62). The words I want are of course "the two parts of the world *which lie open to* [*man's*] *use*" (*duo merōn tōn es khrēsin phanerōn*). In Pericles' mouth they apply to a particular situation and their scope is limited. There is nothing here of the showy impiety of Xerxes scourging and yoking "the sacred Hellespont, God's stream," as Aeschylus puts it (*Persae* 745-746; see also Herodotus 7.35, 8.109). And yet perhaps this calm assertion of man's control of the elements is more far-reaching.

The power of Athens, Pericles says a little later (2.64), is the greatest that has ever existed up to our time. Even if Athens should decay, "the memory of this greatness will be left to posterity forever" (*es aidion tois epigignomenois . . . mnēmē kataleleipsetai*). Simonides had said that a man's fame lives after him for a while "like a splendid funerary monument, [but] in the end it sinks below the earth."[68] Pericles makes a stronger claim, for the tense he uses (*kataleleipsetai*) points to a permanent future condition. And he goes even further. Do not worry if men hate you, he tells the Athenians. Hatred does not last long, but

ἡ δὲ παραυτίκα λαμπρότης καὶ ἐς τὸ ἔπειτα δόξα
αἰείμνηστος καταλείπεται.

"The brilliance of the present moment remains even in days to come, a glory that will always be remembered." What gives this claim its power, *griechisch gedacht*, is that present brilliance, whether in the literal sense or used metaphorically of high achievement, is of all things what least can endure. It can last on one condition, as Pindar often tells us: when the act is joined to the praising word. But Pericles has already rejected this prop ("We need no Homer to praise us," 2.41). The only brilliance that can possibly last is the brilliance (*aiglē*) of Olympus in which the gods enjoy their eternal felicity (*Odyssey* 6.45-46). Pericles' claim is that the human act alone can, at its greatest, burst through the limits imposed on it and reach into the sphere of the permanent, which in Greek means the divine.

These high claims are, to our sense, undercut, sometimes almost comically, by the inadequacy of the means available for their realization. Thucydides faithfully records the humble seasonal necessities to which Greek warfare and imperial ambition had to submit. At 3.15, for example: "The rest of the allies gathered slowly, for they were busy getting in the harvest and had no spirit for campaigning." The means were however soon to be found, in the next century, in the place where one would least think to look and where no one before Heidegger did systematically look: in Greek metaphysics. Hans-Georg Gadamer, speaking of what he calls a "recent discovery of Heidegger," writes:

> I am convinced that Heidegger's discovery will later become part of the common knowledge of humanity, for we see with increasing clarity today—as he has taught us to see—that Greek metaphysics is the beginning of modern technology. Concept formation, born of western philosophy, has held, throughout a long history, that mastery is the fundamental experience of reality.[69]

It is with Plato, wholly against his conscious intention, Heidegger has shown, that the process begins which would allow man to set himself at the center of things, things that in time would become objects represented to himself as subject, thinks that still later become mere objects submitted to his will, to be refashioned or disposed of as he sees fit.[70] The possibilities hidden in this new attitude were not to be worked out in Greek culture and indeed could not be until they were combined with the dynamic Judeo-Christian conception of history as a meaningful evolutionary process. Man now acquired a far greater role than Greece had ever assigned to him: he was no longer the spectator of an unchanging, perfect cosmos but an actor required to reshape an imperfect world and direct it toward its goal. And something else was needed, the development of modern natural science and the realization of its powers through technology.

3

Hermeneutics must start from the position that a person seeking to understand something has a relation to the object that comes into language in the transmitted text and has, or acquires, a connection with the tradition out of which the text speaks.... Every age has to understand a transmitted text in its own way, for the text is part of the whole of the tradition in which the age takes an objective interest and in which it seeks to understand itself. The real meaning of a text, as it speaks to the interpreter, does not depend on the contingencies of the author and whom he originally wrote for. It is certainly not identical with them, for it is always partly determined also by the historical situation of the interpreter and hence by the totality of the objective course of history.[71]

Today the goal has been reached, or very nearly, and we see what it is, what perhaps it has always been: the subjection of the earth and all its creatures, and now nearer space, to man's will, a project of absolute dominion which, as we are starting to realize, is also directed against man. He too is so much plastic raw material to be reshaped and programmed, by unlimited social conditioning and eventually genetic manipulation, into whatever form the project may require.

I approached the *Trakhiniai* from the angle I did, from a current question about man's relation to nature, not necessarily in the hope that it would tell us something about today's world but simply in order to let it reveal its present meaning, a meaning "partly determined...by the historical situation of the interpreter and...by the totality of the objective course of history." It so happens, however, that a contemporary crisis makes the *Trakhiniai*—originally a response to the critically rapid advance of Athenian civilization, I argued—look very timely today. For defeated nature now really does seem to be turning on its conqueror, turning rather ugly here and there; moreover, there are voices in our midst telling us that modern life has become too artificial and that we ought to "go back to nature." (Deianeira made two attempts to do this. The first didn't work and the second proved disastrous.) The full proportions of the environmental crisis are not yet clear. So far they appear to be manageable, though no one knows how much abuse the delicate structure of the ecosystem can take and an insatiable demand for more energy may prompt mankind to take irreversible steps. Short of outright catastrophe, however, the prospect of outraged nature taking its revenge is unlikely to bring any change in our thinking. We will continue to confront it, in the proper objective way, as one more problem for technology to overcome. Mastery remains the fundamental form of our experience of reality.

The real threat is coming from a different quarter, not from the natural world but from human nature. Suppose that someone wanted to film the *Trakhiniai* and deciding that its mythological framework was no longer meaningful set about rewriting the play in contemporary terms. The great culture hero becomes a Nobel Prize scientist—a mousy little person, not at all Heraklean in his behavior. His mind, though, is full of projects of dominion which would have shocked his Greek predecessor into a state of catatonic *apragmosunē*. He is walking late one evening in New York (rearrange the plot as you will) musing on his latest scheme—he proposes to bulldoze moon dirt into orbit and construct a floating garden suburb—when a deranged teenager jumps out from a dark corner and knifes him in the back, making off with a few dollars. A banal encounter and yet, if you come to think of it, as modally discordant as Deianeira's with the river Akheloos. For *this* is the form that the *selvaggio* now takes, whether it is the carnival dance of released, unsublimated instincts (our new healthy sexuality and so forth) playing havoc with the inherited structure of civilization, an interlocking system of shared beliefs, conventions, ceremonies, repressions (what Philip Rieff calls the interdicts), or whether it issues in conduct still admitted to be unsocial, the middle-class boy smashing a school window "because it is there" or the bemused patriot blowing up a plane to bring freedom to someone or other. Our social contraption is falling apart so fast that unless you are actually hit by one of the pieces you hardly notice the wild comedy of discords proposed by every day's news. On the one hand, austerely conceived plans to extend our dominion in any and every direction—mapping Mars, burning and hacking a way through the vast rain forests of Amazonia,[72] prolonging human life indefinitely or thereabouts, devastating Alaska for the sake of a few more years of gas. On the other hand, crowding signs that the elementary forms of living together have almost broken down. It is safer to travel to the moon than walk our streets after dark.

Disturbances in the natural world we can take in our stride. But that man should elect to go mad, now of all times, after so many laborious schemes for his betterment, really does threaten our project, and wise heads wagging in committee confess that they don't know what to do about it. The counterculturists a decade ago had their explanation and answer. Abstract rationalism has compelled the joyfully anarchic energies of life into its own rigid schemata. So smash the schemata, put flowers in your hair, and let yourself grow green again, and all will be well. Dostoevski said some of the same thing (and a good deal else) much better a century ago. That two plus two must always equal four, his underground man saw, is tyranny and the beginning of death. However comfortable you make him, "out of sheer spite and ingratitude, man will play a dirty trick on you. He'll even risk his cake for the sake of the most glaring stupidity, for the most economically unsound nonsense, just to inject into all the soundness and sense surrounding him some of his own disastrous lethal fancies."[73] The other, official side sticks to its guns (which are heavier) and insisting that man's dignity depends on the maintenance of reason deplores the spread of irrational conduct and the retreat from sober modes of inquiry.

The trouble with all such debates is that both sides remain firmly within the forms of thought that have dominated our tradition for so long, perhaps ever since the Athenian breakthrough in the fifth century B.C. This thinking is radically anthropocentric, *humanist*. One side of man has unduly gained the upper hand, so let us, by a dialectical reversal that reverses nothing except our direction along the familiar tramlines, give a boost to the other side of man. We can understand our situation in no other way. And yet in the long reach of its memory the Western tradition preserves traces of a different kind of thinking which might introduce a real change of direction, if only we could let the past address us, in a living communion, and not deaden it into an object of knowledge.

We were in fact led to the possibility of another kind of thinking by Sophocles. The *Antigone* ode, the first major statement of
the Western project, proposed, as Hannah Arendt beautifully
saw, not a conflict between two sides of man (the mastering, say,
and the sparing) but between purposeful "human activities" and
the eternal quiet of "being-forever." (A quiet that man must
nonetheless violate, to be man. We have still found no way to
understand this.) We were sent to that ode by puzzling features
in the *Trakhiniai*. That play shows nature striking back at its
conqueror and almost defeating him. Herakles eventually triumphs but his triumph is painful and bitter, won at very great
cost. Why the pain and cost, I keep asking, if what he confronts
is bestial, hated by gods and men alike? The *Antigone* ode hints
at an answer, but the vision of the other which it still preserves
was being submerged in the Greek world, so I turned to the older
Babylonian poem. Where *Beowulf*, intensifying and darkening
the *Trakhiniai*'s vision of the *selvaggio*, sees only the irruption of
violent evil which it is the hero's mission to repel, the more profound *Enuma Elish* looks behind civilization's favorite theme of
order versus chaos and sees original repose disturbed into aggression by the emergence of ordering will. To understand this, I
drew on Freud's hypothesis of a death instinct working alongside
and against the life instinct and struggling to restore the primal
quiescence. Freud, an inveterate dualist, never suggested that the
death instinct must (or can) be rooted out. It is part of the equation. If one side, say the life instinct, grows too strong, the other
must strike back and redress the balance. He said as much in
grand mythological terms at the end of *Civilization and Its Discontents*, though he put it the other way round. Dramatically
picturing the struggle between Eros and Thanatos, he expressed
the hope that "eternal Eros will make an effort to assert himself
in the struggle with his equally immortal adversary."

The terms are loaded, of course. If love is fighting death, we
are bound to hope that love will win. The polar rhythm of night
and day in the *Trakhiniai*, as I interpret it, provides a more equa-
ble way of depicting the struggle. Freud chose the terms he did, I
suspect, because he remained within the old Western conception
of a conflict between man's higher and lower nature.[74] He can
only tell us of two sides of man in conflict. We may however
understand his powerful dualism in another way. We may think
of "love," the instinct that joins life into ever larger units and

111

creates civilization—in the form that civilization takes today, the will to absolute dominion—and hear in "death" Apsu's cry for the restoration of quiet, a quiet that embraces more than man.

A quiet that man must nonetheless violate, to be man.

And yet perhaps to put it like this is in itself a pointer to another way of thinking. For who talks of violation today? What is there to violate? Few question our right to deal with nature as we see fit—although we have learned that we must use our (*our*) resources more wisely—or to deal with the emergent *selvaggio* in man as best we can. And even if we agree with Freud's view of civilization as a system of repressions, what is being repressed is after all a part of ourselves, *cosa nostra*. The humanist circle is drawn tight and we are inside it.

Help can come only from outside, from some region beyond the restrictions of our culture. It can come from our tradition, if we will let it speak to us. The *Trakhiniai*, presenting an early phase of the *mission civilisatrice*, saw man's triumph as bitter and painful: a necessary violation leading to a painful triumph. Something outside the humanist circle still speaks here.

To realize his own mode of being in the world, man must transcend and do violence to nature. To forgive himself for what he has to do, he turns nature into the enemy. Divine *phusis*, transformed into Hydra or Grendel, strikes back. Apsu's cry for the restoration of quiet can now no longer be directly heard. It can be experienced only as threatening disorder, chaos. His conscience clear, man goes ahead, bit by bit enlarging the bounds of his empire.

Man's will to dominion has today grown so absolute that we would expect the other side to strike back and redress the balance. Something is striking back and our project is not in good shape, but the threat does not come from the natural world, at least not yet. It cannot do so, for man no longer experiences nature as the "other." There is no other. Wherever he turns, man now confronts only himself, Heisenberg said. So the other emerges, as the *selvaggio*, not in nature but in man.

Following the pattern at work in the poems we have studied, we recognize the other which, transformed into the *selvaggio*, confronts us today.

Primal repose speaking through the hoodlum, the bombing patriot, the proletarian dance of the liberated instincts?

It is always hard to discern Apsu in Grendel. It is now harder than ever, when limitless will has so suppressed and disfigured his old adversary. Probably it would be impossible to see anything opposing the will, except misery and confusion, if the other had not chosen to address us directly in his own high voice.

In a meditation on the nature of dwelling, Heidegger finds that man dwells truly when he plays his part in a fourfold unity composed of earth and sky, divinities and mortals:

> Mortals dwell in that they save the earth—taking the word [*retten*] in the old sense still known to Lessing. Saving does not only snatch something from danger. To save really means to set something free into its own presencing [*etwas in sein eigenes Wesen freilassen*]. To save the earth is more than to exploit it or even wear it out. Saving the earth does not master the earth and does not subjugate it, which is merely one step from spoliation.
>
> Mortals dwell in that they receive the sky as sky. They leave to the sun and the moon their journey, to stars their courses, to the seasons their blessing and their inclemency; they do not turn night into day nor day into a harassed unrest.
>
> Mortals dwell in that they await the divinities as divinities. In hope they hold up to the divinities what is unhoped for. They wait for intimations of their coming and do not mistake the signs of their absence. They do not make their gods for themselves and do not worship idols. In the very depth of misfortune they wait for the weal that has been withdrawn. [*Im Unheil noch warten sie des entzogenen Heils.*]
>
> Mortals dwell in that they initiate their own nature—their being capable of death as death—into the use and practice of this capacity, so that there may be a good death. To initiate mortals into the nature of death in no way means to make death, as empty Nothing, the goal. Nor does it mean to darken dwelling by blindly staring toward the end.[75]

Though it speaks from our own tormented century, the voice seems to come from a great distance; it is saying things that have not been heard in the Western world for a very long time. And yet Heidegger spent his life within the Western tradition, searching in its origins for recoverable possibilities, and it is from our own forgotten origins that he speaks here. In the third *Iliad* Helen stands on the walls of Troy beside old Priam and he asks her to identify the leaders of the Greek army down below. She describes them one by one but can see no sign of her brothers, Kastor and Polydeukes. Perhaps they were ashamed to come? The poet's own voice answers her:

ὡς φάτο, τοὺς δ᾽ ἤδη κάτεχεν φυσίζοος αἶα
ἐν Λακεδαίμονι αὖθι, φίλῃ ἐν πατρίδι γαίῃ.

So Helen spoke. But her brothers—by now life-giving earth held them, in Lakedaimon, the dear land of their fathers.

The scene is marvelously full of human diversity and suffering and emotion, yet as it comes to a close silence falls and for a moment we stand before the great calm of enfolding nature—a "moment" that lasts through the poem, grounded as it is in the contrast between man's brief passionate course and the being-forever of the divine, elemental powers. Here, at the beginning of our tradition, which like all great things starts with its highest achievement, the two sides of the equation are in perfect harmony. They were not to remain so for long.

Heidegger's view of dwelling, it may be said, is no doubt very poetic, but it is too withdrawn and quietist to help busy people like ourselves live our lives. As it happens, Heidegger anticipates this response a page or so before the passage quoted earlier: "When we speak of dwelling we usually think of an activity that man performs alongside many other activities. We work here and dwell there. We do not merely dwell—that would be virtual inactivity [*Untätigkeit*, i.e., *apragmosunē*]—we practice a profession, we do business, we travel and lodge on the way, now here, now there."[76] No, the danger of our lapsing into a classic fatigue is not very grave. Quiet will never break out here for long. Herakles and Marduk and Beowulf will come marching back soon enough. But at least, if we could hear what addresses us through Heidegger's voice, they would not have things all their own way. Our doing would recover a nobility it has lost if it were seen as rising up from, rising up against, the stability and tranquillity of being, if we were able to recover the tension of a conflict that may be endemic in the Western world and perhaps part of the human condition everywhere. (An "immortal" spirit that transcends time and space lodged in a dying animal.) The stretched will is great in Sophocles because it is up against the limits imposed on man's action. Think of the ode Sophocles could have written on the exploration of space: a man-made object set among the heavenly bodies, the most dazzling of transgressions! Whereas the machine that transports our gadgets to Mars is merely the poor first of a long series, a Model T space-

114

ship dwarfed before it even takes off by the better and better spaceships of tomorrow reaching farther and farther, ruining along the illimitable inane.

To learn to move once more within the given space of our mortality may now be too much to hope for. But it would be a step in the right direction if, helped by material breakdown, we could start to recover the tension between man and what is not man, between man and the other. It doesn't sound like much, and yet we have spent some of our best years between the horns of the great dualisms.

BIBLIOGRAPHICAL NOTE

I usually follow A. C. Pearson's Oxford text (1971), though at 831-837 I print Jebb's. I have used the commentaries by R. C. Jebb (*Sophocles: The Trachiniae*, Pt. 5 [Cambridge, 1892]); J. C. Kamerbeek (*The Plays of Sophocles*, Pt. II, *The Trachiniae* [Leiden, 1959]); and less often that by Lewis Campbell (*Sophocles* [Oxford, 1879], II). I have also profited from the translation by Paul Mazon (*Sophocle*, I, Collection des universités de France [Paris, 1967]), The scholia are quoted from *Scholia in Sophoclis Tragoedias Vetera*, ed. P. N. Papageorgius (Leipzig, 1888).

IV

DANTE ANTAGONISTES

As our culture grows less and less Christian, the question of how
we should read the classics of Christian literature becomes unmistakably urgent, even if the academic community is content to
act as though this were not so. The large doctrinal ignorance that
most readers now bring to *Paradise Lost* is putting a good deal of
the text at an awkward distance. So many beliefs have to be
playacted, so much background knowledge mugged up before
we can get to the poem. With *Paradise Lost* the modern reader's
difficulties are mitigated by the way Milton too sometimes seems
to be struggling with his religion. The unbeliever can take comfort from the thought that perhaps Milton himself was not an
anima *naturaliter* christiana. But what of Dante, the chief imagination of Christendom, as Yeats called him? A late starter on the
road to classic status, Dante stands very high today. The modernist masters and critics joined in paying him homage. His status in the literary and academic world is unquestioned. Here,
apparently, the religious obstacle causes no discomfort. And yet
the leading Dantista in America, Charles S. Singleton, is uneasy
about the place of the *Divine Comedy* in our culture. "For some
time now," he wrote in 1958, "we have been reading the great
work in what amounts to an amputated version. It is not that the
text of the poem...suffers from any serious lacunae.... The
lacunae are rather in us, the readers, and reside in that deficient
knowledge and lack of awareness which we continue to bring to
our reading of the poem."[1]

Professor Singleton states the problem very honestly and,

since he has devoted a lifetime of scholarship to overcoming it, he may serve as the spokesman for one very influential approach to our classical Christian literature. Call it, using the term neutrally, the academic approach. What we must do, Singleton says, is "reinstate...in our minds" a whole body of doctrine. This is a large undertaking but there is no other course if we are to become "such readers as Dante expected us to be." The task of scholarship has been to piece together the "recoverable context" of the poem, not merely a multiplicity of facts about people and places and events but "the dominant modes of thought and feeling, the master patterns of the Christian mind and imagination that had come to prevail through the Christian centuries," patterns that Dante could assume were public property.[2]

To recover not simply knowledge but modes of thought and feeling, modes that our minds have, historically, not mislaid but rejected: this, it might seem, could lead only to formal response, academic in the pejorative, limiting sense. Yet no one could be content to see the *Comedy* simply as a historical document and certainly Singleton does not see it in this way. The difficulty, as he here and there grants, is that not merely ignorance stands between Dante and ourselves. There are metaphysical obstacles. Thanks to the Renaissance, "our faith in the ability of the word to contain a changeless truth continues to diminish." Before long, we may have "completely lost the belief in the possibility of transcending the world of change."[3] And there are religious obstacles. The *Comedy* is addressed to the unquiet heart of the Christian pilgrim who knows that the world is only a place of transit. And yet this conception, as Singleton himself tells us, was already starting to fail six centuries ago, with Boccaccio.

More than our ignorance is at issue. Unavoidably the question of belief crops up, and no one has found anything very helpful to say about it. Eliot declared in the famous essay that "you are not called upon to believe what Dante believed, for your belief will not give you a groat's worth more of understanding and appreciation."[4] And went on to contradict himself handsomely: "I cannot, in practice, wholly separate my poetic appreciation from my personal beliefs." He tried again with the aid of Coleridge, distinguishing between "philosophical belief" and "poetic assent." Singleton takes a similar tack. To read the *Comedy* properly we must be converted: not of course a religious conversion but "a necessary conversion of our *imagination*."[5]

117

Most readers do not in fact feel the need to go as far as this and contrive to make themselves at home in Dante's poem by silently translating it into a more familiar language, psychological or existential. "The action of the *Purgatorio*," Francis Fergusson writes, "has a natural source which is not too difficult to identify in one's own experience. After some deep fright, some nightmare-intuition of being nowhere, hope returns, and with hope the disquieting naïveté of the bare forked animal who needs to know who he is, where he is, and what he is trying to do."[6] A reading of this sort will work up to a point, yet it is open to the objection the young German theologian Wolfhart Pannenberg has raised against Bultmann's interpretation of Scripture. If you put "the question of human existence" to the text (biblical or Dantesque) it will speak to you only partially since its answer is framed in terms of a larger whole that includes the world, society, history, and God. The trouble with fastening this "anthropological constriction" onto a religious work, Pannenberg argues, is that only "the possibilities of human existence" become relevant for your interpretation. Much of what the text has to say is inevitably toned down or ignored.[7]

Another influential approach, one that brings its own lasting satisfactions, is open to different objections. Call it the poet's way of reading Dante and let R. P. Blackmur speak for it. Claiming that "there is a part of Dante which never came to life until our own time," he maintains that

> When criticism some six hundred years old comes suddenly to life, and relevant life, in a new context, that new life cannot be destroyed even if it can be shown to be based on a misunderstanding of the life in the original text. We have a right—we literary critics with a little bent for poetry—to whatever life we can find.[8]

The strength of the literary approach is in its care for the present, and the presence, of a past text. When scholarship intervenes, as it must, and shows what the text is *really* saying, the danger is that part of its vitality may be lost. It happened with Donne. He was "kidnapped" by the literary gentry, as Professor Douglas Bush put it, and made over "in the likeness of a modern intellectual." So scholarship had to sound its *rappel à l'ordre* and correct this "distortion of the real Donne" by setting him in "a much richer and clearer historical setting."[9] The unfortunate result has

118

been that Donne, a powerful poetic force in the earlier decades of this century, has withdrawn into history and become simply one more figure in the literary tradition. The same fate could befall even Dante.

It is disagreeable, though, to commit oneself to a reading grounded in bad scholarship—"based on a misunderstanding," as Blackmur candidly allows—and before falling back on these literary or psychological byways it is only sensible to try the main thoroughfare to the great poem which scholarship has constructed. We cannot do better than take Singleton as our guide, drawing not only on his numerous publications on Dante but on the monumental commentary that has put us forever in his debt.[10] Let us take a few steps, then, along the *via regia*. Of the fifth canto of the *Inferno* Singleton writes:

> Here are Francesca and Paolo, forever without peace, tossed on an infernal storm. This is the simple and literal fact, such is their state after death. But in the literal fact we may behold the justice of God: for their state, which is a punishment, bears witness to its sufficient reason, its justice. The passion of lust is itself such a storm; peace is forever denied it. It is proper, it is just, that the condition of the lustful after death should be the condition of lust itself.... [This is not] offered as a justification of God's ways to men. Here is no pleading of a case for God. In His will these things are so, and that is our peace if not always theirs.[11]

Singleton's usual strategy is to speak as though from inside Dante's world. It is hard in such passages to be sure (so closely has he identified himself with his author) if we are to hear the dramatic utterance of the exegete or an expression of personal belief. No doubt it is impertinent to inquire and anyway not to my point, which is that our recovery of Dante's world has taught us a rather cloistered way of talking about his poem. Santayana, an unreconstructed though not unintelligent reader of Dante, spoke more bluntly some years ago of this matter of eternal damnation. "The damned are damned for the glory of God," as he put it. He went on:

> This doctrine, I cannot help thinking, is a great disgrace to human nature. It shows how desperate, at heart, is the folly of an egotistic or anthropocentric philosophy. This philosophy begins by assuring us that everything is obviously created to serve our needs; it then main-

119

tains that everything serves our ideals; and in the end, it reveals that everything serves our blind hatreds and superstitious qualms. Because my instinct taboos something, the whole universe, with insane intensity, shall taboo it for ever.[12]

We have come a long way since these words were written, even if an unregenerate poet-critic like William Empson can still complain of the way scholarship is forcing the reader of older literature to "enter an alien world called 'historical' from which his own conscience and knowledge of life are excluded."[13]

2

Move forward many thousands of lines to a serener region, the sphere of Mercury in paradise where Dante has just heard Justinian deliver a splendid, impassioned speech on the providential course of Roman history. He is puzzled by one thing, the point where Justinian tells how under Titus the Roman standard, "inspired by the living Justice," sped forward to "do vengeance for the vengeance of the ancient sin" (*Paradiso* 6.92-93). Dante understands, as we may not, that the emperor was referring to the destruction of Jerusalem in A.D. 70. What he does not understand (as Beatrice perceives) is how a just vengeance could be justly avenged (7.20-21). So Beatrice has to remind him that when Adam sinned he damned himself and all his progeny until God chose through an act of love to make himself man, in human form atoning for (avenging) the primal human offense. "Christ's death on the Cross therefore *justly* atoned for original sin in Adam," Singleton explains. "Nothing was ever so just." The destruction of Jerusalem was also just since "even though the Crucifixion of Christ was part of God's plan, the Jews are nonetheless accountable for their terrible deed." A passage from Aquinas is cited in confirmation of this malignant argument: "It must, however, be understood that their ignorance did not excuse them from crime, because it was, as it were [*quodammodo*], affected ignorance. For they saw manifest signs of his Godhead; yet they perverted them out of hatred and envy of Christ: neither would they believe His words, whereby He avowed that He was the Son of God."

With less learning John D. Sinclair, in his commentary, played the role of mediator to the extent of recognizing that such passages may be difficult for us ("indeed a singular historical judgment . . ."). We might hope that Singleton too would pause here and explain not simply the logic of Dante's case but the compulsions that led him to it, the satisfactions he found there, with perhaps even a hint of what it felt like to look at the world in this way. But no. The prevailing fiction of Singleton's commentary is that we stand with him inside Dante's world and require not so much mediation or persuasion (the "pleading of a case for God") as instruction. This does raise questions. Under the immediate spell of Dante's verse we can accept almost anything he proposes and grant "imaginative" truth to matter we might otherwise find repellent. This however is likely to involve no more than poetic assent. It is one of Singleton's great services that he forces us to go into the prose of it, the hard small print, and realize what it is we are being asked to assent to. The question is how far we *can* "reinstate" in our minds the beliefs that Dante shared with his age. And what happens to our minds, and hearts and consciences, when we have performed this operation? There is a story about an actor who was to play the part of a gorilla. To get inside the animal's skin—metaphorically, before he did so literally—he visited a zoo every day for some weeks and studied a particular gorilla so closely that in the end he felt he had become one. Later he went mad.

For the fact remains that with poetry of this order a purely aesthetic response (if indeed there is such a thing) must be inadequate. "The accuracy of accurate letters is an accuracy with respect to the structure of reality," Stevens said grandly, and the *Comedy*, if any poem ever did, aims at this final accuracy. It requires a response as serious as we can give. We must bring to it our fullest sense of life, our deepest beliefs and unbeliefs. "Poetic assent," a term that raises more questions than it settles, will hardly do. Nor can we come to this poem in borrowed robes, fancy-dress medieval Christians imaginatively accepting much that we vigorously reject.

Bring to it, *not* impose upon it. The first step toward a genuine encounter must I think be to decline the alternatives that Singleton would press on us. Either, he says, "by an effort of the imagination we . . . again achieve" Dante's view of life, or we "shall be forever recasting Dante and his world into the image of our own."[14] Certainly we are not to fasten our categories upon

Dante; on the other hand we can understand only from within our own horizon of experience which, though it may be transcended (but never denied), is very distant from Dante's. We need to devise a means of bridging this distance which does not demand wholesale capitulation on our part, a capitulation likely to be damaging to any real sincerity of response. We ought to recognize that this demand, although made in the name of historical scholarship, is itself naively unhistorical since it fails to perceive the historicality of all understanding. It assumes that a text has a single "real" meaning that exists independently of every act of understanding it, a changeless timeless identity which we must "go back" to recover.

3

The *Geschichtlichkeit des Verstehens* is of course a central pillar of the hermeneutic theory of understanding advanced by Hans-Georg Gadamer in *Wahrheit und Methode*, and it may be in these terms that we can now best approach the *Divine Comedy*.[15] It might offer a means of overcoming some of the contradictions and evasive stratagems (particularly those related to the problem of belief) that have hitherto stood in our way. There is nonetheless a great deal that we must first know— knowledge that can come only from scholarship—before we can hope to understand. The proper contribution of scholarship is suggested by Paul Ricoeur in a paper called "What Is a Text?" with the Diltheyan subtitle, "Explanation and Interpretation."[16] Dilthey saw the two terms as belonging to different areas of inquiry, the first to natural sciences, the second to the *Geisteswissenschaften* or humanities. Ricoeur would apply both to the study of texts, overcoming their opposition by setting them in a sequential, complementary relation. Explanation, in this sense, seeks to suspend the text's reference to the world and the reader's subjectivity, bracketing the question of its truth in order to concentrate on the interplay of its internal relations, its structure. The model Ricoeur proposes is in fact French structuralism. As he makes clear, the ideal rigor of this procedure must be something of a fiction since no text worth studying can be reduced to the pure play of its constitutive elements. Rather, explanation fruitfully *postpones* the full hermeneutic encounter with the text until such time as its structure has been laid bare. So far as I know, a structuralist reading of the *Comedy* has not been attempted. It might throw valuable light on the poem's central patterns and polarities, but with a work of such dense intellectual complexity something more is surely needed. We still need historical scholarship, provided that it is recognized as constituting only the first "explanatory" stage.

Its limits reached and task accomplished, explanation yields to interpretation. The brackets are now removed and the text can address me. The *text*, it is well to insist (not Dante), understood not in terms of an individual life but of what is said there: "Detached from the contingencies of its origin, what is put down in writing is freed for new relations of meaning exceeding those which may have been intended by the author."[17] It follows that what concerns me now is not the text as it ("really") was but as it addresses me now in the event of understanding. And yet how can I hope to understand a work so culturally remote as the *Comedy*? By seeking to enter into a relation that at first resembles a conversation. I find that I have a question to put to it, a question arising from my own experience of life and yet set in motion by my preliminary grasp of what the text has to say. Gradually I discover that it is answering me and that my initial question is being transformed by this answer.

The process of understanding which allows this to happen Gadamer calls the fusion of horizons.[18] At first the horizons of text and interpreter seem wholly dissimilar. The distance, and the challenge, the tension, of this distance must be accepted; a great work from the past should break disturbingly into my present existence. At the same time there is some common ground, for my cultural horizon has been formed by countless elements from the past, that past from which the text has been handed over to me by the tradition. This holds out the hope of constructing a new more comprehensive horizon within which the text and interpreter, while retaining their otherness, can both stand.

However, the possibility of entering into such a relation at all depends on my initial question. A bad question will be met only with silence. Since the *Comedy* is a religious poem, it must in some sense be a religious question and it is here that the real difficulty starts. For although this is presumably the greatest religious poem in our tradition, it has become, from a religious point of view, among the least approachable. Hölderlin, at the beginning of the modern period, spoke of "God's default," *Gottes Fehl*, not so much a blank nothing-there as a pregnant absence or missing presence which, he said, "helps"—helps, I suppose, to keep us discontent, keeps us searching for the traces of the fugitive gods, as Heidegger puts it. Religious experience today is likely to be paradoxical and fragmentary, "hints followed by guesses," guesses at an unknown holy which has no place in a profane, despoiled world and which is nonetheless to be sought *here*, in this world, if anywhere. Dante's universe, however, is rigorously two-tiered, the here of earthly existence vertically related to a transcendent reality *there*, in the next life. It is a real question how far the *Comedy* can still be a *religious* poem for those whose experience is "sealed off against any transcendental ingression from without" (in Nathan Scott's phrase)[19] and whose gods are at best absent. Dante's poem speaks from a world that, however sinful, bears the impress of the divine intention everywhere. Even in the infernal realm where God cannot be named, his absence is in no sense problematic.

The trouble is that nothing in the *Comedy* is finally problematic, for although Dante the poet provides Dante the pilgrim with much to puzzle him (Why is A damned and B saved? Why did God choose to save us in this way rather than that? and so on), they both know there is always an answer. The pilgrim, at the beginning, is lost but he knows where he ought to be going; his difficulty is how to get there. Even the most perplexing matter of all, Dante's long questioning of God's justice in regard to the damnation of the virtuous heathens (*Paradiso* 19.67 ff.), is finally laid to rest by the discourse of the eagle. God's justice is like the ocean; man's eye cannot see to the bottom yet he knows that there must be one. This is not an answer that would have satisfied Milton,[20] nor is it meant to be an answer. Singleton comments: "The reply of the eagle to the troubling question . . . is actually no reply at all, but an outburst against man's very pride and presumption in asking such a question in the first place." If Singleton is right, even the possibility of the problematic is excluded. More than any other great work of the imagination the *Comedy* confronts us with a world that is ordered and meaningful from top to bottom. A recurring phrase of Singleton's is "It is no accident that . . ." One sometimes wishes it were. What Dante says in paradise, "casüal punto non puote aver sito" (32.53), is true of his poem as a whole: there is no place there for a particle of chance, for the randomness of things. No place, then, for the unexplained gift of the moment when, in Stevens's words, "Life's nonsense pierces us with strange relation."[21] The relations are all there, plotted in advance, waiting only for reason to discover them or grace to reveal them.

4

There are those who claim to feel nostalgic about this world of vanished certainties. I do not share their emotion; Homer's sane world of chance and change strikes me as far more habitable. Nor can I think nostalgia a proper frame of mind in which to approach this unyielding text. Unyielding and, for some readers finally, excluding. Perhaps the best hope of finding a way in would be to come on a chink in the armor, some flaw or imperfection. The *Comedy*'s reputation is now so great that the reader feels almost helpless before it. Any difficulties he has are always his fault, due to his ignorance or spiritual obtuseness; they never point to some failure in the poem. It might be helpful to recognize that the *Comedy* is not quite so unapproachably perfect nor so all-encompassing as we have been claiming for the last few generations. Reflect, with the *Iliad* in mind, that Dante's theological scheme allows him to say nothing important about death. The gravity of this great human event cannot be acknowledged; it is reduced to a mere moment of transit, to damnation or salvation (*Inferno* 27.112 ff., *Purgatorio* 5.94 ff.). Again, though Dante's world is very large, poetically and also I think intellectually it suffers from not having enough to overcome. Its truths have to contend only with human backsliding. Compare the treatment of the atonement in *Paradiso* 7 and in Book 3 of *Paradise Lost*. Milton's God the Father, speaking in the doctrinally neutral air of a latter-day Olympus, has to make a fighting defense of what is evidently a difficult case, whereas in Dante's scene all the cards are stacked in God's favor in advance. (Coleridge, we may recall, thought that in the "combination of poetry with doctrines . . . Dante has not succeeded . . . nearly so well as Milton.")[22] It would do no harm to allow, as Croce did, that even the famous, marvelous diction has its occasional flaws.[23] "I would have a corollary mantle you," for example, in *Paradiso* 8.138. If this occurred anywhere else, it would surely be censured

125

as a lamentable attempt to enliven a theological argument with a touch of "poetry." Again, imagine the outcry if we found an ungainly Latinism like "umbriferous prefaces" in Milton. Yet "umbriferi prefazi" passes without comment in Dante (*Paradiso* 30.78). Later in the same canto we are given "come *clivo* in acqua di suo *imo.*" What sort of Italian is that?

However, the flaws I have in mind and think might prove helpful are of a different kind. I mean rather some fault in the design or fertile contradiction which probably did not seem contradictory in Dante's time but which *has since become so.* There is a moment in *Paradiso* 22 which may, from this point of view, be worth glancing at. Dante has now ascended to the sphere of the fixed stars and Beatrice tells him to look back at the great distance he has come. So he gazes down through the seven planetary spheres and sees our earth, "tal, ch'io sorrisi del suo vil sembiante" (such that I smiled at its paltry aspect). In its achieved context the utterance feels dramatically right; at this height the human tension between Here and There has been fully resolved. It is only if we step back for a moment and hear the line from our perspective that it can sound a little outrageous. A medieval Christian, we suppose, would not have felt this. Or is there, even from Dante's perspective, a slight though concealed sense of strain here? Has he quite earned that smile? His heaven, after all, must wear our colors or go naked, and even his god is composed, by inspired *bricolage*, from bits and pieces of man's earthly endeavor—a geometer's puzzle, scraps of ancient myth and cult.

This line can be related (from the point of view I am pursuing) to a much earlier scene, in *Purgatorio* 13. Dante sees a group of penitents approaching and asks if there are any Italians among them. "Each one of us is citizen of a true city," comes the reproachful reply. "You mean—did any of us live as pilgrims in Italy?" The souls in purgatory, Singleton comments, "no longer indulge in those lingering attachments to the world of the living that were characteristic of souls in Antepurgatory," and on the next page he refers to the verse in Hebrews 11.13 which reminds us that we should be "strangers and pilgrims on the earth." The fact that this conception of life is now hardly more than a historical curiosity, even for Christians, need not concern us on our first, explanatory reading. There, the question of the poem's truth does not arise and we listen neutrally when Singleton tells us that "in this life it is our proper condition as Christians to be as pilgrims"[24] or when Augustine, at his behest, explains why we must use rather than enjoy the things of this world:

> Suppose... we were wanderers in a strange country, and could not live happily away from our fatherland... and wishing to put an end to our misery, determined to return home.... But the beauty of the country through which we pass, and the very pleasure of the motion, charm our hearts, and turning these things which we ought to use into objects of enjoyment, we became unwilling to hasten the end of our journey.... Such is a picture of our condition in this life of mortality. We have wandered far from God; and if we wish to return to our Father's home, this world must be used, not enjoyed, so that the invisible things of God may be clearly seen.[25]

It is very different, though, when we are trying to interpret the poem and must let it enter our lives and address us. Interpretation of course acknowledges the challenging distance of the text; at the same time there has to be some common ground and it is hard to know where to find it if the *Comedy* does indeed present human life in the terms proposed by Augustine, which are far too remote to be seriously challenging.

Dante's poem, however, challenges us continually. It is true that the poet calls on us to detach ourselves from the things of this world, but he manages to combine this call with a passionate attachment to their every aspect which he recreates with unsurpassed splendor. It may seem that we have come on a real contradiction here, but Singleton can explain, with the aid of another great medieval theme, that it is not really one. The things of this world deserve our closest attention not only because they are God's handiwork but because they are *signs*. Every *res* exists truly here and is at the same time a *signum* pointing there, to the invisible things of God.

These things, Singleton gets Augustine to tell us, are to be *used*, not *enjoyed*. Is this really what the *Comedy* has to say?

Only a generation or so after Dante's death we find Boccaccio no longer able to understand the allegory of the pilgrim's unquiet heart. In the same period Petrarch, a man of religious temper as Boccaccio was not, bears more significant witness. His *Rime* can be read as the record of the long struggle of a heart no less unquiet than Dante's, if in a different way (*nusquam integer, nusquam totus*),[26] to achieve a unity of being grounded in Christian

127

submission. A struggle whose outcome is left open and problematic, despite the final penitential canzone which seems imposed on the work by an act of will rather than rising organically from it.

The great synthesis that held all the sign-things of this world in a pattern whose meaning could be discovered only in the next failed soon after Dante's death. Is it quite certain that we have our dating right? Or did the failure begin a little earlier, *within Dante's mind and Dante's poem?* Perhaps after all it is not wholly on the far side of the great divide. If so, can the immense energy of its structure be understood at least in part as a last-ditch attempt to hold the day and as a premonition of coming defeat?

What—to take a bolder step forward—if the poem is trying to say something that could not be said then but was soon to be said and that we, from our perspective, can *help it to say*? As Singleton reads the *Comedy* it points back to "what is already conceptually elaborated and established in Christian doctrine."[27] During the first, explanatory stage we too must look back, with the poem, to the doctrine upon which it is built. This is a necessary step, but it is only the first one. We should also allow the poem to point *forward*. We pay the *Comedy* a dubious compliment if we suppose that its life and rage for truth were cut short at the year 1321. Instead of protectively putting it out of time's way, we should let it collaborate with, or struggle against, its own future and grant it what all other great poems possess, a genuine *Fortleben*, the power of entering into new relations of meaning beyond those its creator could have foreseen or intended. For a moment, remove the Aquinas map we have exhumed from the theological library, detach the *signa* from the *res* and let them stand in their own terminal right. For a moment, let the poem suffer the shock of its own dissolution. Then of course it must come together again, but subtly a change has taken place. The text's intentionality (the text's, not Dante's) has not been destroyed. Rather, it has been released from the timeless limbo to which scholarship would confine it and thus strengthened. It has been brought back into time and history, returned to the tradition (with all its hazards) to which we too belong, and it can stand before us in its challenging presence as we put our question to it. For to read a great work of the past does not mean "going back" to some frozen as-it-was-then. True reading, as Gadamer says, "is not a repetition of something past but a participation in a present meaning."[28]

5

I do not know what sort of *Comedy* would emerge from the reading I am struggling to point to. It would hardly be the whole poem, but then we don't have the whole poem today, despite the enthusiasm of the literati, nor can historical scholarship give it to us. Great wholes, poetic or intellectual, seldom pass intact through the ages. Better living parts, though (which does not mean *momenti lirici*), than a mummified *texte intégral*.

What can I make of the *Inferno*? It should today be the most approachable of Dante's three realms. Clearly it must not be reduced to a series of human encounters set in an irrelevant theological framework, and to call it a prolonged metaphor for alienation or loss is too easy. Even to see it, like *Lear* or the *Iliad*, as a facing of the ultimate cruelty of things—rather than of the cruelty or "justice" of God—is shirking the text's statement. This is hell, eternal Belsen, a compound image of the evil man is capable of, including the evil of imagining the possibility of hell, and beyond that a guess at some metaphysical black hole of the universe large enough to contain all our hopes and fears. I doubt I can go further than that.

The *Purgatorio* and *Paradiso* are, from a religious point of view, more intractable: the absent god has bafflingly returned. Even so, much of purgatory is still accessible as the record of a long, painful schooling, a relearning of the words of celebration in order to return to the Garden and then venture on to the more arduous joys of paradise. (An honest reading would I think sometimes simply black out here, leaving a discontinuous, fragmentary heaven, as in Pound's later cantos, rather than this steady crescendo of light.) And beyond that again to the vision of the ultimate good. We must take it for what it is. At the same time we may wish that we could find there the makings of a less anthropomorphic center of reality, some radiant, abounding core of being ("It was everything bulging and blazing and big in itself"), rather than the circling light within which *our image* is depicted.

Probably this would not be possible nor is it certain that the poem can teach us the lost art of celebration. "We do not know how to celebrate," Peter Brook said of his dealings with Shakespearean comedy, "because we do not know what to celebrate."[29] Dante's divine comedy speaks abundantly of the "what" but its terms are not ours and we cannot simply take them over. Perhaps what is required is to recover the "how" of celebration without knowing, or knowing only dimly, what there is to celebrate, if anything. As it happens, the text can speak to this question and raise another. At the end of *Purgatorio* 28 Matelda says of the pagan poets who in Parnassus sang the age of gold and its happy state that perhaps they were dreaming of the Christian Garden. These final cantos of the *Purgatorio*, among the densest of the poem for all their early morning splendors, can be read as Dante's attempt to build into an enduring structure poetry's ancient, inextinguishable vision of joy. But poetry, loyal to the bounds of earthly existence even when it remembers the age of gold and its eternal spring, speaks of transitory joy. Pindar's god-given brightness is subject to vicissitude; Milton's paradise is shaped by our knowledge of its necessary brevity and loss. What Dante wants is steady on-and-on-forever joy. The poem tests us fiercely here, challenging a deep if perhaps quite recent (or recovered?) sense that to judge value by duration is unworthy and even vulgar. Despite the pain of loss and death, I can find in myself no desire for permanence, for a state in which things do not pass, since the pain of death is precisely its affront to this existence against which the desire for some other form of existence is an even graver affront. Yet Christian Dante will hear nothing of this and tells us, from his paradise: "It is right that he should grieve without end ["'suffer eternal torment' in Hell," Singleton glosses, lest we take this for a mere *façon de parler*] who robs himself of [God's] love for the love of what does not endure" (15.10-12). The words are hateful, and yet this is how the religious conscience of the West spoke for centuries and a religious reading of this great Christian masterpiece cannot ignore them, even if it must seek to overcome them and struggle to lead back the poem's eternal longings (if only that were possible!) into the clear round and measure of finitude.

For to read this poem should mean to struggle with it, and my complaint against the current approaches is that in different ways they play down the tension between the poem's horizon and our own. The literary (and psychological) approach assimilates the poem far too easily, bringing it into reach by overlooking whatever is alien. To delight in the paradisal imagery of the last third of the *Comedy* and forget the grim infernal soil from which it grows is simply not honest. The scholarly approach recognizes and indeed insists on Dante's distance, but by denying both the text's historicality and our own it eliminates the possibility of any real encounter. This is a poem that should challenge us from first line to last and the supreme challenge or difficulty it now presents I take to be: Will it allow us to find in the Christian pilgrimage the directives for a different but no less religious journey? Would it be possible to interpret the sign-things of this poem so that they no longer point from here to there, from this world to the "true" world, but rather to a different way of human being on this earth? In his reading of a poem by Georg Trakl, Heidegger writes, drawing on an essential line of Hölderlin: "[Trakl] calls the soul 'something strange on the earth.' The earth is that very place which the soul's wandering could not reach so far. The soul only *seeks* the earth; it does not flee from it. This fulfills the soul's being: in her wandering to seek the earth so that she may poetically build and dwell upon it, and thus may be able to save the earth *as* earth."[30]

Could Dante's poem speak to a religious quest of this sort? It is older and no less venerable than his own and may in some form be struggling to reemerge. For if Heidegger's words look back to the earlier piety of Greece, they also look forward to the possibility of recovering, on our ruined earth, a new sense of the holiness of earthly dwelling.

It would be worth putting this antipodal question to the text only if it left the text free to return its own answer. Let Dante strike back at us, as savagely as in the poem he strikes at everything that stands in the way of *his* truth. Let him ask: "Where does this 'holy' you would recover for earthly dwelling come from if not from my holy God? And when you have lost Him altogether, will not the last vestige of the holy vanish from your earth?" Or let him put Nietzsche's question: "You have abolished the true world: what world is left?" And return Nietzsche's answer: "The world of appearance, perhaps? No! With the true world you have also abolished the world of appearance."

What the outcome of this agon would be I do not know. It might not even prove possible. Perhaps the *Comedy*, unlike the other masterpieces of our tradition, is locked so fiercely into its doctrinal armature that it has only one meaning which it must endlessly repeat. And yet surely the attempt is worth making, the attempt to achieve a genuine if partial encounter, before this great central text which presents itself to us as truth is finally handed over to scholarship. And poetry.

V

DARK WITH EXCESSIVE BRIGHT:
FOUR WAYS OF LOOKING AT GÓNGORA

1

It is easier to recover a writer from neglect than to keep him in circulation. I start with this generalization, which will startle no one, as a means of putting a general question, a question that can be pursued in the light of a particular author, Don Luis de Góngora y Argote. After his great initial fame, Góngora passed into the shadows where he remained for about two hundred years. In the earlier decades of this century he came back once more into favor, a process that culminated in 1927 with the celebrations marking the tercentenary of his birth. On May 23 of that year in Madrid three prominent Gongorists publicly committed to the flames all books considered injurious to their author. These Spanish happenings served their purpose: Góngora now stands in the literary histories and on the library shelves as a classic of European poetry. All is well, then. But what life in the world today, in America, does a classic text have? That is the question proposed by my generalization. Who does it belong to? Are some classics now read in ways and places that are the least likely to release whatever it is that makes them worth reading? And of course these general questions raise the specific question: Is Góngora worth reading? What claim does this Spanish poet of the late Renaissance have on the person who is not a professional Hispanist?

These are questions that criticism should take care of, though often it fails to. Perhaps translation which as we all know is a special form of criticism can handle them better. It so happens that two accomplished versions of Góngora's *Soledades* recently appeared, within the space of twelve months: one by E. M. Wilson, professor of Spanish at Cambridge, first published in 1931 and now tidied up here and there;[1] one by Gilbert F. Cunningham, who also translated Góngora's other major poem, the *Fábula de Polifemo y Galatea*, an amateur in the old and honorable sense of the word, a man at home in many languages and literatures.[2]

This is a matter of more than local interest. For modern verse translation, which has brought the ancient world into our time, China hardly less than Greece, and moves easily across the frontiers of Western literacy in pursuit of whatever is being written today, has made little account of the Renaissance. Roy Campbell's remarkable versions of St. John of the Cross apart, this period has not been well served by contemporary translators. Petrarch, the founding father, has proved singularly resistant to the modern manner; the great province of Renaissance epic, Italian and Portuguese, lies well off our poetic trade routes. No poet has been drawn to the *Orlando Furioso*, to the *Gerusalemme Liberata* or *Os Lusiadas*. Even the French have been relatively neglected. If the *Pléiade* is rather out of range at the moment, poets like Théophile de Viau and even more d'Aubigné would seem to have something to say to us. But they have not found their translators. A glance at the contents page of George Steiner's *Modern Verse Translation* (Penguin Books, 1966) reveals no Renaissance work by a writer born in this century (except Campbell).[3]

A failure of translation is always a failure of reading, of sympathy, and there is no doubt that the Renaissance is still under a cloud. The period has not recovered from its nineteenth-century glorification and the various twentieth-century attacks. A variety of scruples, aesthetic, moral, and religious, prevent us from feeling at home in this period which for several centuries provided the Western imagination with one of its standards of excellence, a "golden age." Of the two other traditional golden ages, Augustan Rome and Periclean Athens, the first has probably gone for good, but the second shows signs of surviving the educational changes that have deprived most people of a formal classical training. Even if we are no longer Periclean, Greece is standing up pretty well. The Renaissance is much worse off. At present it is in the hands of professional scholars and popularizers. The scholars address one another and though we may profitably eavesdrop, we know that their communications are not meant for us. The popularizers write those introductions to the Christmas tabletop books in which it seems as though nothing had happened to the Renaissance since the death of Burckhardt. What is lacking is the man in the middle, the middleman or interpreter who can tell us whether this particular golden age has served its turn or whether it still has something to offer. And if so, what.

Since an interpreter is a kind of translator, we are back with the question proposed just now: Why has translation, which has established good working relations with China and the more distant regions of the modern world, been unable to open up communications with the Renaissance? The immediate obstacle is the *language.* Listen to Ezra Pound advising the novice to "consider the definiteness of Dante's presentation, as compared with Milton's rhetoric." ("The great aim is accurate, precise, and definite description," said T. E. Hulme, a famous anti-Renaissance man.) There is of course no valid sense in which Dante is less "rhetorical" than Milton, but we know what Pound means. Although the modern movement in poetry did not, like the modern movement in painting, propose a direct challenge to Renaissance values, nonetheless much that was found objectionable in the literary tradition could be attributed to the Renaissance. "Undoubtedly," Eliot remarked, translating Pound's advice into a more oracular idiom, "there is an opacity, or inspissation of poetic style throughout Europe after the Renaissance." Take a typical modernist manifesto like Marianne Moore's: "the natural order of words, subject, predicate, object; the active voice where possible; a ban on dead words, rhymes synonymous with gusto." And set it against the opening lines of Góngora's *Soledades:*

> Era del año la estación florida
> en que el mentido robador de Europa . . .

At once, an offensive inversion and a dead-looking phrase, "the flowery season of the year" (one can imagine Pound's blue pencil going through that). What hold can the translator get on a poetic style so far removed from his own? The modern movement may itself now be part of literary history, but many of its bans remain in force and still stand in the way of a sympathetic reading of much sixteenth- and seventeenth-century poetry.

The fact that its diction and expressive devices are not felt to be "modern" would in itself not matter—neither are those of ancient Greek or Chinese poetry and yet both are distinctly in fashion—were it not for a curious fact that might repay investigation. There is a body of literature, starting somewhere between the time of *Beowulf* (say) and the *Divine Comedy* and lasting until at least the Romantic period, which seems to resist translation into a contemporary idiom. You may modernize Homer and he still remains Homer, as Christopher Logue has shown. But modernize Dante and still more Racine (as Robert Lowell has shown) and most readers will feel you have destroyed their identity. The poetry of Greece and ancient China is far enough away to be "out of time" and hence has the freedom of time. It can lodge in our own time and talk more or less as we talk. The classical literature of western Europe belongs to its particular point of known, historical time and is apparently disnatured when it is removed from it. In translation at least, Hamlet cannot wear jeans and remain Hamlet.

Dante, nonetheless, is important to us, even if we cannot translate him. We read him, in a way that we don't now read Ariosto or Tasso or Góngora or for that matter Milton, in whom so many of the deepest ambitions of Renaissance poetry assume their grandest form.[4] There is something in all these poets that puts us off. They seem to stand at the wrong angle to the universe. Consider a famous sentence echoed in one way or another by a great deal of Renaissance literature and art: "But man is a noble animal, splendid in ashes, and pompous in the grave." Such pride of utterance has no place in our world. Even Christian humility is easier to take, and certainly the *sermo humilis* of the Middle Ages is nearer our own speech habits that the grand style of so many Renaissance writers. The "rhetoric" to which Pound and others objected is more than a matter of language, yet it *is* a matter of language and of attitudes to language, and it is at this level that I want to look at it. Take these lines of Ariosto, written at the very heart of the period, the "golden age" of Leo X:

Come purpureo fior languendo muore,
che 'l vomere al passar tagliato lassa;
o come carco di superchio umore
il papaver ne l'orto il capo abbassa:

così, giù de la faccia ogni colore
cadendo, Dardinel di vita passa;
passa di vita, e fa passar con lui
l'ardire e la virtù de tutti i sui.[5]

What is striking about the language here is its *adequacy*. Though
the stanza is dense with elect memories, the tone grave and ceremonious, the writing extremely formal, nonetheless the action
and the feelings which the action proposes toward itself fit into
the linguistic encasement as snugly as a young body fits into its
skin. The apparently effortless harmony of the construction (4:4,
with each quatrain again falling into two balancing and related
parts) seems to reflect an equally harmonious relation between
the means of expression and that which is to be expressed, between gesture and emotion. This is, in Hegel's sense, a genuinely
classical poetry. One may say of these lines that they show a
great confidence in language's power to render and "stand for"
human experience. One could also say that it takes a great confidence in life to be able to dispose the bits and pieces of experience into so nobly harmonious a structure. We think differently
about living, and about dying, and as a result feel excluded by
Ariosto's lines. It is hard to imagine that anyone could now
translate them into living poetry.

Move forward some seventy years and listen to another poet,
the young Góngora. He speaks the same language but the accent
has changed:

Ilustre y hermosísima María,
mientras se dejan ver a cualquier hora
en tus mejillas la rosada Aurora,
Febo en tus ojos y en tu frente el día,

y mientras con gentil descortesía
mueve el viento la hebra voladora
que la Arabia en sus venas atesora
y el rico Tajo en sus arenas cría;

antes que de la edad Febo eclipsado

137

y el claro día vuelto en noche obscura
huya la Aurora del mortal nublado;

antes que lo que hoy es rubio tesoro
venza a la blanca nieve su blancura,
goza, goza el color, la luz, el oro.[6]

Wallace Stevens said of the Colleoni statue in Venice that "there, on the edge of the world in which we live today, [Verrocchio] established a form of such nobility that it has never ceased to magnify us in our own eyes." It is however a nobility we cannot now realize, since "the apposition between the imagination and reality is too favorable to the imagination." Verrocchio's noble rider has come to seem "no longer quite the appropriate thing outdoors . . . a little overpowering, a little magnificent."[7] I think we respond to Góngora's poem, if we read it hard enough to make it blaze on the senses, in much the same way. We may admire but we are affronted by its intolerable swagger. Our sense of reality is crushed by this vaulting imagination and we lay the poem aside. Splendid, perhaps, but irrelevant, even damaging, to the business of being alive today. And totally untranslatable.

The obvious difference between this poem and the lines from Ariosto is that Góngora's language draws much more attention to itself. We read badly if we do not respond to the syntactical bravura with which the fourteen-line sentence is composed, the octet built around the two *mientras* clauses, the sestet around the two *ante* clauses, and the two sections related in various ways. To say that the means of expression is becoming more important than that which is to be expressed would be to point very crudely to the fact that, whereas in Ariosto the language relates firmly to an action going on outside itself, the "objects" in Góngora's poem, the lady's cheeks, eyes, and hair, gold, snow, day, and night, have a much less obvious external reference. They belong not to nature (to which the translator, if he used the words that Góngora used, would be bound to relate them) but to the Renaissance poetic tradition. They cannot, since the poem is furiously "about" something—the vision of light beating on some elemental landscape, the horror of that light's eclipse—be called conventional poetic properties and it might seem best to say that Góngora is writing in a more visionary manner than Ariosto. No doubt he is. We could also say that he is already moving toward that kind of poetry which Damaso Alonso had in mind when he suggested, making the point a shade bluntly, that in the *Sole-dades* "nature has become no more than a procession of beautiful names: *silver, crystal, ivory, mother-of-pearl, marble.*"[8] Jorge Guillén said much the same thing in a more impressionistic way when he described Góngora as the kind of poet for whom "language . . . is itself the marvelous goal. All his energy [is] concentrated on exploiting the inexhaustible mine of words. Their potential expressive power lies waiting there for anyone who can utter them; then these words, like a magic incantation pronounced in a rite, will bring about no less an effect than the creation of a world."[9]

In an earlier critical day, it is interesting to note, the language of *Paradise Lost* was described in much the same way though from a different point of view. Milton, F. R. Leavis said, "seems to be focussing rather upon words than upon perceptions. . . . He exhibits a feeling *for* words rather than a capacity for feeling *through* words."[10] Elsewhere in the same essay, comparing a passage from Donne's third satire with some lines from *Lycidas,* Leavis complains that although Milton's words do so much less work than Donne's, "they seem to value themselves more highly —they seem, comparatively, to be occupied with valuing themselves rather than with doing anything." Whatever one may think about the critical adequacy of Leavis's position, he has put his finger on something in Milton's poetry which many people in this century have disliked. What is objectionable is *the way the language behaves.* The words on the page are extraordinarily sure of themselves. Instead of being "the offspring of passion" (to turn Coleridge's distinction to different ends) they seem to have become "the adopted children of power." A similar use of language is found in early sixteenth-century writers like Bembo and Della Casa; it is very marked in Góngora and occurs in one form or another in many of the "Latin-nourished" styles of the time. "What weight and what authority in thy speech," Jonson said of the English antiquary Camden, exactly catching the note. It sounds very strongly in Milton:

> I saw when at his Word the formless Mass,
> This world's material mould, came to a heap:
> Confusion heard his voice, and wild uproar
> Stood rul'd, stood vast infinitude confin'd.

139

Stood rul'd, stood vast. There is a supreme assurance in the echoing syllables. Milton's word behaves as though it were God's, itself imposing order on chaos. The poet's task is always to order experience, but his ordering is felt to be worth little if it has not first submitted to experience, in all its obduracy and variety. What those who dislike Milton's kind of verse miss is the pressure of sensuous particularity forcing the language into shape. Another way of making the same point would be to say that the relation it establishes between the imagination and reality is, in Stevens's sense, too favorable to the imagination.[11]

It may be no accident that most if not all of the writers who use language in this way were influenced by the momentous decision to bring their vernaculars to the "perfection and elevation of Latin," as Góngora put it. Latinization may in itself have brought a different attitude to language. Whatever the Romans felt about Latin, to the outsider it seems to possess a particular solidity, something builded, *architecturé,* which Greek for instance does not possess and which the European vernaculars do not naturally possess. The syntax seems to exert a peculiar control over the things designated by the words. Latin is a monumental language, we say, and the cliché had for the Renaissance mind the special sense that, restored to what was felt to be its proper form, it appeared to be proof against time. It had survived the wreck of the civilization to which it belonged and shown itself capable of preserving from the flux whatever was entrusted to its care. The vernaculars, reformed and made to approximate as far as possible to Latin, could surely share something of the same power. Purged of its imperfections, language does not (as a great modern poet complained) "slip, slide, perish." On the contrary, words may stand for ever, like blocks of marble.

Such a view leads naturally to a great pride in, and of, language. It also suggests a relation between language and reality, or between mind and nature, at the furthest remove from our own. It opens a radical distinction between the matter to be treated and the verbal medium, a distinction implicit in traditional rhetorical theory. Sidney in a well-known passage confessed himself "moved more than with a trumpet" by the old poem of Percy and Douglas, even though it was "so evil appareled in the dust and cobwebs of that uncivil age." How much greater it would be, he thought, "trimmed in the gorgeous eloquence of Pindar." For us such a distinction is critically a scandal and philosophically something worse, and it remains so even after we have listened to Rosemond Tuve warning us that we should not be so naive as to take this old metaphor at its face value. (Style, she explains, provides a "garment in the sense that the flesh is the soul's garment, its bodying-forth or manifestation.")[12] Nonetheless, in one form or another Renaissance poetic theory—whether it distinguished between the sensible and the intellectual world, or between the particular and the universal— assumed that "mere" reality, the immediate stuff of experience, had to be ordered into higher significance before it could be admitted into poetry. It is an assumption that to modern if not to Renaissance eyes bespeaks a great confidence in the mind's authority over nature. Modern poetry starts, in the Romantic period, with the fall from nature, a fall into apartness and hence into self-consciousness, and has devoted much attention to the mind's struggle to return. By an act of knowledge, which is also an act of love, the poet's mind seeks to penetrate "into the confidence of things." in Rilke's phrase, and bring subjective and objective, internal and external, into an "intimate coalescence" that dissolves the distinction between them. This painful distinction vanishes completely when word and thing coalesce so completely that the poem becomes "the cry of its occasion, / Part of the res itself and not about it."

The great interest of Góngora, for the present inquiry, is that his major poems exhibit in the highest degree a use of language which most modern readers have found objectionable. The balance they propose between imagination and reality strikes us as grossly partial to imagination. And the relation between mind and nature, far from suggesting a loving penetration into the confidence of things, looks more like a tyrannous subjugation. And yet, strangely, the literary history of the last eighty years or so lends support to Damaso Alonso's claim (made at a time when Góngora's position in Spanish poetry was comparable to what Donne's then was in English) that "one step further and he would have been the first modern poet." He was found interesting by later nineteenth-century French poets, even if they did not much read him, and Mallarmé's belief that poetry must provide "l'explication orphique de la Terre" offers a suggestive approach to the *Soledades* and *Polifemo*. It is not absurd but merely unhistorical to say of Góngora (as Wallace Fowlie said of Mallarmé)

that "he saw language as a force capable of destroying the world
in order to rebuild the world that it might be interpreted differently."[13] Again, it is possible to read into Góngora's work the
hostility to nature felt by some Symbolists and to imagine him
agreeing with Wilde that "Nature has good intentions . . . but she
cannot carry them out. Art is our spirited protest, our gallant
attempt to teach Nature her proper place." Although in his two
great poems Góngora celebrates the energies of the natural
world with a power unsurpassed in European literature, he is in
one sense not concerned with nature at all but only with the artistic representations of nature found in Greco-Roman and Renaissance poetry. This poetry is his "nature," a secondary nature
providing him with the raw materials from which to fashion yet
another nature, more perfect, more amenable to our instincts.
Working at so many removes from the sensible world, his poetry
ought to be precious, etiolated. Criticism has often found it so.
So no doubt it would be, were it not for something primitive and
elemental and even ponderous which moves there.

It is time to look at the two poems.

2

A young man and a young woman (call them so: Góngora calls
them Acis and Galatea) are alone in the country (in Sicily, the
poem says, a mythological pleasance seen *sous un flot antique de
lumière* by a poet whose eyes are ancient as humanity and full of
learned memories).[14] He is amorous; she is not, as yet, disposed
to yield:

> Entre las ondas y la fruta, imita
> Acis al siempre ayuno en penas graves:
> que, en tanta gloria, enfierno son no breve,
> fugitivo cristal, pomos de nieve.

Acis, in this celestial torment, is like Tantalus, mocked by the
water that slides from his lips, by the apples that elude his grasp.
By a marvelous subversion of the familiar myth, the waves and
the fruit of the first line are Galatea's white body, and become in
the last line, as she pretends to resist and evade him, "fugitive

crystal, apples of snow." Using traditional similes and metaphors in his customary way, Góngora suppresses the tenors, with their unwelcome reference to the everyday world, and concentrates on the vehicles that, freed from their grosser parts and hence at liberty to set up subsidiary relations of their own, create that poetry of the second term which characterizes the *Polifemo* and the *Soledades*. Not of course that this practice is peculiar to Góngora. His contemporary Marino employs it and it is found here and there in much poetry. Eliot's "the river's tent is broken" is a partial Gongorism, so is Virgil's "in lento luctantur marmore tonsae." The oars struggle in water that is smooth and heavy as marble, but since this metaphor is familiar in Greco-Roman poetry, the water need not be named and the oars can be said to struggle "in slow marble." Góngora, however, would have gone one step further and suppressed the oars as well, replacing them with an appropriate metaphorical vehicle, as he did in the line Alonso used to analyze this procedure, where a boat is described as "treading blue crystal with swift feet." In the present passage Góngora takes advantage of the fact that in his literary tradition both water and a girl's body may be compared to crystal and omits all direct reference to Galatea's person. She—her cool, naked body—appears simply as "las ondas," and her breasts (by an easier route) as "la fruta." The living girl has become her attributes—running water, apples, crystal, snow—a flickering sequence of lovely images which woman's beauty has suggested to the Mediterranean imagination. By a similar process of reduction, or *intensification*, Acis vanishes into his mythological paradigm, Tantalus, emblem of eternally unsatisfied desire.[15]

This abstract, rigorously stylized poetry possesses great sensual intensity. The images here suggest, with the utmost economy, the solace to parched lips of flowing, rippling water and cool fruit. What they plainly do not offer is "the reek of the human" and if you insist on that, then Góngora is not your man. The central stanzas of the *Polifemo* present sexuality *à l'état pur*, purged of its grosser accidents. (A floral sexuality, Lorca called it, "a sexuality of stamen and pistil and the spring theft of pollen.") The elements in these lines—wave, fruit, crystal, snow— are derived from the world of nature but they have been transfixed into *words*, and these words, secluded as far as possible from their normal field of reference, have been used to create what is essentially a formal composition. Góngora disintegrates the phenomenal world in order to recompose it (art's final power over nature) in images of elect clarity.

And the *Polifemo* offers examples of an even more radical stylization. Some stanzas before the one I have discussed, Galatea, flying from her lovers, comes to a shady grove beside a spring and lies down:

> La fugitiva ninfa, en tanto, donde
> hurta un laurel su tronco al sol ardiente,
> tantos jazmines cuanta hierba esconde
> la nieve de sus miembros, da a una fuente.

The fact that it is a laurel by which she pauses starts a familiar myth into action. The laurel that "steals its trunk from the burning sun" recalls Daphne who escaped from the hot pursuit of her lover, the sun-god Apollo: just as Galatea is escaping from her lovers. Daphne was transformed into a laurel; Galatea, too, is about to be transformed, first into jasmines and then into snow.

This flowerlike creature now lies down to rest. So an ordinary writer might have put it. But Góngora again suppresses all reference to her person and says instead, keeping to the secondary, metaphorical terms: "She gives to a spring as many jasmines as the snow of her limbs hides grass." That is, probably, she lies down beside the spring and where there once was grass, only snowy jasmines—her white body—are now to be seen. (Some commentators have thought that she gives the *reflection* of her jasmines to the spring.) Acis then appears on the scene and washes his hands in the water. Galatea, hearing the sound made by "the sonorous silver of the stream," at once—but we must have Góngora's words:

> La ninfa, pues, la sonorosa plata
> bullir sintió del arroyuelo apenas,
> cuando, a los verdes márgenes ingrata,
> segur se hizo de sus azucenas.

Showing a lack of gratitude to the green borders of the spring which had sheltered her, Galatea "made herself the sickle of her lilies." That is, Alonso and Vilanova both agree, she got up and

144

thus detached the lilies (of her body) from the grass. This is certainly what happens, but perhaps the image has greater visual energy. Since sickling is a vigorous business, we are surely invited to contemplate the moment when the white flowers fall beneath the blade: to see the abrupt transformation of the still, white surface of Galatea's body into an agitated complex of planes as she not merely gets up but jumps up.

It might be said of such passages that Góngora, by presenting the elements of our visual experience in startlingly new ways, has forced us to see more clearly than we do in ordinary life—or in ordinary literature. There are times, however, when his methods are so extreme that we are tempted to say, not that he makes us visualize more clearly, but that he has created a world that must be visualized differently. Near the beginning of the *Soledades* he describes how a traveler observes in the distance the "brief trembling splendor" of a light that, on closer view, proves to be so large that "a sturdy oak tree lies in it, moth dissolved in cinders":

> y la que desviada
> luz poca pareció, tanta es vecina,
> que yace en ella la robusta encina,
> mariposa en cenizas desatada.

There is, to start simply, the sense that the fire is so big that it makes a tree look as tiny as a moth. More interestingly, the reference to the moth serves to suggest the fire's attractive power which has drawn the traveler to it. Visually, however, a huge log in no way resembles a moth, not even if one does as most translators do and insists, unlike Góngora, on its size (Wilson: "huge butterfly in cinders lay untied"; Cunningham: "as some great moth disintegrates in flame"; Alonso: "deshecha en cenizas como enorme mariposa"). The point is surely that the "vacilante breve esplendor" of the light, when the traveler first saw it, did look like some tiny fluttering creature. (Ariosto says of someone seeing a distant light, "lontan vide un splendor batter le penne" [*Orlando Furioso*, 12.86].) The parallel with cubism, however unhistorical, is hard to resist. Just as a cubist painter takes the separate surfaces or profiles of a three-dimensional object and presents them simultaneously, so Góngora has taken the successive visual images of the fire and, removing them from the chronological sequence in which they were seen by the traveler, presented them in the same moment of time.[16]

In isolation, such passages might seem merely the exercises of a rabidly analogical wit at large in a world of correspondences. But they are not isolated. In Góngora's major poetry, in the *Polifemo* and the *Soledades*, they are almost continuous. Ordinary discourse has very nearly vanished. In a "normal" metaphysical or baroque poet, the reading of God's analogical book and the search for the correspondences hidden there are a means of penetrating the nature of reality and discovering the divine plan. But although in his magnificent later sonnets Góngora shows a grave sense of our mortality which is Christian enough, these two poems make the minimal reference to God's workaday world. The analogies that matter are the analogies between the secondary terms of art with which Góngora builds his poetic universe. And yet, the paradox remains: if he moves away from nature, it is in order to come closer to it. For all the exquisite indirections provided by the great tradition along which he lived, he is celebrating the primal energies of the natural world.

3

In discussing the difficulties of translating Renaissance and later sixteenth-century poetry, I mentioned three interesting performances in this field: Gilbert Cunningham's *Polifemo* and *Soledades*, and the revised *Soledades* by E. M. Wilson. Between them, these translations should show what access we have to Góngora today. If Wilson's success is due to his skill in finding a "present moment" for Góngora, an aspect of his poetry which has some relation to contemporary poetic interests (or did have when his translation was first written, in the later twenties), Cunningham succeeds by writing as though the problem of turning Góngora's gorgeously intricate Spanish into modern English were no problem at all. The explanation is that Cunningham does not write modern English. He has a robust faith in the resources of the English poetic tradition and considerable skill in handling them. The trouble is, of course, that, while Góngora can strike us as "modern," Cunningham belongs unmistakably to an earlier day. And yet there are no octaves in English like the

octavas reales of the *Polifemo* and Cunningham, closely following the literal sense of the original while preserving the tight
weave of the stanza, has brought something new into English. At
the least, someone with no Spanish can get from his version a
fuller sense of how Góngora works than he has any right to hope
for. Here are some lines from the opening of the poem, the por-
tentous description of the Cyclopean landscape which provides
Polyphemus with his appropriate setting and throws its shadows
forward to the paradisal brightness of the central stanzas:

> Where, as it treads on the Sicilian surge,
> Marsala's foot is shod with silver foam
> (Either a vault that houses Vulcan's forge,
> Or serves the bones of Typhon for a tomb)
> Upon an ashy plain pale signs emerge
> From this one's sacrilegious wish, or from
> The other's toil, and there a lofty rock
> Muzzles a cave, whose mouth it seems to block.
>
> For garniture some rugged tree trunks grow
> Round this hard boulder, to whose matted hair
> Even less the cave's recesses seem to owe
> Than to the rock for light and purer air;
> Above the murky den, as if to show
> What black and midnight depths are hidden there,
> A flock of nightly birds defiles the skies
> With ponderous wings and melancholy cries.
>
> Earth, yawning hugely, leaves a dismal space
> Which makes the terror of the countryside,
> The Cyclops, a barbaric dwelling-place.[17]

At its best, Cunningham's version of the *Soledades* has the
same old-world confidence and also considerable grace, as in
this description of a rustic *fête champêtre*:

> Her homely linen Ceres here unrolled,
> Laden with fruit, preserved in hay, so sweet,
> The apples might have been a curb of gold
>   For Atalanta's feet.[18]

The metrical address that showed to such advantage in his handling of the *Polifemo*'s octave stanza does not, however, serve

him so well with the free combination of seven- and eleven-syllable lines Góngora employs in the *Soledades*. Cunningham follows the verse and rhyme scheme exactly, but since Spanish rhyme is much less emphatic than English, his rhyme sounds sometimes fall rather heavily on the ear. More serious, he often makes the mistake of simplifying, and expanding, Góngora's diction and unraveling his tightly woven syntax. Thus he writes of a boat "whitening the surge with frost," whereas Góngora, his eye on the boat's passage, uses only three words: "las ondas escarchando." English can provide three words as good (Wilson has "frosting over waters") and such metaphorical compressions are common in modern poetry. Again, at 1.54-55 ff. Góngora describes country girls dancing beside a stream that, literally, "stole"

> pedazos de cristal, que el movimiento
> libra en la falda, en el coturno ella.

Wilson writes:

> it took...
> The crystal fragments that their movements freed
> Between the skirt and buskin,

whereas Cunningham has the stream (my italics)

> *mirroring*
> *Flashes* of crystal, which the moving knee
> Released between the skirt and buskin.

The water reflects the flashing limbs—a conventional enough picture. But Góngora, who regularly alters the relations between things and elsewhere makes the sea a centaur assaulting the shore, offers something odder: a river, on the way to embodiment, reaching out toward girls who have been turned into statues, into fragmentary sculptured objects. One more example: in an earlier passage from the first *Solitude* (353-355) Góngora speaks of a rustic lover resting his head

> sobre la grana que se viste fina,
> su bella amada, deponiendo amante
> en las vestidas rosas su cuidado.

("...on the fine scarlet that his beloved wears, laying down on the clothed [or worn] roses the cares of love.") Cunningham translates:

> Against the crimson dress his sweetheart wore,
> To find repose for weary limbs and rest
> His amorous yearnings on a rosy bed.

Rather poor verse, I am afraid, and a weak response to the branching implications of the Spanish. "Las vestidas rosas" means *clothed* roses, since the girl's rosy flesh is concealed by her dress, and also *worn* roses, since the dress she wears is read. The hyperbaton that inserts the roses between "cuidado" and its modifier "amante" suggests the way the young couple seem in their amorous fatigue to melt into each other, a typically Gongoresque fusion of abstraction (*cuidado*), artifact (*vestidas*, referring to clothes), and living substance (*rosas*, both flower and flesh). Góngora's Latinate constructions often look pedantic but are really poetic: they evade the fixities of ordinary syntax in a way that is common in classical poetry (in Pindar, above all: the two masters illuminate each other, in the splendor of their formal means and to some extent in their spirit).[19] It is however very rare in traditional European poetry and yet Wilson manages to convey at least a hint of what is going on in the original:

> Upon his loved one's dress of scarlet fine;
> The lover leaving there,
> In roses clad his care.

(Perhaps the rhetorical comma at the end of the second line is a mistake.)

Cunningham's *Soledades* is nonetheless an accomplished performance and it is only the reissue of E. M. Wilson's version which allows one to make this or that complaint. Damaso Alonso described Wilson's translation as "bordering on the miraculous," and even if this is the voice of a foreign scholar rather than a connoisseur of English poetry, it remains true that Professor Wilson has performed a notable service for Góngora. The way to read him is to keep an eye on the Spanish and pause to ask yourself how in the world anyone could translate *that*— and then look across the page to see how much not merely of the

sense but of the poetry Wilson has brought across. Like Cunningham, he is not afraid of archaisms and in his 1965 preface he
imperiously motions away readers who "refuse to tolerate inver-
sions and contractions, thous and thees, 'adust' and 'hydroptic.'"
His use of the last word shows his method to advantage. At
1.108-109 Góngora writes:

> No en ti la ambición mora
> hidrópica de viento,

which Cunningham translates:

> Here is no lust for power,
> No thirst for windy fame.

Wilson, however, keeps both the seventeenth-century wit and
the seventeenth-century word (fortified, perhaps, by the example of his friend William Empson, whose name stands with
Alonso's in the dedication)[20] and translates:

> Here no ambitious care
> Can dwell, hydroptic of the empty air.

Writing in the later twenties, Wilson would naturally have been
conscious of the parallel between the recent Spanish recovery of
Góngora and the full English recovery of the metaphysical poets;
in this sense his translation, when it appeared, was related to
contemporary poetic interests in a way it may not seem to be
today. He writes with an ear on Marvell and makes skillful use
of the final couplet of his Horatian stanza:

> One hundred birds, in crimson leather shod,
> That here, among uncultivated hills,
> Insult the Berber's state,
> Whose garb they imitate.

Even when it stands by itself Wilson's six-syllable line has often a
Marvellian ring, bringing passage after passage to a close with a
perfect cadence, as in this description of two boats racing, one of
Góngora's most astonishing relations between the most remote
beauty (2.61-68):

The greater, frosting over waters, flew;
The lesser with more slothful movement bore
Onward to meet the sea, whose foamy hoar,
    Of the sharp, dark prow had made
The splendid throat of the Peruvian queen,
To whom the South its hourly tribute paid:
    A hundred ropes of pearls.

We have become rather resigned to the thought that verse translation, if it is any good, will play fast and loose with the original.
Wilson shows that it need not do so:

Aquél, las ondas escarchando, vuela;
éste, con perezoso movimiento,
el mar encuentra, cuya espuma cana
    su parda aguda prora
    resplandeciente cuello
hace de augusta Coya peruana,
a quien hilos el Sol tributó ciento
    de perlas cada hora.

4

These three translations, all more handsome than we had any
right to expect, might be taken as the final stage of that great act
of recovery (whose earlier stages included the inspired scholarship of Alonso, Lorca's magnificent essay, and Alberti's third
Solitude) which brought Góngora back to life after two centuries
of neglect. He is, once again, accessible. And of course academically he is now thoroughly respectable. There is no longer any
argument about his work, Alonso remarks in a note, dated 1956,
attached to his forty-year-old essay on the *Soledades*: "He has
been incorporated into the normal framework of European literature." Then Professor Alonso adds three disquieting words:
"That is all" (*Eso es todo*). What exactly does this mean? What
happens to a poet when he is incorporated into European literature?

Ideally, every poem should be read as though it had just been
written. A poet may be capable of reading in this way but most
people cannot and scholarship has to provide enough information to allow us to get the poem into proper focus. R. O. Jones,

in his useful Cambridge paperback, *Poems of Góngora* (1966), pays attention to the poet's relation to his society and finds a contrast between the island paradise of the *Soledades* and the failing world of imperial Spain. "Unless the historical background to Góngora's poetry is borne in mind," Jones tells us, "the poetry loses much of its point." Two questions. First, can poetry of this order ever "lose its point," whatever our historical ignorance? Second, an earthly paradise may always carry an implicit criticism of the corruptions of the real world, but although such criticisms may have been specially called for at this period it is hard to believe that a poet creates a genuine paradise in order to criticize society. In an article in which he develops his argument at greater length, Jones describes the *Soledades*, rather oddly, as "anti-commercial pastoral" and defends the poet against the charge of being an escapist, "a literary playboy writing poetry primarily as a display of literary self-importance" (a charge surely too vulgar to be worth refuting) on the grounds of his supposed concern with "the social evils of his day."[21] The poem, we are told, can be fully appreciated only when it is set against the "seventeenth-century Spanish background of economic decline, excessive urbanisation and contempt of manual work." No. These are doubtless interesting subjects in themselves but by no means a necessary prelude to a reading of the *Soledades*. Filling in the historical background all too easily results in obscuring the poetic foreground.

Scholarship may also have to help us with an author's beliefs. Most of the older literature of Europe was written by Christians; the modern reader may not be a Christian at all and even if he is a believer he may be doctrinally ill informed. He needs help, but possibly not quite so much help as he is getting. If we found ourselves in seventeenth-century Europe we should no doubt be impressed by the degree to which Christianity permeated every aspect of life. Probably we would also find areas where it had not taken hold so firmly, patches of unreclaimed territory that struck us as neutral or even "pagan." We cannot at any rate be sure, and it seems to me that much modern scholarship—innocent perhaps of Christian belief but resolved to be historically minded—makes the mistake of Christianizing the past so completely that it is pushed almost out of reach. This is a recent tendency. The Renaissance, certainly, was once seen, and often admired, as a great moment of liberation from the prison of dog-matic Christianity. We now learn that it was a very Christian period indeed and that although a number of pagan authors may have been printed they were outnumbered by editions of the Church Fathers and other improving writers. The piety of Machiavelli and Leonardo is still, I gather, questionable, but very likely we shall come to think of them as pillars of the Church. Montaigne once seemed a subversive figure and Pascal, who presumably saw some way into the matter, thought him a serious danger to the faith. ("Il inspire une nonchalance du salut, sans crainte et sans repentir" [*Pensées* II.63]). Montaigne's substantial orthodoxy is apparently now well established. Shelley thought that in *Paradise Lost* Milton presented a god who was morally inferior to the devil, but the Milton of much modern criticism is a character so excessively pious that one sometimes wonders how he stole for his poetry the time he would sooner have spent on his prayers. Even Dante has had to be defended from the charge of dangerous thinking. It used to be taken as a great sign of generosity that he did not deprive his damned of all their human virtues and could allow the heretic Farinata to lift up his head "as though he entertained great scorn of hell." A sinner presuming to scorn the hell created by God's love is however too much for the learned piety of our time and a recent critic, the devout Miss Irma Brandeis, sternly warns us that "to scorn Hell when one is in it is to scorn the condition of one's own soul, the source of one's anguish."[22]

In his later sonnets Góngora wrote, very grandly, as a Spanish Catholic Christian, but at the full stretch of his imagination, in the *Polifemo* and the *Soledades*, he created a world of such enormous vitality and self-sufficiency that it leaves no room for the Christian god. ("Góngora, the poet, is not a Christian," Octavio Paz remarks.)[23] This is something that contemporary criticism does not readily tolerate, and Jones attempts to take remedial action. It would not be easy to Christianize these two poems, but where Christ fails Plato will always serve, and Jones discovers that Góngora was influenced by Neoplatonism. Armed with an obscure remark in a letter to the effect that the reader who looks below the surface of the *Soledades* will find something called "la primera verdad," Jones argues that Góngora's "vision of a Nature brimming with life, ruled by a harmony in which all discord is resolved, suggests that his thought had a Neoplatonic cast." This is reassuring news, but there is one difficulty: "True, the core of Neoplatonism—the emanations that radiate from God down, from level to level, through all creation—is absent." If the *core* of Neoplatonism is absent, why does Góngora have to be a Neoplatonist? Serious professional interests are obviously involved, for Jones returns to the subject at the end of the introduction to his edition of the poems. "Perhaps Plotinus can have the last word," he suggests. "Imagining the universe as a tree rooted in its creator, he describes the manifold branching out into all the diverse forms of created things." Since Jones admits that his author may not have known the *Enneads* or any other Neoplatonic treatise, it is curious that the last word should be with Plotinus rather than Góngora. And the difficulty of attributing to Góngora the thought that the universe is a tree rooted in its creator is that, while spending a great deal of time celebrating the abounding foliage of the tree, he omits any reference to its creator, a feature of the Christianized Neoplatonic universe which even this master of indirection would surely not have left out altogether.

The explanation of Jones's attachment to his thesis, I suggest, is that a seventeenth-century poet who writes a poem purporting to lead readers to "la primera verdad" and yet fails to make any mention of God is, academically, a scandal. It is offensive to that historical sense which scholarship prides itself on and which has reached out to claim Góngora for its own. On his recovery he was treated as a modern poet, and Lorca, in his 1927 address, "The Poetic Image in Góngora," speaks of him quite as a contemporary. So more recently did Jorge Guillén, only to be cracked over the knuckles by a reviewer in the *Bulletin of Hispanic Studies*.[24] Góngora has however now been incorporated into the normal framework of European literature and must be provided with an appropriate historical dress. Neoplatonism may not fit particularly well but it serves to cover his nakedness.

Mr. Jones does at least show some enterprise in the way he puts Góngora in his historical place. Some of his colleagues are less ambitious. Alexander Parker, of the University of Edinburgh, remarks in his introduction to Cunningham's translation of the *Polifemo* that "there are few poems more subtly and pervasively erotic," adding quickly, "in the very best sense of the word." Certainly one wants only the very best eroticism. He goes on to say:

Góngora, however, is no neo-pagan sensualist; nor is he an aesthete worshipping beauty through art. His mind was too open to experience for him to do that. Nature and life in this world can be loved but not worshipped, because they are inherently imperfect.

Góngora a neopagan sensualist? Certainly not! He was a well-conducted member of the literary tradition, worthy of being studied at places like the University of Edinburgh. There was however some loose talk of this kind a few decades ago and it is still possible that you, *hypocrite lecteur*, if you do not take the proper precautions, may find that your response to the poem turns *you* into a neopagan sensualist. The claim that, for Góngora, nature and life "in this world" (a Sunday morning reminder of our mortal estate) may be loved but not worshiped "because they are inherently imperfect" does not seem to me to square with the poem as it stands. No demonstration is offered, and after some brief remarks about ugliness and death we are led to a safer theme, the baroque style of the *Polifemo*.

Parker's cautious persuasions are directed against the unsettling claims made for Góngora in the first years of his recovery when his work was praised for its "purely poetic" qualities. He created a world "illuminated not only by the light of day but by its own inner radiance," Alonso wrote in 1927. A world of "*claritas*. Hyperluminosity. Aesthetic light." But aesthetic light fails as life moves toward the shadows, and in recent years Alonso has written less fervently of Góngora. It seems that he has not quite survived the test of time, and Fray Luis and St. John of the Cross now speak more directly. British criticism, without ever having experienced the first raptures, accepts, as we have seen, this more chastened estimate, and in America the poet's fortunes appear to be at a rather low ebb. Elias Rivers, in his introduction to Cunningham's translation of the *Soledades*, complains of "ignorance of Góngora's poetry in the universities of the English-speaking world" and suggests that it should be attributed primarily to "the critical inertia of American Hispanism." Not being an American Hispanist myself I cannot speak to this point, but I wonder if the ignorance of which Professor Rivers complains (I take him to mean that his colleagues and students are not really inward with Góngora) is not simply an instance of what happens to the great literature of the past when it becomes the object of academic study—an instance the more vivid since we can so easily compare the way poets spoke of this author forty years ago with the way the learned speak of him now. After two centuries of exile and a decade or two of glory, Góngora has sailed into his rest. He has entered the tradition: that charnel house where professors grub for bones.

—*This is unjust. And unreasonable. Where else should a dead poet go? What home can he have except the classroom and the library and the books of the learned?*

—He would sooner say *Volito vivus per ora virum.*

—*Men's lips have other words to speak. Besides, Góngora is very difficult. Who will read him except the learned?*

—The *Polifemo* is no harder than *Notes toward a Supreme Fiction.*

—*But Stevens is of our time; he belongs to us. Góngora does not.*

—Yes, that is the question. It should be asked periodically of every old writer. Do we need him? What does he offer that justifies the time it takes to read him?

—*What does Góngora have to offer?*

—I admit . . .

—*A bad start. What do you admit?*

— . . . that his poetry can only speak to someone who has made himself at home in the tradition.

—*So we may talk of tradition?*

—Of course, if we talk properly. To read Góngora, you must first make yourself at home with a good deal of classical and Renaissance poetry, Italian and Spanish. You must be able not merely to identify the mythological allusions but to recapture his way of thinking with myth. You must recognize the figures of rhetoric.

—*And where are these abilities to come from except the classroom and the library and the books of the learned?*

—Certainly. But there is poet's learning and professor's.

—*Say we become learned in poetry. You have merely pushed the question one stage further back, not answered it. What does Góngora have to offer now?*

—I consider his two major poems doctrinal and exemplary to our time.

—*Try to express yourself more plainly.*

—I will do my best. Remember, though, that the critic's true business is with the formal qualities of a poem. If he wants to go on to speak of its value he has to move outside literature, and hence outside criticism.

—*Value judgments are implicit in all good criticism.*

—Stevens said: "The great poems of heaven and hell have been written. The great poem of earth remains to be written." My claim for Góngora is that in the *Polifemo* and the *Soledades* he composed some of the necessary stanzas.

Góngora—the Góngora I am concerned with, the Góngora of the two absolute poems—is remote from us in many ways. His poetry (as Eliot said of Milton) is "poetry at the extreme limit from prose." He does not take our care of the antipoetic, indeed he virtually excludes it, for the ugly here becomes aesthetically beautiful. He does not believe that language is all-encompassing and that any word may belong to poetry. His lexicon is aristocratic, purged, excluding. The balance he sets up between the imagination and reality is, in our eyes, too favorable to the imagination. When he writes of paradise, he seems to write from within paradise instead of making his poetry out of the struggle to return. He does not convey much of the texture of everyday experience and his poetry has little of the reek of the human, for though it is deeply sensual it is a distilled, perfected sensuality. Celebration, at this intensity, burns away the boundaries of individual consciousness; vitality is diffused everywhere and is perhaps stronger in his natural and animal forms than in his human figures. Finally, he demands of us considerable poetic learning of a kind we do not possess, since we have either forgotten his masters or read them in different ways.

Yet in the very daring and extremity of his formal means and his vision of the world there is something that speaks out to us from the seventeenth century, and the Symbolists were not altogether wrong in seeing him as a kindred spirit. The Symbolist movement has run its course, but it is the last great poetic tradition to which we have direct access and we should use our instinctive understanding of its procedures to help us with Góngora.

In his two major poems he sets the scene in the "ever-early candor" (the phrase is his—"el candor primero"—as well as Stevens's) of a Mediterranean paradise. The tone is ruder than in

157

the usual Renaissance idyll and, as Professor Wilson notes, admits earthy, realistic details that were normally excluded. Violence finds a place there and violent death, particularly in the second part of the *Soledades*. This is not a world where the animals live at peace with one another and with man. The old fisherman's description of his daughters' fishing exploits is, at least to modern tastes, distinctly bloodthirsty, and in the magnificent hawking scene the poet stresses the power and cruelty of the greater birds in harshly syllabled lines: "El neblí que, relámpago su pluma, / rayo su garra."[25] And yet, as most critics have seen, both poems are hymns to love and beauty. Violence is present because it is a special form of energy, and death may be admitted because it does not point outside the poetic universe to some other realm but is rather a part of the ceaseless round of life.

There is another unusual feature of this paradise, at least in the *Polifemo*; its part in the unfinished *Soledades* can only be conjectured. Our deepest intuition about the earthly paradise is that it does not last. Milton's title exactly fits our sense of things, and he ministered to an equally profound need by holding out the promise, at least, of a new and better paradise to come, "a paradise within thee, happier far." Without this eschatological hope, the portrayal of paradise, of the good place, must be tragic or profoundly ironic, as it is in *Beowulf* where the building of Heorot serves at once to release the destructive energies of the evil spirit, Grendel. The *Polifemo*, from one aspect, presents the traditional myth of the loss of paradise in its purest form. Góngora's Polyphemus is associated with the sea (like Leviathan and the Mithgarth Serpent) and with the darkness below the earth (like Satan and Typhon). He is a demonic creature who lusts after a goddess of nature and destroys the happiness he cannot know himself. Góngora, however, makes the myth say something very unusual. The *Polifemo* begins and ends with the sea. It begins by associating the sea with the destructive power of the giant (in the *Soledades* too the sea is at first the hostile element from which the traveler escapes); the poem ends by associating it with the gracious marine deity Doris who welcomes Acis, after his death at Polyphemus's hands, as a son-in-law. The sea is the destroyer; it is also the source of all being, the vital continuum to which Acis returns and from which he will obviously emerge to

love Galatea once more and once more be destroyed by Polyphemus:

> Courons à l'onde en rejaillir vivant!

A similar pattern can be observed in the *Soledades,* as in the
beautiful lines about the two swans:

> y mientras dulce aquél su muerte anuncia
> entre la verde juncia,
> sus pollos éste al mar conduce nuevos.[26]

For Góngora, then, paradise is not lost. The *Polifemo,* structurally and through the enforcing suggestions of panic energy
and fertility present in almost every stanza, is a circular poem. It
celebrates a cyclical view of reality, a world of eternal recurrence
in which life is self-fulfilled and self-fulfilling and in which death
is not fearful since it is simply a stage in the ceaseless process of
life. Moreover, there is no fallen world outside the poem to
which man may be exiled and no supersensible heaven to which
he must aspire. With an intensity unsurpassed in European
poetry, Góngora propounds "the minimum fiction, that of the
brilliant earth."[27] *Perhaps this is what he now means* (whatever
he may have meant in the seventeenth century) by "la primera
verdad."

The *Polifemo* and—even in its incompleteness—the *Soledades*
are what Stevens calls poems of the earth. In a secular age, such
work should be understood readily enough. In fact, it may have
been more easily accepted in a Christian period. The traditional
Christian reader, his central concerns taken care of elsewhere,
could give himself to Góngora's vitalistic paradise without fear.
He could always claim that he was merely taking an aesthetic
holiday and would be reporting back for duty on Monday morning. The post-Christian reader is in a more exposed position.
Whether or not he quite admits it, he lays upon literature the
explicatory burden that was once carried by religion. To be inward with a great writer is to run the risk of acquiring a new
theory of life. Hence one has to inquire very closely what that
theory may be. And if the ordinary reader has his difficulties (or
would have, if he tried reading Góngora), the academic reader's

special interests keep him away from any very direct exposure to the texts. I stressed the point, perhaps at undue length, because Góngora's not altogether deserved reputation for desperate obscurity means that he is largely left in the hands of the learned. And because I believe his major poetry is, or could be, so valuable—the value being directly related to the apparent difficulty of its acceptance—that every effort should be made to get it on the better reading lists.

As poems of the earth, the *Polifemo* and the *Soledades* should be able to stand in the direct light of such sentences as these from *Zarathustra:*

> Stay loyal to the earth, my brothers, with the power of your virtue! May your bestowing love and your knowledge serve towards the meaning of the earth! Thus I beg and entreat you.
>
> Do not let it fly away from the things of earth and beat with its wings against the eternal walls! Alas, there has always been much virtue that has flown away!
>
> Lead, as I do, the flown-away virtue back to earth—yes, back to body and life: that it may give the earth its meaning, a human meaning![28]

To this one might add the sentence in which Nietzsche presses on us the "value of the briefest and most ephemeral, the seductive gold glistening on the belly of the serpent *vita.*"

This is heady stuff, of course, and Nietzsche did not altogether or always believe it. He saw deeper in the brief gnomic section from *Twilight of the Idols:* "We have abolished the true world: what world is left? The phenomenal world, perhaps? . . . No! With the true world we have also abolished the phenomenal world." That is, as Hannah Arendt paraphrases: "The sensuous loses its very raison d'être when it is deprived of its background of the suprasensuous and transcendent."[29] And yet poetry remains bound to the sensuous, however devalued, and although Platonists and Christians have tried lecturing it into wisdom, it has across the ages conducted a long, desperate love affair with what the old woman in Euripides' play calls "this thing that glitters on the earth, whatever it is."

The strength of poetry's case is the difficulty of what it proposes, a difficulty compounded by the fact that it seems to be proposing something easy. Christianity has traditionally held that man is naturally attached to this world and can only with difficulty be persuaded to turn his attention to the next one. Nietzsche, and Góngora as I am reading him, thus appear to be offering the easy, natural way. Or perhaps they have been *made* to appear so; this may be one of the Enemy's tricks. For the loyalty to the things of this world which Nietzsche urges upon us, faith in the brilliant here and now, is in fact very demanding, at least after the first ardors of youth. As Christianity realized, it takes a saint to live in the moment, what Kierkegaard called "the moment as eternity." To attribute supreme value to the moment for what it is, not for where it leads to, lays on us the burden of living that moment supremely well. It also seems to deny any purpose to our lives. Man likes to think that his life has a meaning, and this is most easily understood in terms of direction toward a goal. The linear view is comforting: things may be better elsewhere, farther along the line. Remove that goal and substitute for it the absolute present and you are likely to arrive at some version of the hard doctrine of eternal recurrence: live so that you may wish to live this moment again and again. The cyclical view of reality has great aesthetic beauty, particularly when it succeeds in associating man's brief passage with the eternally creating, eternally destroying, process of nature. It speaks directly to those who reject and are rejected by Platonic-Christian transcendence. But viewed coldly as a way of life it calls for more heroism, more resolve, and more joy than most of us can command. Moreover, the brilliant here and now does not, a great deal of the time, seem very brilliant. To the question of Camus's chaplain, "Aimez-vous donc cette terre à ce point?" one has very often to answer no.

The difficulties of preserving loyalty to the earth are heightened by the enemy's skill in showing that such loyalty is really disloyalty to something higher. The older forms of his argument having worn thin, he now presents them in new forms and in recent years he has often been found disguised as a Buddhist. Forgetting that he once found the world good, he is now telling a generation repelled by industrial exploitation that the great obstacle is "materialism" and preaching the renunciation that in the end leads to freedom, what Philip Rieff nicely calls "the Oriental idea of salvation through self-contemplative manipulation." *The wise man becomes weary of the eye, he becomes weary of the knowledge of the visible, he becomes weary of the contact of the visible.* It is a seductive song, but as usual there is a verbal trick. Materialism is now a very rude word, meaning the acquisite itch for a third car, a new and larger refrigerator. (For certain delicate spirits, a French critic remarks, "être matérialiste, c'est avoir un peu de ventre.") But materialism may also be a perfectly respectable belief concerning the goodness of matter.

In a not dissimilar vein the enemy may be discovered repeating the words he once whispered to Hegel and luring us away from the sensible world, which can no longer provide a home for the spirit, into the infinite recesses of *Innerlichkeit*. Come inside with me, he says, sight work is done, the reign of things (that is, materialism) is over. And once he has us inside, in the pure vacuity of the spirit, we are helpless, for that is his hunting ground. We are very much better able to resist when we are out in the open ("Kill us in the light," Ajax prayed to Zeus), attached as closely as possible to the visible, sensible world. Nietzsche saw through the subjective stratagem and counterattacked with the Greeks who, he said, knew how to "stop at the surface, the fold, the skin; to adore appearance; to believe in forms, tones, words, the whole Olympus of appearance! Those Greeks were superficial—*out of profundity!*" The enemy, no doubt appreciating the paradox, is quick to reply that unfortunately the Olympus of appearance is not what it was when the Greeks beheld it. The visible world has been so corrupted that much of it is now genuinely inhospitable to the spirit. And this is true—the enemy often makes use of the truth. The greatest single task that faces us is to recover a sense of the holiness of the forms of the natural world.

What Hegel called "the secularization of spirituality" provides him with another powerful ally. Modern spirituality is "religious" in so fluid a sense that it cannot be called in question since it cannot be defined, and so accommodating that it will keep any sort of company. (We are all "companions of the Holy Spirit," Allen Ginsberg told readers of *Playboy* some years ago; "*everybody* is really inhabited by the Holy Spirit.") Often identified with something called "true Christianity," spirituality is becoming the mark of the superior person, the sign of a rich and interesting inner life. For the less spiritually gifted he has simpler approaches. A few decades ago he was busy recapturing those who had left him for the political god that, predictably, failed. Why not give the Rock of Ages another try? he asked people who by that time were ready to try anything. Another effective device is the announcement that he no longer exists. On the grounds that *de mortuis nil nisi bonum*, it has come to seem uncharitable to dislike Christianity. A gracious old system of belief that once filled the world with beautiful churches and interesting theological doctrines and offered the questing heart a certainty that we, unfortunately, can no longer afford—surely no one could be opposed to *that*? An old-fashioned humanist like William Empson may complain that although "by this time we seem pretty well inoculated against its more virulent forms, . . . it is not sensible to talk about Christianity so cosily as is now usual, ignoring its theoretical evil, ignoring its consequent use of rack, boot, thumbscrew and slow fire."[30] Such outbursts are greeted with relaxed amusement. Poor old Empson! A brilliant man, of course, but quite mad.

My own view is that Empson is right but distinctly too optimistic. The enemy is as active among us as ever and considerably less vulnerable to argument than he used to be. He was once to some extent confined within a body of doctrine which, however impenetrable and contradictory (= paradoxical), could in a measure be understood and hence attacked, at whatever personal risk. He has now shed his incommodious doctrines and can drape himself in any attractive idea that happens to be fashionable. Given the variety of Christian thought over a long span of time and the even greater variety of ways in which neo-Christians now feel free to interpret that thought, it is almost impossible to question any aspect of Christianity without being told that you have not understood its profundity or have failed to appreciate the paradox. You object, on moral grounds, to the doctrine of eternal damnation? "But what has morality to do with it? This is *poetry*, a marvelous way of expressing (negatively, to be sure) the enormity of God's love!" If you complain that Christianity tormented men's sexual lives for nearly two thousand years, you are told that there was nothing Christ cared about so deeply as a vital, healthy sexuality. If you then protest that, this being so, he chose a most curious way of coming into the world, you are told that there is a paradox here which you have not understood. It is impossible to win.[31]

A number of powerful objections to the enemy's activities are nonetheless on record and he has found different ways of dealing with them. Voltaire's attacks are easily made to look rather ridiculous since Christians are no longer allowed to do the things he disliked, such as condemning a boy to death by torture for ridiculing the Virgin Mary. By a very neat stroke, Voltaire's attitude to Christianity has been made to look bigoted. Goethe, who in an unpopular epigram listed Christ (or perhaps Christians) along with bedbugs, garlic, and tobacco smoke as things he could not abide,[32] presents in his major work and even more in his life an ideal of human wholeness and self-sufficiency which leaves Christianity no point of entry. But Goethe is no longer a danger, for he has become a bogus Olympian humanist read mainly by professional Germanists. Nietzsche, although he has been embraced by some Christian existentialists as one of their number, is a more troubling problem. The two best ways of dealing with him are to maintain (a) that he didn't mean what he said or (b) that he did not understand what he was attacking. Jaspers adopts the second line when he remarks, rather too casually, one may feel, that Nietzsche "never penetrated the profundities of Christian theology."[33] Walter Kaufmann prefers the first, more cautious, line. Discussing the question of "Nietzsche's repudiation of Christ," he suggests, amid many agonizing attempts to be tactful, that what Nietzsche "denounces is not sincere Christianity, but insincere Christianity . . . what he proposes instead may well be closer to true Christianity than what he denounces as 'Christian.' "[34]

The problem is less acute today when attacking Christianity is considered unnecessary and/or uncharitable, unscholarly and of course superficial, but the case of Wallace Stevens still deserves note. Stevens writes as that now very rare creature, a convinced atheist. He does not argue; he does something much more damaging, simply saying again and again—with all the persuasive power of a major poet—how good the earth feels when it has been cleared of the Christian god:

It seems
As if the health of the world might be enough.

It seems as if the honey of common summer
Might be enough, as if the gold combs
Were part of a sustenance itself enough,

As if hell, so modified, had disappeared,
As if pain, no longer satanic mimicry,
Could be borne, as if we were sure to find our way.[35]

The lines from Stevens bring us back to Góngora. Both poets can be seen as belonging to the same spiritual tradition. Both composed some of the necessary poetry of the earth; both wrote the words that could help to "restore to the earth its aim and to man his hope" and to lead to "the redemption of reality from the curse laid upon it by the ideal which has prevailed up to now" (*Genealogy of Morals*, II.24). If Stevens matters now, Góngora —less directly—should too.

This may seem a lot to expect from poetry. For has it not rather let us down? We began about a hundred years ago asking it to save us and here we are, as unsaved as ever. Perhaps, although we take it very seriously, we take it with the wrong kind of seriousness. Our critical habits will not allow it to teach, yet poetry, when it is not entertaining (a most proper thing for it to do), is always teaching, is always, in Milton's words, doctrinal and exemplary. When Stevens praises the goodness of a world without the Christian god, we suppose that he must be saying something much more abstruse. Like the allegorists, we disregard the surface (not the verbal surface, which we have been trained to scrutinize, but the declarative surface) for the hidden persuasions that lie beneath. But perhaps this is really what Stevens is saying, with the indirections needed for the reception of so difficult a doctrine.

Poetry cannot save us and yet the poets could do a great deal to redirect our minds and senses back to the proper object of their love. To look for a recovery of natural piety now, when the earth has been profaned apparently beyond redemption, will seem a forlorn hope. And yet eyes schooled by the poets, as they look out on the ravaged landscape of our world, might rediscover there the lineaments of a sacred that man has not made and is not licensed to disfigure or destroy. The very extent of the outrage we are committing might, paradoxically, sharpen our perception of *what* is being violated. The first stirrings must come from us, but the poets could quicken them and provide the forms of worship. All poetry is from the enemy's point of view a profane activity—that is, from the point of view proposed here, a sacred activity—even the poetry that seems to take his side. Poetry is in love with the world, even when it claims to deny it. All true poetry can help in our present need but the poets who could do most are those of the Mediterranean tradition: Homer above all and after him, Pindar. The Mediterranean genius has never withdrawn allegiance from the brilliance of the visible, and even today, despite the violence of an unrestrained and desperate technological assault, natural objects have preserved something of their sacred aspect there. It is significant that Pound, who has done so much to suggest the forms for a recovered natural piety, should have spent his life in Italy.

The claim I make for Góngora is that he belongs to this company. His formal mannerisms, the intense stylization that frightens some readers away, the sovereign power with which he commands every artifice of classical and Renaissance poetry: all this may seem to confine him within his particular historical period. But he uses these tricks of his trade, as no one else did, to present a vision of nature uncorrupted and self-renewing, existing in its own right and its own immortal round. He has little to say about man's fate; he does not unravel our perplexities. Yet in recreating the imagery of paradise, the landscape

del mejor mundo, del candor primero,

he too played his part in the task of redeeming reality from the curse laid upon it by the Enemy.

BIBLIOGRAPHICAL NOTE

Quotations from Góngora are from Damaso Alonso's *Góngora y el "Polifemo"* (Madrid, 1961), and his *Soledades*, 3d ed. (Madrid, 1956).

VI

LEOPARDI: THE POET IN A TIME OF NEED

ἐπάμεροι· τί δέ τις; τί δ' οὔ τις; σκιᾶς ὄναρ
ἄνθρωπος. ἀλλ' ὅταν αἴγλα διόσδοτος ἔλθῃ,
λαμπρὸν φέγγος ἔπεστιν ἀνδρῶν καὶ μείλιχος αἰών.

Pindar, Pythian 8

Tagwesen. Was aber ist einer? was aber ist einer nicht?
Der Schatten Traum, sind Menschen. Aber wenn der Glanz,
Der gottgegebene, kommt,
Leuchtend Licht ist bei den Männern
Und liebliches Leben.

Trans. Hölderlin

1

If Leopardi's poetry does not, in the English-speaking world, quite belong to what a critic calls contemporary literacy, there is some agreement (more perhaps in England than America?) that he is important, an author one "ought" to have read. Everyone has such names on his list and Leopardi probably appears on a number of them. It is not quite easy, though, to get a clear sense of his quality. The poetry, occupying no more than 132 pages in the standard Mondadori edition, reaches out into a large body of prose, much of it not yet translated. Moreover, Leopardi is housed very deeply in his tradition and in his language which, though it has sometimes an angelic candor, can also be very difficult, with a verbal, syntactical difficulty that one does not expect from a poet of the Romantic period. Struggling with these

167

difficulties, the English-speaking reader may miss what matters most because, as Santayana says, "without familiarity with the Italian language and sympathy with the classic temperament it is incommunicable: I mean the poignant accent, the divine elevation of this poet."[1]

Since he lies a little off the main track, it is likely to be chance that directs a new reader to Leopardi. Suppose that a few lines quoted in a critical essay have caught his attention and sent him to the source, *Giacomo Leopardi: Canti*.[2] The poems are arranged in a sequence as considered as that of *The Tower* or *The Winding Stair*, but for today's reader it is an uncomfortable sequence since it begins with nine very formal canzoni which introduce him not so much to Leopardi the great lyric poet as to Leopardi the *grand rhétoriqueur*. Master, by the age of twenty, of the tradition of high Mediterranean lyric, the first poem, "All'Italia," shows him already in full control of the intricate canzone form.[3] It is a stiff, handsome piece, public poetry (Leopardi never quite abandoned, and never fully realized, the classical conception of the poet as *utilis urbi*) full of a patriotic ardor that made his name sacred to the warriors of risorgimento. Its companion, "Sopra il monumento di Dante," has the vices but few of the virtues of "All'Italia"; warmed into life by no community of spirit between the young poet and the laureled bard he commemorates ("O dell' etrusco metro inclito padre"), it has the marble blankness of an effigy in Santa Croce. The third poem, forbiddingly titled "To Angelo Mai on His Discovery of the Manuscript of Cicero's *De Republica*," offers more. Cardinal Mai's scholarly find leads Leopardi to imagine that a series of great figures from Italy's past are returning to life and rebuking its torpid present. This is still ostensibly public poetry but behind the denunciation of Italy's degenerate condition we hear very clearly Leopardi's private despair. He tries artificially to combine the two elements, following the praise of each figure with thoughts on the present, a device that allows him to introduce some of the permanent themes of his poetry. Thus, having praised Columbus, he reflects that the more thoroughly the world is known the smaller and more arid it becomes: "discoprendo, / solo il nulla s'accresce." Only the void—"il nulla," the nothing that haunted Leopardi for so much of his life—grows. Then comes the first poetic statement of an obsessive theme:

> a noi ti vieta
> il vero appena è giunto,
> o caro immaginar.

Truth, once it has appeared, forever denies us the blessed powers of the imagination.

"On the Marriage of His Sister Paolina" is encased in an obdurate rhetoric that makes access difficult, though there is an energy of moral posture one may seek to admire in the way this twenty-three-year-old poet reads his twenty-one-year-old sister a lesson in ancient virtu. And for a moment the rhetorical structure dissolves and the language becomes supple and tender, allowing Leopardi's true voice to sound:

> Eri pur vaga, ed eri
> nella stagion ch'ai dolci sogni invita.[4]

"To a Victor in the Ball-Game" is an exercise in seventeenth-century Italian Pindaricks which the freshman reader decides to skip; perhaps he will also give a miss to the next poem, "Bruto Minore." (Later he reads it and is astounded by this attempt to recover, in a clamorous silver Latin diction and the highly romantic mode that Leopardi's Italian critics are pleased to call "titanic," the violence of antique heroism.)

The reader I am imagining has now traversed twenty-five pages, in the Mondadori plain text edition, and having fought his way through periods that make the tougher passages of *Paradise Lost* sound colloquial is probably deciding that Leopardi is a very special study. Is this poet really one of the great, if somewhat neglected, figures of European Romanticism? Does he belong to the modern world at all? The next poem (the reader decides) will be the test case. It is called "Alla primavera o delle favole antiche" ("To Spring, or on the Ancient Fables"). The first nineteen lines, Leopardi at his most formidably involuted, nearly prove the last straw, but then, just in time, the voice speaks again:

> Vivi tu, vivi, o santa
> natura? vivi e il dissueto orecchio
> della materna voce il suono accoglie?

169

The question, one that other poets of this period were moved to ask, strikes home, and for once the language is perfectly simple despite the Latinism *dissueto* ("and does the unaccustomed ear catch the sound of nature's maternal voice?") which Leopardi was moved to defend in a playful note. The lines that follow—first a Latin picture, then a more romantic picture growing stroke by stroke from Latinate word order—provide a strategic point from which to tackle the difficulties of Leopardi's language (one of his languages, at least), since old poetic resources are being used for what look like new purposes:

> Già di candide ninfe i rivi albergo,
> placido albergo e specchio
> furo i liquidi fonti. Arcane danze
> d'immortal piede i ruinosi gioghi
> scossero e l'ardue selve (oggi romito
> nido de' venti).[5]

If this is difficult, it is not with the difficulty of "Sans marquer par quel art ensemble détala / Trop d'hymen souhaité de qui cherche le *la.*" What is likely to hold up the modern reader is that Leopardi is thinking and feeling in Latin; he sees this scene as Horace might have seen it. One does not need to be "a good Latinist" to enjoy what the poet is doing, but one must at some time have taken pleasure in the disposition of words in a Latin sentence—that "mosaic of words where each word, as sound, as position, as concept, pours forth its power to right and left over the whole":

> iam pastor umbras cum grege languido
> rivumque fessus quaerit et horridi
> dumeta Silvani, caretque
> ripa vagis taciturna ventis.[6]

"This minimum in the range and number of signs which achieves the maximum energy of the signs"—in short, the special Latin virtues that made Nietzsche claim that no poet gave him the same artistic delight that he received from an ode of Horace.[7]

The brief parenthesis ("oggi romito / nido de' venti"), apparently no more than an aside, reveals the direction of Leopardi's thought. The peaks where once immortal feet danced are now

haunted only by the winds. Something is missing. The conclusion of the passage is no less Latinate, but there is a visionary
quality in the writing which suggests, more clearly than before,
that new energies are stirring within the old form:

> ...e il pastorel ch'all'ombre
> meridiane incerte ed al fiorito
> margo adducea de' fiumi
> le sitibonde agnelle, arguto carme
> sonar d'agresti Pani
> udí lungo le ripe; e tremar l'onda
> vide, e stupí, che non palese al guardo
> la faretrata Diva
> scendea ne' caldi flutti, e dall'immonda
> polve tergea della sanguigna caccia
> il niveo lato e le virginee braccia.[8]

What is missing is the power to see these visions. Leopardi is
lamenting, as Keats had done more ambiguously three years
before in *Lamia*, that "cold philosophy" has emptied the haunted
air and banished the poetry of earth, turning the old vital universe into a universe of death. Leopardi, however, is saying this
"in Latin," hence we need to be attentive to the way he says it,
the building of this long periodic sentence out of three cola or
clauses, each with a verb in the past definite tense. The first two
("*udí* carme sonar"; "*vide* tremar l'onda') both employ an infini-
tive construction, though they differ in length and articulation.
With the third colon ("e *stupí*, che...") the construction changes
and expands to encompass the vision of the goddess Diana to
which, though it is not granted him directly, the shepherd boy
responds in the old way, with wonder or awe.[9] Without attending closely to the language and syntax we are likely to miss the
point, and the grave paradoxical wit, of this poem on a great
Romantic theme, the death or absence of the gods. The language
that once celebrated their presence, the dense Latin of an earlier
imagination, is now mourning their absence. Leopardi's classical
learning does not after all disqualify him from membership in
the modern world, even if it makes him come at it obliquely.

In his major poetry Leopardi will find more powerful ways of
expressing this theme. The mythological framework will go, the
Latin armature dissolve and the language become freer and seem

more modern, or perhaps we should say more Greek.[10] The
accent will often be so poignant and sound so personal that we
may not recognize that the theme remains the same.

2

Il passero solitario

D'in su la vetta della torre antica,
passero solitario, alla campagna
cantando vai finché non more il giorno;
ed erra l'armonia per questa valle.
Primavera dintorno   5
brilla nell'aria, e per li campi esulta,
sí ch'a mirarla intenerisce il core.
Odi greggi belar, muggire armenti;
gli altri augelli contenti, a gara insieme
per lo libero ciel fan mille giri,   10
pur festeggiando il lor tempo migliore:
tu pensoso in disparte il tutto miri;
non compagni, non voli,
non ti cal d'allegria, schivi gli spassi;
canti, e cosí trapassi   15
dell'anno e di tua vita il piú bel fiore.

Oimè, quanto somiglia
al tuo costume il mio! Sollazzo e riso,
della novella età dolce famiglia,
e te german di giovinezza, amore,   20
sospiro acerbo de' provetti giorni,
non curo, io non so come; anzi da loro
quasi fuggo lontano;
quasi romito, e strano
al mio loco natio,   25
passo del viver mio la primavera.
Questo giorno, ch'omai cede alla sera,
festeggiar si costuma al nostro borgo.
Odi per lo sereno un suon di squilla,
odi spesso un tonar di ferree canne,   30
che rimbomba lontan di villa in villa.
Tutta vestita a festa
la gioventú del loco

lascia le case, e per le vie si spande;
e mira ed è mirata, e in cor s'allegra.   35

Io solitario in questa
rimota parte alla campagna uscendo,
ogni diletto e gioco
indugio in altro tempo: e intanto il guardo
steso nell'aria aprica   40
mi fere il Sol che tra lontani monti,
dopo il giorno sereno,
cadendo si dilegua, e par che dica
che la beata gioventú vien meno.

Tu, solingo augellin, venuto a sera   45
del viver che daranno a te le stelle,
certo del tuo costume
non ti dorrai; che di natura è frutto
ogni vostra vaghezza.
A me, se di vecchiezza   50
la detestata soglia
evitar non impetro,
quando muti questi occhi all'altrui core,
e lor fia vòto il mondo, e il dí futuro
del dí presente piú noioso e tetro,   55
che parrà di tal voglia?
che di quest'anni miei? che di me stesso?
Ahi pentirommi, e spesso,
ma sconsolato, volgerommi indietro.[11]

Of the two clusters of poems on which Leopardi's fame chiefly depends, the first, the so-called *primi idilli*, was written between 1819 and 1821 when he was in his early twenties (that is, within the period of the nine canzoni which span the years 1818-1822). The muse then left him—this seems the proper expression for a poet so dependent on her visitations—and he turned to prose, to the dialogues or *Operette Morali* most of which were written in 1824 ("A book of poetic dreams, or melancholy inventions and caprices, or an expression of the author's unhappiness").[12] In November 1827 he went to Pisa and at once fell in love with the town. It was the only place that he positively liked. There he began, and finished at home in Recanati, the handful of poems that (though he wrote other great poems of a different kind) give him his place among the supreme lyric poets of the world: "A Silvia," "Le ricordanze," "Canto notturno," "La quiete dopo la tempesta," "Il sabato del villaggio." The poem I have printed was most probably written during this second period but it appears in the *Canti* as the first of the *primi idilli*. By way of introduction we may look at some lines from a poem of the second period, "Le ricordanze," which speak from the region to which all Leopardi's finest poetry belongs:

> Piú non ti vede
> questa Terra natal: quella finestra,
> ond'eri usata favellarmi, ed onde
> mesto riluce delle stelle il raggio,
> è deserta.

The lines are addressed to a girl to whom Leopardi gives the pastoral name of Nerina, poetic sister to the Silvia of another poem of the Pisan period. Whatever light biographical reality these girls possess, they have become purely symbolic figures and what matters about them is that they died young and now bring back, in memory, a season that memory has transfigured. There were two occasions, Leopardi held, when man lived in a vital universe. The first was during the youth of the world, as Greek poetry remembers it for us, the second during our own youth, "since what the ancients were we have all been, and what the world was for some centuries we were for some years, I mean children."[13] So Leopardi wrote in his early polemical essay on Romantic poetry. He continued, recalling the time

when thunder and winds and sun and stars and animals and plants and the walls of our home all seemed friends or enemies, none of them indifferent, none inanimate; when everything we saw seemed somehow to beckon to us and almost to wish to speak [*favellare*] to us; when, nowhere alone, we questioned images and walls and trees and flowers and clouds and embraced stones and sticks, . . . when wonder [*maraviglia*] . . . possessed us all the time. . . . How great our imagination was then, how often and how readily it took fire, . . . how it enlarged small things and adorned bare things and lit up dark things; what living breathing images, what blessed dreams, what indescribable ramblings of fancy . . . what stuff for poetry, what richness, vigor, strength, emotion, delight. I myself recall having had in childhood the sense of a sound sweeter than any heard in this world. I remember how I looked up at shepherds with their flocks painted on the ceiling of my room and imagined a pastoral life so beautiful that were such a life granted to us, this would not be earth but paradise, home not of men but of gods. I would think myself . . . a divine poet could I truthfully recreate in my writing the images I saw and the emotions I felt in my childhood and arouse them, as it were, in other people.

His wish was granted but on the hardest terms. The price of the momentary returns to or intimations of paradise which his best poetry enacts was a condition of exile or loss, loss of all the common good of life. Only from utter destitution could the radiance that once shone on all things shine again.

Nerina, dying in the flower of her youth, returns—in memory. Her native earth sees her no more and is now desolate; yet something remains of her, the place from which she spoke, *that* window. We may think of it as a source. "Speak" is the uppermost meaning, in older or poetic Italian, of the verb *favellare*, but Leopardi has in mind the whole history of this and related words to which he devoted several philological notes in his *Zibaldone* or commonplace book.[14] The primary sense of Latin *fabula* (yielding the verb *fabulari*) is narration, discourse; from this the secondary sense develops of *false* narration or fiction, hence Italian *favola*, fable (and in the form *fola*, which Leopardi uses a number of times, idle fancy).[15] The verb *favellare* remembers this development here and with great concentration expresses one of Leopardi's central themes. What Nerina spoke, from the poet's and the world's youth, are the fables telling of our home in a vital universe that, with the appearance of truth, has become a universe of death. They are now mere fables, or illusions, and yet we live by them. Nerina is dead. That window is empty, the window from which (*onde*) she used to speak or fable and from which (*onde*), now, is reflected only the sad glitter of the stars. Sad, because though they still glitter, the stars have become meaningless points of light. The heavens are as dead as the earth. And yet the source remains and Nerina may in memory return, bringing back the radiant world in which she moved:

> Ivi danzando; in fronte
> la gioia ti splendea, splendea negli occhi
> quel confidente immaginar, quel lume
> di gioventú.[16]

175

Keats wrote in a famous letter: "I am certain of nothing but of the holiness of the Heart's affections and the truth of Imagination—What the imagination seizes as Beauty must be truth."[17] To the first part of this proposition Leopardi would fervently have assented; the second he had sadly to reject. Intellectually he was in most ways a child of the Enlightenment, and he accepted in all its rigor, as truth, the material universe as philosophy since Descartes had fashioned it. Man is lodged in an alien, inanimate world governed by mechanical laws. Wordsworth's filial or marriage bond that relates mind and nature was, as he saw it, one of the illusions or fictions that philosophic truth had forever banished: a blessed fiction without which the spirit languishes and dies, but still a fiction. Imagination, for Leopardi, is a *facoltà ingannatrice,* an organ of deception that tells us beautiful lies about reality; it has been implanted in us by a kindly nature (later he took a darker view of nature) which wishes us to think of it as a means to knowledge, a *facoltà conoscitrice.*[18] This war between truth and the imagination's fictions is Leopardi's most obsessive theme; he never develops it, and never leaves it. A character in one of his dialogues says:

> I never cease to deplore...the study of that wretched cold truth, knowledge of which is the source of indifference and sloth, or of meanness of mind, wicked actions and perverse customs. Whereas on the contrary I praise and exalt those opinions, although they are false, which generate noble, strong, magnanimous, virtuous actions and thoughts that serve the public and private good; those fine and happy imaginings which, even if they are idle, give value to life; the illusions that are natural to the mind; in short, the ancient errors.[19]

Philosophically, and humanly, this is a sterile position, yet Leopardi had the wisdom to seek no speculative solution. He knew that he must live in this impasse; it allowed him to keep faith with his deepest intuition.

Perhaps the first question about "Il passero solitario" (if one may trouble the calm surface of this poem with a question or so) is: What is the relation between the singer, bird or poet, and the scene? We may also have to ask, though clearly the bird is a figure of the poet, what their relation is. The bird, sitting apart from its fellows, fulfills its being through song. Everything it does is entirely natural (48-49). No less naturally the human scene fulfills itself on this joyful occasion. People ring bells and shoot off guns and the young men and women in their holiday best enjoy one another. But surely all this could happen without the presence of the bird (and certainly without the dark figure of the poet)? If so, the thrush is no more than a poetic ornament, even if the other birds do play a part in the plot, as the vehicle of a simile: they enjoy their best season ("pur festeggiando il lor tempo migliore," 11) just as the townspeople do ("Questo giorno, . . . festeggiar si costuma al nostro borgo," 27-28). What the poem provides, on this reading, is a slightly idealized picture of a little country town on a happy festal day. The sad figure of the poet serves to bring into relief the happiness of everyone else.

But according to Leopardi life is not happy now. Man has been separated from nature and is like a tree pulled up by the roots; he has been utterly disnatured ("uno snaturamento senza limiti")[20] and corrupted by the habit of reflection. ("'Tout homme qui pense est un être corrompu,' dice il Rousseau, e noi siamo già tali.")[21] Even though this is less true of country people and peasants, they too suffer from the central corruption of modern times. It does not seem likely, then, that Leopardi is giving us a genre picture of Recanati ("nostro borgo," 28) on the evening of a holiday. Apart from anything else the tone is too visionary for that. And yet the scene is not visionary in the sense of being unreal or insubstantial. The poem presents a complete human world, even though it is done in very few strokes: the little town with its ancient tower and thronged streets, the people in their holiday dress, the fields all around and the distant mountain; we know the time of day and the season of the year. But what reality, what ontological status, does this scene have? The poet might reply in words he used on another occasion: "je ne le considérais pas d'après ce qu'il était; je le contemplais dans mon imagination."[22] In that event we could say that although there really is such a place, with festivals of this kind celebrated there, the poet's imagination has recreated it, bringing to its depiction something that the scene does not in itself possess. This recreative power is of course one that poets of the Romantic period often claim for the imagination. Coleridge writes in the "Dejection" ode:

> Ah! from the soul itself must issue forth
> A light, a glory, a fair luminous cloud
> Enveloping the Earth—

For Coleridge, imagination really has this power. For Leopardi, it does not. The function of the *caro immaginar* is to clothe with its beautiful fictions a reality that philosophic truth has left forlorn and loveless. Is that how we should see this scene, as an "inanimate cold world" lit by a luminous but illusory cloud issuing from the poet's soul? The question had better be left open for the present.

We have anyway been forgetting that there is another poet or singer here, the bird, who seems to belong to the scene in a much more direct way. The bird is a figure of the poet, resembling him but also contrasted with him. The bird simply sings. The poet does not sing; he grieves and reflects. What is the relation between bird and poet?

The bird is a figure of the poet not as he is now but as he once was. Once, the poet stood open to things, and sang. This happy adhesion, however, has become impossible since things no longer speak (*favellare*) to us; hence the modern poet cannot do what poets did in earlier ages of the world, imitating nature in such a way that they seem to be transporting natural objects directly into their verse, so vividly that as we read we seem to see and feel the things they have imitated.[23] Man today is cut off from nature, and the poet, feeling this alienation more keenly than other men, has grown reflective and sorrowful. Poetry must now be written against the grain, at very high cost; it may not even be possible anymore. And yet the poet, as poet, must still sing; or rather, part of him sings while another part watches himself sing and wonders at the song. For the poet's is now a divided consciousness; there are two poets, separated by an ironic distance. The relation of bird to poet enacts, by the simplest and most traditional of means, the new complex situation of poetry in modern times.

No less economically, the opening lines establish the bird as a figure of the traditional poet and tell us certain things about his vocation which are true for the modern poet in a different, more painful sense. The tower on which the sparrow perches is ancient, and literary allusion at once associates him with older singers: with Petrarch ("Passer mai solitario in alcun tetto / non fu quant'io," *Rime* 226) and with the psalmist ("Vigilavi et factus sum sicut passer solitarius in tecto," Psalms 102, 8). The bird sings "finché non more il giorno," until day dies (the first of the poem's many references to the passing of time), in another allu-

sion, to a famous passage from Dante.[24] Dante's lines are the
vehicle of a submerged simile whose tenor is the poet's pilgrimage to God. The pilgrim leaves his native place to go on a journey required by his Christian calling; it is a momentous departure but one that his culture fully understood and accepted. He
still feels a momentary sadness as he hears his familiar church
bell ring (wasting nothing, Leopardi picks up this bell, "squilla,"
at 29) and his heart is moved, "intenerisce il core." Leopardi bor-
rows this phrase too, but it is not at once clear to what end.
Whose heart is moved? It cannot be the bird's; he is too much a
part of nature for that. It must be the poet's since he is the only
center of consciousness in the poem. But what is it exactly which
moves his heart to tenderness as he gazes at (or wonders at—perhaps we should hear Latin *mirari* here) spring shining in the air
and exulting through the fields? (Certainly we should mark the
intensity, emphasized by rhythm, of the two verbs that frame
line 6.) Dante's lines tell us: because he is leaving home. In what
sense is that true here? In one sense it has always been true of the
poet who must stand aside from the immediate business of life,
contemplating it at a necessary distance in order to turn it into
song. Homer understood this. The detachment of the bard singing of the Trojan War at the remote Phaiakian court is thrown
into a relief that is already potentially ironic by the presence of
Odysseus, who played a painful part in the events that for the
bard are simply matter for distanced song. The traditional poet's
detachment, however, was felt to be as unforced as that of the
singing bird, or of Dante's pilgrim, whereas the modern poet's
pilgrimage, still required of him by his calling, is performed at
heavy human cost. It is not so much pilgrimage as bitter exile,
and using another religious metaphor the poet describes himself
as

> quasi romito, e strano
> al mio loco natio

"almost a hermit, a stranger to my native place." The modern
poet must suffer this estrangement because, as Hegel expressed
it, "during the period of romantic art, the spirit knows that its
truth does not consist in immersing itself in corporeality; on the
contrary, it assures itself of its truth only by leading itself from
the external back into its own internality, positing exterior reality as a form of existence which is inadequate for it."[25] The spirit

may still use the things of the external world but must first impart to them, from its own inwardness, a life they no longer have. Whereas the bird, the old poet, lives in the flesh of reality, his song reaching out into the natural world to which he belongs, the modern poet contemplates nature sadly since he is well aware that he no longer has a home there.

Hegel's words throw light on the theme of exile here; whether they adequately describe the full statement this poem is making remains to be seen. In any event Leopardi was hardly touched by the new thought that had arisen in Germany[26] and had to face the modern situation—the poet's plight in a destitute time—in his own very old Mediterranean terms. The wonder is that his ancient tradition should have been able to provide everything he needed. Let Leopardi, then, describe the poet's exile:

> Being divided from mankind and almost from life itself has this advantage: even though a man is tired of the world, even though experience has enlightened him and put him out of love with human affairs, yet little by little he grows used to gazing at them once more from a distance [mirarle da lungi], whence they appear far more beautiful and valuable than from close at hand. He forgets their vanity and wretchedness and begins to form and almost create the world after his own fashion.[27]

The poet is quite out of love (disamorato) with a world where the blessed fictions have failed and cold truth prevails. There is no place for him there and he withdraws from it. From a distance, however, he gazes (wonders) at it again and finds it beautiful: a world he has formed and almost created from the resources of his own spirit.

Since imagination is an organ of deception, a facoltà ingannatrice granting neither knowledge nor truth, this world that the poet "almost" creates is then a fiction? The question must still remain open.

With the second movement the poem turns, on the word oimè, alas, from bird to poet and the action is replayed in human terms, or rather in modern terms. To catch the utter simplicity of the lines addressed to the thrush (12-16),

tu pensoso in disparte il tutto miri . . . ,

a simplicity Leopardi achieved by the hardest of routes, via the rhetorical elaboration of much of his earlier work, it may help to recall the lavish eloquence that Shelley directed at his skylark. There is certainly, in Leopardi, a superior tact (talking to birds, even in a poem, can be faintly ridiculous), but more important is the wonder, even awe, with which he contemplates the old un-selfconscious absorption in the poetic task, the singer so vanishing in his song that he *is* the song, whereas (17-26) the modern poet, even though his acts are so similar, is eaten up by hopeless regrets, bitterly aware that his calling requires him to desolate his life.

"Passo del viver mio la primavera" (26), the passage ends, exactly balancing but with how different an intonation the conclusion of the lines to the thrush ("cosí trapassi / dell'anno e di tua vita il piú bel fiore").

The next section (27-35), on the festa itself, paralleling but not contrasting with the description of the freewheeling happiness of the other birds, begins with yet another reference to time passing: "This day which is now yielding to evening." The scene is not described; a few details suffice to present it: the bell sounding through the clear air, the reverberation of distant shots, the young people coming on to a dance step in the two seven-syllable lines followed by the energetic line in falling (dactylo-trochaic) rhythm framed by its two verbs which show them leaving their homes and scattering through the streets, then the long slow wondering vowels of line 35 bringing the passage to a close.

The central action of this poem which so insists on time's passing is the festa. The festal day is now yielding to evening but another one will dawn. The young people who celebrate it will grow up and grow old and die, but they will beget children who will celebrate their festal days. The festa, a recurrence that has its being in becoming, holds its celebrants in a stance we feel to be timeless.

The festa is an emblem of the work of art. Works of art, however, poems, are made by poets who live in time. Leopardi is on to an old painful paradox—the stone image survives after its maker has crumbled to dust; timeless beauty is created by a being immersed in the temporal flux—but he gives it his own twist: the modern artist is subject to time in more than its usual rigor for his work demands that he give up the common good of life, the ordinary joys that mitigate the cruelty of time's passage.

He must go into exile; his art can grow only from suffering and loss.

So (36 ff.), a shadow falling across this innocent joy:

Io solitario . . . .

Greek might signal the abrupt disjunction by asyndeton. A poet like Laforgue would introduce his mournful person with a stroke of self-mockery, but that is not Leopardi's way. The irony that shapes his structure must not be allowed to disrupt the verbal surface, which must be seamless, classical. The final passage of this movement (36-44) develops and brings into full focus the first seven lines of the poem (recalled by verbal echoes, *solitario*, *alla campagna*) which laid the ground for the theme of exile without yet stating it. The poet turns his back on the festa and walks out into the fields. Lines 39-44, the second part of a sentence starting at 36, are the most intensely written in the poem and are worth taking very slowly. Though Leopardi's mastery of the periodic sentence may, in the early canzoni, sometimes seem no more than technical virtuosity, here it serves purely poetic, thematic ends. The syntax first. We see quickly that "guardo" is the object and that the construction is "il sole mi fere il guardo," the sun strikes (literally, wounds) my gaze. But the word order suggests a second construction whereby "il guardo steso nell'aria aprica" is a genitive or ablative absolute, a clause in indefinite time standing loose from the rest of the sentence which records a temporal process. Temporal and timeless, then, interact in the syntax too. But there are more important things to notice. The poet's gaze is "steso" (stretched) into the air. Bickersteth's "straining against" may be going too far, but there is certainly tension here: a tensed, even adversary, relation between this stretched gaze and the sun that strikes (wounds) it. The opening lines of the poem propose a very different mind-nature relation, the old graceful adhesion to things when the spirit could still immerse itself in the flesh of reality. The bird sang to the open country and the harmony of its song wandered through the valley. Looking at the countryside in its springtime joy the heart (of the separated poet) was moved to tenderness, and perhaps there is a hint of the same mood in the adjective *aprica*. Roman writers, in prose as well as verse, use *apricus* of gardens or hills or fields exposed to the sun; in Italian the word is poetic and is often used when nature is seen in its happiest light—the blond serenity of fulfilled summer, as in Ariosto's lovely stanza ending:

> Quinci il gran mare, e quindi ne l'apriche
> valli vede ondeggiar le bionde spiche.[28]

The sun, as it sets, strikes on the poet's gaze and seems to say something ("par che dica")—*seems*, because the elemental powers no longer address us directly as they did in youth, the world's and our own. And in fact what the sun is saying or seems to say is precisely that the time ("il giorno sereno") of the old communion between mind and nature is ending. These lines, which sound so personal, are more than a lament for the poet's wasted youth. They mourn the passing of a blessed season in the life of the world.

The final movement begins:

> Tu, solingo augellin . . .

Leopardi often turns in this way and very tenderly once more addresses a personage in the poem.[29] In translation these words say nothing. Why are they so moving in Italian? This is hard to discuss but something must be said about the continuous linguistic miracle, of a kind hardly found elsewhere, which marks Leopardi's best writing. He often praised Italian for not abandoning its old resources (as he thought French was doing) and claimed that many words found in the Italian classics could still be used with no affectation and in such a way that they sound quite natural and are immediately comprehensible even to the reader who has no idea of their provenance. He compared such words to fruit preserved in wax which emerges, long after its season, as fresh and vividly colored as though it had just been picked.[30] Here, the word *solingo* (found, e.g., at *Purgatorio* 1.118, "noi andavam per lo solingo piano") is quite archaic; so too is *augello* (in place of *uccello*) which acquires a further slight patina of age from the omission of the last letter of the diminutive. The effect of this language, which is constant in Leopardi,[31] is that while the themes of his poetry are timely the diction appears at once timeless and charged with centuries of life and feeling. His old/new words sound as pliant and natural as the words of everyday speech, yet with none of its contingent triviality.

The poem ends by bringing the bird, which occupied the first movement, and the poet, occupying the second, into a relation that reveals the distance between the two singers. For one, a graceful apartness; for the other, bitter exclusion. The desolate final lines spell out the full extent of the sacrifice now demanded by art, as the poet looks ahead to a time when his vital powers will have failed and he will see behind him only the ruin of his life. However remote Leopardi's early canzoni may seem from the modern world, his mature poetry is governed by great Romantic themes that in one form and another carry through the nineteenth century and into the twentieth.

In his youth the poet moves in a radiant world he is so much a part of that he knows his blessedness no more than do the young people celebrating their festa. To know or possess this blessedness he must first lose it and then, through some rebirth of the spirit, recover it, a rebirth that will be followed by a death of the spirit, whether temporary or permanent. Leopardi's was a lucid mind and he charted these ups and downs carefully. In 1825, from the period of poetic silence which followed the *primi idilli*, he wrote: "This is the first time I grieve at having said farewell to the muses, or rather I grieve that they have entirely abandoned me, leaving my mind cold and occupied only by ennui and melancholy."[32] The rebirth that granted his greatest poems came at Pisa and from there, in February 1828, he wrote to his sister: "I have here a certain delightful road that I call *road of memories*; I stroll there when I want to dream with open eyes." And a few months later: "This April I have written some verses, verses really in the old way [*all'antica*] and with that heart I once had."[33] He had in fact just completed the poem, the first of the Pisan cycle, which formally announces the news of his recovery. This seems a fair way to describe "Il risorgimento," a far too schematic program poem in an elegant, artificial meter Leopardi borrowed from Metastasio and never used elsewhere.[34] Ten neatly packed *strofette* record the various stages of the death or lifeless stupor of his spirit, ten more little strophes record its rebirth:

> Meco ritorna a vivere
> la piaggia, il bosco, il monte;
> parla al mio core il fonte,
> meco favella il mar.[35]

Coleridge's "Dejection" ode (which Leopardi had certainly not read) comes to mind again, one of the clearest statements in Romantic poetry of "the dependence of nature's life on the inner life of man":[36]

> O lady! we receive but what we give,
> And in our life alone does Nature live:
> Ours is her wedding garment, ours her shroud!

and the lines that follow. Yet as we saw, the similarity conceals a profound difference. What Coleridge laments is the loss of a proper, innate power, the "shaping spirit of imagination" which actively collaborates with the data it receives from the external world and recreates them into a new whole. Leopardi, however, has no doctrine of the creative imagination, in the Coleridgian or Wordsworthian sense, and what he celebrates here is the return of the illusions—blessed illusions ("sí beato errore," 44)—but still illusions:

> Pur sento in me rivivere
> gl'inganni aperti e noti.

"And yet [though I know the bitter truth about reality] I feel revive within me the illusions, which are now recognized as such." Recognized, but still potent, strong enough to allow imagination to resume its old task of spinning the life-giving fictions around nature which remains exactly as it was: an inanimate cold world governed by mechanical laws.

There should I think be a question of how, from so sterile a position, great poetry could ever arise. It is sometimes said that any position will do so long as the poet entertains it ardently, but before falling back on that dispiriting view I want to look again at a suggestion I made earlier. Leopardi, I said, knew instinctively that he must not seek a way out of the impasse into which his thinking led him, for this impasse allowed him to keep faith with his deepest intuition. This I take to be a sense of irreparable loss. We need a new perspective from which to look at his work.

Any recurrent theme or image may lead to a poet's central region, and we might find the way to a new perspective by noticing how many poems are set on the occasion of a festa or refer to a festa.[37] In "Il sabato del villaggio" Leopardi writes of the evening of the day before the holiday:

> Or la squilla dà segno
> della festa che viene;
> ed a quel suon diresti
> che il cor si riconforta.[38]

The festa, perhaps we may say, is a recurrent occasion when happiness or joy breaks through;[39] it is a kind of public equivalent of the poet's more privileged moments when the $αἴγλα$ shines. This however is merely my own tentative explanation, not Leopardi's. Though an extremely self-conscious poet who endlessly analyzed the themes that drove him, he nowhere explains, to my knowledge, *why* the festa plays so important a role in his poetry. If he were asked exactly what a festa *is*, I suspect he might not have been able to reply. Suppose that we put the question instead to his older contemporary Hölderlin, in whose poem "Wie wenn am Feiertage" ("As on a Holiday") these lines occur:

> Jetzt aber tagts! Ich harrt und sah es kommen,
> Und was ich sah, das Heilige sei mein Wort.[40]

Leopardi has no such word. For Hölderlin, as Heidegger interprets him, the festa (*die Feier*) is not a holiday, a pleasant relief from the week's work, but a holy day, a day (see the second epigraph to this book) when man is transported to a region where his being receives its essential determination, a day when he stands open in astonishment before the inhabitual, the other. The festa is the day when a rift opens in the close-packed set of everyday life and the divine shines through. (The festa is an emblem of the work of art.) But Leopardi knows none of this or rather, perhaps, he cannot say it. To use another phrase of Hölderlin's, in his poetry *es fehlen heilige Nahmen* ("sacred names are lacking"). Leopardi's inherited Catholicism, which he had rejected, gave him no access to a sacred, nor, great Hellenist though he was, could he find one in Greece, for he lacked the new German sense of Greece. The early poem to spring looked back to the time when nature was alive and full of divine presences, but in his mature poetry there are no such presences.

Instead, he speaks poignantly of loss. Loss of the blessed fictions, he explains. I want at this point to make a distinction between the intuition and the explanation, even though the explanation occurs not only in the discursive prose but repeatedly in the poetry, and claim that Leopardi's explanation is not on the same level as his intuition. I want to argue that, because he lacked "sacred names," he cannot truly say what this loss he felt so profoundly was loss *of*.

Perhaps Hölderlin can help. At the end of "The Poet's Vocation" he speaks of the poet standing fearless and, if need be, alone before God "until God's failure helps" (*bis Gottes Fehl hilft.*) Two earlier versions of the enigmatic last line—"so long as the God remains close to us," "so long as the God does not fail"[41] —suggest that the divine "failure" or default is dialectically related to nearness or presence: absence may be a kind of presence. In the seventh section of his elegy "Bread and Wine," after a rapturous vision of the Greek world when man stood open to the divine, Hölderlin turns to the present and speaks this time not of the failure but of the distance of the gods:

> Aber Freund! wir kommen zu spät. Zwar leben die Götter,
> Aber über dem Haupt droben in anderer Welt.
> Endlos wirken sie da und scheinens wenig zu achten,
> Ob wir leben, so sehr schonen die Himmlischen uns.
> Denn nicht immer vermag ein schwaches Gefäss sie zu fassen,
> Nur zu Zeiten erträgt göttliche Fülle der Mensch.
> Traum von ihnen ist drauf das Leben. Aber das Irrsal
> Hilft, wie Schlummer, und stark machet die Not und die Nacht,
> Bis dass Helden genug in der ehernen Wiege gewachsen,
> Herzen an Kraft, wie sonst, ähnlich den Himmlischen sind.
> Donnernd kommen sie drauf. Indessen dünket mir öfters
> Besser zu schlafen, wie so ohne Genossen zu sein,
> So zu harren, und was zu tun indes und zu sagen,
> Weiss ich nicht, und wozu Dichter in dürftiger Zeit.
> Aber sie sind, sagst du, wie des Weingotts heilige Priester,
> Welche von Lande zu Land zogen in heiliger Nacht.[42]

We live in a *dürftiger Zeit*, a time of need or lack, a destitute time when the gods have withdrawn and poets do not seem to be called for. And yet the gods may return. And poets may still have a role. Perhaps their task is to prepare for that return. They are like priests of Dionysos (the *Freudengott*) who travel the earth during this night, a holy night upon which a dawn may yet break.

To suggest that Leopardi's sense of loss points in this direction —to a loss or absence of "the gods"—is (once again) to go against the poet's own account of his work. He was annoyed when a German critic found a "religious tendency" in his writing[43] and maintained that his view of life was grounded in serious philosophic thinking. (". . .étant amené par mes recherches à une philosophie désespérante, je n'ai pas hésité à l'embrasser toute entière.")[44] Let us listen, though, to the way he speaks of his most profound experience, the condition of emptiness which he called *noia* (ennui):

> *Noia* is in some sense the most sublime of human emotions. Not that I believe that the examination of this emotion yields the consequences that many philosophers have thought to derive from it. And yet our inability to be satisfied by any earthly thing or even by the entire earth . . .; to imagine the infinite number of worlds and the infinite universe and feel that our minds and desires would still be greater than such a universe; always to accuse things of insufficiency and nothingness and to suffer the want and the void—this seems to me the best proof of the grandeur and nobility of human nature.[45]

It might almost be Pascal. Certainly it is hard not to put a religious, indeed a Christian, interpretation on such words. Yet Leopardi will not have it. "The sense of the nothingness of all things," he tells us, "and our inclination toward an infinite we do not understand has perhaps a very simple explanation which is material rather than spiritual."[46] This infinite and never fully satisfied desire for happiness arises from amour propre, from the instinct for self-preservation implanted in us by nature.[47] But surely this hand-me-down stuff is quite unworthy of the experience upon which it has been imposed. Leopardi's explanation of *noia* and the sense of devouring nothingness that afflicted him[48] does, however, reach deeper. *Noia* he understood as the desire for happiness *à l'état pur*, neither satisfied nor directly opposed by what contravenes happiness. Poised in this blank interregnum the mind achieves "la cognizione del gran nulla," the knowledge that all is nothing.[49] Leopardi is here trying to describe an experience that again must be called religious, though it points toward Buddhism (I would suppose) rather than Christianity. It comes to expression in the beautiful second section of "La vita solitaria" ("Talor m'assido in solitaria parte . . .") where a series of negatives leads to a region or condition beyond negation, a pure, perhaps blessed, void. What is not, at this intensity, dissolves into what is. Nothingness reveals itself as the other face of being.

Such states of mystical ecstasy are, however, comparatively rare in Leopardi; what concerns me is a different but no less religious kind of experience. Though he has a great deal to say in his prose, and in his poetry too, about *noia* and *il nulla*, what distinguishes his finest work is joy, joy experienced negatively as the absence of joy or, more positively, as the memory of joy: joy that once irradiated the earth like a blessed presence. It may be diffused over a whole scene, as in "Il passero solitario," or concentrated in a single figure, most often the figure of a dead girl. The lines to Nerina from "Le ricordanze" speak of a time when joy shone on her brow, *in fronte / la gioia ti splendea*, and was then lost: *spegneali il fato, / e giacevi.* Joy was extinguished by "fate"; the blessed presence withdrew. Yet not entirely: a devout poet may still discern its afterglow. The same pattern informs the companion poem to Silvia. It begins as memory returns to the time when beauty shone (*splendea*) in her laughing, fugitive eyes as she went about her daily tasks, singing while she worked at the loom, and the young poet paused from his studies to listen to her. The scene, sketched with an even greater chastity of detail than in "Il passero solitario," is in itself quite ordinary. This is everyday life, transfigured:

> Mirava il ciel sereno,
> le vie dorate e gli orti,
> e quinci il mar da lungi, e quindi il monte.
> Lingua mortal non dice
> quel ch'io sentiva in seno.[50]

But soon the golden light, the *aigla*, failed, and with supreme tenderness the poet turns again to the dead girl:

> Tu pria che l'erbe inaridisse il verno,
> da chiuso morbo combattuta e vinta,
> perivi, o tenerella.[51]

Here is Leopardi's central territory: the vision of a momentary radiance, the steadfast mourning for loss. He had to stay close to this loss that was granted him and preserve it as pure loss, hence he could accept no doctrine of the creative imagination which would seem to repair, and in repairing conceal, the loss. A nature that depends for its full being on the inner life of man is a nature that can readily be submitted to the will of man. Better to believe, despairingly, that the answer to the question *vivi tu, vivi, o santa natura?* is no, or that nature's life is illusory, than to prepare the way for devastation. So Leopardi kept faith with his sense of loss, even though he could not say what it was loss of. He tried endlessly to understand his experience in terms of the intellectual schemata he derived from the Enlightenment, but though the front of his mind was lodged there, his spirit silently reached back to more sustaining regions. He was what Valéry said the true poet must always be, *un homme très ancien.*[52] Leopardi's poetry requires us to reject most of what he called his system, and even more firmly must we reject any attempt to read his work as the record of personal suffering somehow transformed into "art." This is religious poetry and requires a religious, though not a Christian, interpretation. Inevitably, in Catholic Italy, his thought and still more the expression of that thought were colored by centuries of Catholic Christianity, but the Christian religion did not speak to the deepest needs of his spirit. What he mourns, and in mourning celebrates, is the lost holiness of earthly life.

3

An early poem, since it does not employ the very moving personal terms that have done something to obscure Leopardi's deepest theme, may help to commend the ontological reading I am proposing. Leopardi excluded it from the first edition of the *Canti* (1831), perhaps on stylistic grounds since the artless naïveté of language he tries for has in it something of the *faux-naif*. Or perhaps, in the Italian way, he thought it insufficiently distanced, too direct a transcription of an actual experience.[53] He seems not to have decided on a title. The poem was first called "Il sogno," then "Lo spavento notturno," and in the 1835 edition it appears among the fragments without a title. The second title seems in fact appropriate enough, for the poem describes something frightening that happens at nighttime. Its form is that of a dialogue between two rustic characters. The first says:

Odi, Melisso: io vo' contarti un sogno
di questa notte, che mi torna a mente
in riveder la luna. Io me ne stava
alla finestra che risponde al prato,
guardando in alto: ed ecco all'improvviso
distaccasi la luna; e mi parea
che quanto nel cader s'approssimava,
tanto crescesse al guardo; infin che venne
a dar di colpo in mezzo al prato; ed era
grande quanto una secchia, e di scintille
vomitava una nebbia, che stridea
sí forte come quando un carbon vivo
nell'acqua immergi e spegni. Anzi a quel modo
la luna, come ho detto, in mezzo al prato
si spegneva annerando a poco a poco,
e ne fumavan l'erbe intorno intorno.
Allor mirando in ciel, vidi rimaso
come un barlume, o un'orma, anzi una nicchia,
ond'ella fosse svelta; in cotal guisa,
ch'io n'agghiacciava; e ancor non m'assicuro.⁵⁴

The poem mourns an irremediable hurt done to man's habitat. It records an astounding loss revealed to the innocent eye of wonder: the loss of something that had always, in all human experience and before man came, been there and now has gone. The most familiar and loved of the heavenly bodies has fallen from its accustomed place and the sky above is bare. The earth too has been despoiled, for as the moon sputters out and darkens it burns the grass around it. The gentle luster that once irradiated the earth irradiates it no more. And yet something remains. A glimmer or a trace of the moon's presence can still be discerned.

In an essay with the Hölderlinian title "Wozu Dichter?" ("Why Poets in a Destitute Time?"), Heidegger wrote: "The destitute time is no longer able even to experience its own destitution. That inability, by which even the destitution of the destitute time is obscured, is the time's absolutely destitute character. The destitution is wholly obscured, in that it now appears as nothing more than the need that wants to be met."⁵⁵ It is the poet's task not to satisfy this need but, on the contrary, to preserve and cherish the sense of need. This has become his highest task. He can offer no consolation, yet in attending to what has been lost and preserving absence as true absence, he holds out a kind of hope. "To be a poet in a destitute time," Heidegger says a little later, "means: to attend, singing, to the trace of the fugitive gods. This is why the poet in the time of the world's night utters the holy." He waits ceremoniously upon the elemental energies and watches over the darkened earth, watching for the first signs of a return he can do nothing to bring about. At most he may help to prepare the conditions for a return. "How could there ever be for the god an abode fit for a god," Heidegger asks, "if a splendor of divinity [*ein Glanz von Gottheit*] did not first begin to shine in everything that is?"[56]

Aber wenn der Glanz, der gottgegebene, kommt ... ἀλλ' ὅταν αἴγλα διόσδοτος ἔλθῃ ...

BIBLIOGRAPHICAL NOTE

Quotations from Leopardi's poems are from *Giacomo Leopardi: Canti*, ed. Niccolò Gallo and Cesare Gàrboli (Turin, 1962). For Leopardi's other works I use the complete Mondadori edition, *Tutte le opere di Giacomo Leopardi*, ed. Francesco Flora: *Le poesie e le prose* (1954), 2 vols.; *Zibaldone di pensieri* (1937), 2 vols.; *Le lettere* (1963). I have also drawn on *The Poems of Leopardi*, trans., with introduction, by Geoffrey L. Bickersteth (Cambridge, 1923). The translation in n. 51 is from *Giacomo Leopardi: Selected Prose and Poetry*, ed. and trans. Iris Origo and John Heath-Stubbs (New York, 1966). The latter is a good introductory book for those who hesitate to tackle Leopardi's Italian directly, since the translations of the poems are faced by the originals.

VII

THE MUSIC OF A LOST DYNASTY:
POUND IN THE CLASSROOM

—Mr. G, you brought up an important point last week which I rather brushed aside, in the bad way we people have. The cognoscenti may have settled it, to their own satisfaction; the general reader has not. You said: Is interpretation of the *Cantos* inevitably arbitrary—a matter of making a lucky guess at what EP may have meant by this or that cryptic allusion? Is the poem—this applies specially to the *Pisan Cantos*—irredeemably private, its logic at best the logic of personal association, so that reading Pound means stitching together a poem of one's own out of bits and pieces that catch one's fancy? I wanted to take Canto 81 this afternoon. The opening lines are as good a place as any to pursue G's question. The passage starts with some classical deities and is thus to some degree in the public domain, but then it seems to withdraw into Pound's own private experience. Why doesn't someone read a few lines and get them off the page? Anyone.

X   Zeus lies in Ceres' bosom
       Taishan is attended of loves
               under Cythera, before sunrise
       and he said: "Hay aquí mucho catolicismo—(sounded
                             catoli*th*ismo)
         y muy poco reliHion"
       and he said: "Yo creo que los reyes desaparecen"
       (Kings will, I think, disappear)
       That was Padre José Elizondo
                 in 1906 and in 1917

or about 1917
            and Dolores said: "Come pan, niño," eat
                                    bread, me lad...

—Thank you, hold it there. G, are you ready to shoot?

G   Well yes, I am. So this Elizondo said something that Pound thought important. But what he says here isn't important, that I can see. We just have to guess at what meaning the whole conversation had for Pound. The single remark may be the hook that brings it all back into his mind. It doesn't bring it into mine.

D   We had Elizondo before, though. That helps—

—First perhaps we ought to look at the lines more formally, structurally. There are three sections or moments. The mythological prelude, in Pound's lyrical, cantabile style. One of the many Pisan dawn scenes. Then Padre Elizondo who in fact says two things, not obviously connected, in Spanish. This is in spoken, colloquial style and so is the third moment, also in Spanish, which consists of only one line.

G   Who is Dolores?

—A Spanish lady, I would think. What about the relation between these three moments? Since there's no punctuation at the end of the lines they just flow into each other. "Before sunrise/ *and* he said..." Why "and"?

D   Doesn't Pound often use "and" to join passages that aren't obviously connected?

—To...?

D   ...make us look for the connection, I suppose. Because there really is a connection—and we've lost it?

—I like that way of putting it. Pound distrusts hypotaxis which by subordinating one element to another disposes them in a hierarchical order which tends to weaken their innate force. Para-

194

taxis is more egalitarian. Though that isn't really the point. Pound's typical manoeuvre is to lay his elements side by side. So in the early poem that has become a demonstration piece he writes:

> The apparition of these faces in the crowd;
> Petals on a wet, black bough.[1]

This isn't an elliptical simile. The petals and the faces don't stand in relation of analogy to each other. The two elements in their full strength, their full right, *confront* each other and interact with each other and together make a statement that couldn't be put in any other way.[2] It's a matter—though Pound may not have seen it at the time—of ceasing to treat things as mere objects to be pushed round by an all-important subject. It means giving *things* back their autonomy.

What are the first three lines of Canto 81 saying, do you think, whatever their bearing on the rest of the passage?

X   Zeus lies in Ceres' bosom. Sky and Earth—the sacred marriage, prefigured by the fertility rites in Cantos 39 and 47. Pound usually says Demeter, not Ceres, doesn't he? Taishan, the sacred Chinese mountain, we've had a good many times. It's—

Miss Q   (*who will speak only once more this afternoon*)...an Italian mountain near Pisa transfigured by a piety Pound learned in China.

X   All right. So Greece and China. Pound is always cutting between them.

—In a dark time we may have to draw on all the world's resources. I am not myself convinced that we have a right to other people's resources; Pound thinks we do. All the same, it's a rather Greek China, isn't it, with those attending loves? Then back to Greece proper with Cythera which could be Aphrodite's island but here must mean the goddess herself. It's odd that Taishan is *under* Cythera. Aphrodite is not a sky-goddess. The sacred mountain, anyway, ringed round by loves, and above them Cythera or Aphrodite. And Zeus lies in Ceres' bosom. A kind of mythological flourish to get the canto going, perhaps. Or perhaps not quite that. And this leads somehow to Padre Elizondo. We've met him before, someone said.

D (*rifling back*) Yes, here he is, in Canto 77. "Padre José had understood something or other . . . / learned what the Mass meant, / how one shd / perform it."

—Did we decide what Elizondo had understood?

H I wrote down something you read from some critic. "Pound approves of church ritual"—Catholic ritual, I suppose that is— "in so far as it retains traces of the older pagan meaning." Then change of style, EP speaking: "The Church in sanity RETAINED symbols, look at Easter shows in Siena Cathedral (Egypt etc.) Ceres, Bacchus. . . . "³

—Does that help here?

H Pound probably means—

—Is Pound speaking?

H OK, he makes this Elizondo say—

—Sorry to be difficult but that still isn't right. We are to suppose that Padre Elizondo really did say this. He is a real man who on two occasions said something to Pound in his own Castilian Spanish. It is a cardinal principle of the poem that the materials it presents must be presented exactly as they are or were. A man's actual words, and as far as possible even the sound of his words, must be reported, the date, location, and so on, must be given. As Pound sees it, this is part of the evidence. Elizondo's is one of the poem's countless independent voices that bring their own independent witness, their tithe of understanding or knowledge or memory.

H Well anyway this character says there's a lot of Catholicism —in Spain and I suppose Italy and places like that—but not much religion. Religion meaning the stuff in the first three lines, sacred marriages and what have you. That's what Pound calls religion. Why he thinks it's preserved in Catholicism I can't imagine. If that's what he does think.

X   All Pound says or the critic says is that Catholic ritual retains traces of the older pagan meaning. No more than that. In Catholic countries there may not be much religion, but there is still a bit and that bit retains traces of the older religion. Is that it?

—Don't ask me, ask the poem. Or rather, let it ask you. If our conversation this afternoon is to lead anywhere, it must be the poem that is guiding us.

G   If this is so important to Pound, why doesn't he keep on with it? The stuff that follows about kings disappearing is a new tack altogether.

—I wonder. Anyway, although Pound is didactic in a way no other important modern writer is, at his best he doesn't tell us what to believe. He presents the scattered elements of something, a belief or usage or whatever, and leaves it to us to put the elements together—with the force of a personal discovery. But I don't in fact think Elizondo's second remark is a new tack. I take it there is a distinction here, between the things we had better keep and those we can afford to let go. In a piece called *Patria Mia* written as early as 1912 Pound said: "One wants to find out what sort of things endure, and what sort of things are transient; what sort of things recur . . ."[4] The enduring / the recurrent / the transient: that triple distinction is in fact a governing principle of the poem. So here: the gods endure, the rites or mysteries recur, whereas kingship is a feature of the political and religious life of mankind which Pound as a republican American feels he can do without.

I see a sufficiently clear line that runs from the mythological prelude to Elizondo on religion, with a parenthetical distinction on the subject of monarchy. What about the third moment, though—Dolores' "Come pan, niño"?

R   (*rather stiffly*) Is it meant as some sort of analogue to Communion? At the Last Supper when Jesus broke bread he said, "Take, eat: this is my body." If that is what Pound has in mind, it's pretty blasphemous.

197

—I think you may be right. Not about the blasphemy, though. Pound wouldn't see it like that and I wonder if you need to.

Well, we have been through the passage in a very provisional way. Why don't we play it over again and try to move around inside it more freely? Anyone.

X   Me again?

—You read very well before.

X   Zeus lies in Ceres' bosom
         Taishan is attended of loves
                   under Cythera, before sunrise
         and he said: "Hay aquí mucho catolicismo—(sounded
                                       catoli*th*ismo)
                y muy poco reliHion"
         and he said: "Yo creo que los reyes desaparecen"
         (Kings will, I think, disappear)
         That was Padre José Elizondo
                       in 1906 and in 1917
         or about 1917
                   and Dolores said: "Come pan, niño," eat
                                       bread, me lad . . .

—Thank you. You read more as though it were a whole this time, not a series of new starts. But if it is a whole, as I suspect, a kind of unit within the poem's continuous movement, the thread that links the mythological prelude to Elizondo must somehow lead on to Dolores. R caught an allusion to the sacrament of Communion there. If that's right, we would expect that what Pound is after is a *trace* of the older pagan truth preserved in the Christian sacrament, a trace of "reliHion"—as in the first three lines, presumably—preserved in "catoli*th*ismo." So that "eat bread, me lad" (let's suppose Dolores is speaking to her son), distantly echoing "Take, eat: this is my body" (Christ speaking to his flock), will somehow be related to Zeus lying in Ceres' bosom.

But are we justified in expecting this? Or are we doing what G here objects to, putting our own arbitrary interpretation on fragments that in themselves are quite hermetic? I suppose we should ask: Has the poem done anything to suggest that we should attribute this sort of significance to bread?

Has it had anything to say about bread at all?

198

H   There is some stuff at the beginning of the previous canto where Pound used the same Spanish phrase, "Come pan, niño."

—Good. I think the first page of Canto 80 may well bear on our present passage.

F   And just before that he said, "an era of croissants / then an era of *pains au lait.*" I thought he was referring to a particular period—I suppose around 1900, since Debussy came in just above. Then there is a line that doesn't make any sense at all: "and the eucalyptus bobble is missing." Then, "Come pan, niño."

—Hold the eucalyptus bobble for a moment. How does it go on?

H   that was an era also, and Spanish bread
                    was made out of grain in that era
                 senesco
                        sed amo.

I grow old but I love, right? Then more about bread and grain, then the Latin phrase again. What the Latin has to do with bread . . .

—Hold the Latin for a moment too, along with the eucalyptus bobble. And you'd better hold those croissants as well. We may need them. While we are at it, is there anything else in the poem about bread?

P   There was something earlier on about wild birds not eating white bread. In Canto 74, page 428 in our edition.

—What was the context?

P   It came just before a kind of religious ceremony, Catholic and Chinese mixed up. Oh, he mentions Mount Taishan there too.

—What do you suppose the birds had against white bread?

P   Supermarket pap, maybe, Italian style. Like in the Usura canto:

with usura, sin against nature,
is thy bread ever more of stale rags
is thy bread dry as paper,
with no mountain wheat, no strong flour . . .

—Very good! The perversion of bread there is part of a multiple
perversion of or sin against nature. The canto ends, you remember, with what Pound sees as sexual perversion,

CONTRA NATURAM
They have brought whores for Eleusis

which he admits in a letter is *"very* elliptical." I don't want to get
sidetracked but perhaps we had better follow this up. As we are
coming to see, the *Cantos* work in a cumulative way. You have
somehow to read the single passage with the whole poem in
mind. Whores for Eleusis, Pound explains, "means that in place
of the sacramental————in the Mysteries, you 'ave the 4 and
six-penny 'ore . . . the degradation of the sacrament (which is the
coition and *not* the going to a fatbuttocked priest or registry
office)."[5] And so forth in one of Pound's rather too rugged epis-
tolary styles. In plainer words, uncorrupt sexual union is a sacrament akin to the sacrament of the sacred marriage that formed
part of the mysteries at Eleusis. If this sounds a bit Henry Miller-
ish, reread Canto 47.

Bear up; I've not lost the thread. It is just that there are so
many threads—one has to be very neat-fingered. I am still on
Canto 81 and the phrase I think may be the key phrase—"Come
pan, niño"—which also turns up at the beginning of 80. We have
discovered that there is a good deal about bread in the *Cantos*.
And that may be proper enough, given the aims of the poem. It
is a poem about building the city and it is a religious poem.
(There's a Poundian "and" for you.) It doesn't talk about "spiritual values"; it teaches us the rudiments, about bread, for instance. It teaches us to honor all the ancient makings of man's
hands which are filled with his sense of the holy. Religious people have always taken bread seriously. Christianity certainly did
and so did the Greeks; you can call bread *Dēmētros karpos* in
Greek, the fruit of Demeter. To find out what we have done to
bread—read Giedion if you want the details[6]—and then to
recover bread, the "sense" of bread, the taste of good bread—

this, Pound would say, is a step toward building the city.

(*X is whispering something to H who smiles*)

May we share it?

X   I was just telling him about this Irish character. Someone asks him how can bread be God and he says, "Well, what else would it be?"[7]

—Good for him. Let's take a harder look at the first page of Canto 80 which, as I have said, seems to bear on our passage from 81. There are several things that we set aside just now. First, that eucalyptus bobble. This I admit is pretty cryptic but a poet has a right to a few such properties. The invaluable Mr. Kenner has preserved the story for us.[8] A eucalyptus tree grows on a hillside above Rapallo. Coming down that way in 1945, flanked by two armed partisans, en route to America, to trial and perhaps death, Pound stooped to pick up a eucalyptus pip and took it with him, in memory of a sacred Italian landscape. In *memory*: that's the key notion, and in fact Pound himself tells us earlier, in Canto 74, page 435, all we need to know: "and eucalyptus that is for memory."
   But what do you suppose the eucalyptus pip is doing here, between croissants and *pains au lait* and "Come pan"?

D   Since the eucalyptus pip is *missing*, it must mean...some failure of memory.

—And what has been forgotten?

D   Perhaps that bread—I don't know how to put this—was once a religious sort of thing...

—We don't have the words for this now, I agree. That is why Pound has to be so indirect, why he can't simply tell us.
   Then there is the Latin, "senesco sed amo," and at the start of the period another Latin phrase, "Amo ergo sum, and in just that proportion." Love as the principle or condition of being—a kind of summation of the hymn to Aphrodite in the previous canto. Love and being; love and aging: an oldish man conscious of time

passed and still in love. *Love and time*, perhaps—love resisting the passage of time.

The third thing I asked you to hold was "an era of croissants." What about those croissants?

P   Crescent-shaped rolls, very nice with fresh butter and coffee for breakfast in Paris.

—Pound and his poem would certainly agree with you. Is there anything else, I wonder?

G   Need there be?

—No, but the poem is working at full pressure in these cantos and seemingly random particulars are coming together, building up. Remember the beautiful line at the end of 74, "So light is the urging, so ordered the dark petals of iron." Pound's favorite image of the rose pattern driven into the dead iron filings by the magnet. But now—so light is the urging—no longer *driven*. The filings, the discrete elements of experience—the dark petals—effortlessly take their place in the pattern. The pattern reaches out and claims them. Not that there aren't still plenty of obdurate particles that don't seem to fit in anywhere, though less than earlier readers found. We are learning to see the poem more clearly. And no doubt there is a certain amount of unreclaimable slag. Pound was writing an entirely new kind of poem and had no way of knowing how much to put in.

But here the informing pattern is at work very strongly, so I'm inclined to take a second look at those croissants. Croissant, from *croître*, *crescere*, is in French the crescent moon, the moon in her increase. There is a lot of lunar poetry in the Pisans. The moon—the moon-goddess, Artemis—is one of the divine presences who come to the poet in his cage. There's the Franciscan "sorella la luna" at the start of 74; the moon as "la scalza" in 76, the barefoot girl whose house has been broken (like Isotta's temple at Rimini and other sacred Italian buildings); the moon appears as the muse in the Poundian ideogram at the end of 77, dancing on a sixpence, bringing things into focus; the moon lights up the Pisan tower and baptistery at the start of 79 which culminates in the hymn to Aphrodite. So as I said I'm inclined to think that Pound's sign-seeking, haruspicating eyes found Artemis and her crescent moon in thoise croissants.[9]

202

And if so, there is likely to be some relation here between Artemis and the other goddess who stands behind the Latin words just above, *Amo ergo sum:* Aphrodite, who was invoked so lyrically in the previous canto. Aphrodite and Artemis . . .

G   It strikes me you're just dragging all this in. Or maybe Pound does mean croissant to suggest Artemis and the moon, but how can we possibly be sure?

—If this were a short poem you would be perfectly right, we couldn't. But the passage doesn't exist in isolation; it asks to be read in the light of other, related passages before and after—

G   Did you say *after*?

—Many long poems work this way. They have a spatial as well as a temporal aspect. Temporally, you move through them and A precedes B; spatially, you see the whole poem spread out before you with A and B simultaneously present. When Milton has Adam and Eve pass "hand in hand" before God in the Garden, he wants us to think of the later scene where those hands will come apart and then, at the very end of the poem, be joined once again.

In this same canto, page 500 in our text, the two goddesses are brought into a clear enough relation. There is a strange allegorical passage—it starts with the eucalyptus pip, I hadn't noticed—about the moon and suffering and different attitudes to suffering. Then at the bottom of the page Pound writes, "At Ephesus she had compassion on silversmiths." "She" is Diana of Ephesus, Artemis; that's in the public domain, or was. Silversmiths I suppose are makers, artists in general perhaps. Pound the artist is the center of consciousness in these cantos. And then, apparently in opposition to Artemis, Aphrodite: "Cythera egoista." The compassionate moon-goddess is somehow set against the merciless power of Aphrodite—*saeva*, he calls her elsewhere, harsh, savage. Then ten pages later the two goddesses are lyrically reconciles or united:

> (Cythera, in the moon's barge wither?
> how has thou the crescent for car?

Daniel Pearlman, who discusses this whole canto very thoroughly in *The Barb of Time*, makes the neat suggestion that the open parenthesis serves as a pictogram for the crescent, croissant moon.[10] Pound has always made full use of the typewriter's resources.

Does this seem to bear at all on the lines from 81 we started out with?

(Silence neither unresponsive nor unproductive)

D   Perhaps it explains why Pound speaks of Taishan "attended of loves under Cythera." Cythera, Aphrodite, is now in the moon's barge—she is the moon. The two goddesses are one. Doesn't the planet Venus at certain seasons appear in crescent form?

—The heavens were very much alive for Pound at Pisa. Another of his recoveries. He hadn't much else to look at.

Does this reconciliation or union of the two goddesses convey anything to us? I don't mean: Can we extract some possible significance from it? Of course we can. I mean: What significance does the poem as it is now developing lead us to expect, to look for? Does it, for instance, suggest the reconciliation of discordant forces or elements in the poem, and hence perhaps account for the new serenity that marks the writing of the later *Pisan Cantos?*

(Silence neither unproductive nor unresponsive)

The moon that grows and wanes speaks elegiacally to us of time's passing and the pain of that passing: the inconstant moon, emblem of time that steals from us what we love. "Man is in love and loves what vanishes," Yeats said. And Pound in an early canto (about a lover who tried artificially to arrest time's passing) said, "Time is the evil. Evil." The evil time is linear time that leaves the past behind in a limbo of dead things. But the poem has from the start been trying to uncover another time, organic or seasonal time whose image is not a line but a circle or perhaps a spiral. (This is the argument of Pearlman's book and a very important one, though it may be he makes it explain too much.) Linear time passes, seasonal time returns.

Time becomes an urgent problem for Pound at Pisa. He real-

izes suddenly that he himself is growing old and that the friends
of his youth are dying one by one. The Pisans are full of elegiac,
heroic rollcalls. Their death enforces the sense of irreparable loss
under which these cantos are written, the destruction of so much
of the Europe that Pound loves, the apparent failure of all he has
struggled for. So against the ruinous action of linear time he sets
the power of memory, memory that overcomes time by preserving what we love. And more than that. Memory shows that the
past is not simply passed, gone. Pound somewhere speaks of the
mind, memory, holding resurgent images. Can anyone remember where that comes?

D   At the start of Canto 76 we have:

> And the sun high over horizon hidden in cloud bank
>   lit saffron the cloud ridge
>   dove sta memora

—A morning scene, an hour or so after the dawn scene in 81.
Saffron, Aphrodite's color, then a phrase from the Cavalcanti
Canzone d'Amore, which was incorporated into Canto 36,
"where memory stands."

D   And this draws on a passage six pages earlier quoting another phrase from that poem—I have a mark in the margin...

—Your Ariadne's thread.

D   ...where he wrote:

> and that certain images to be formed in the mind
>   to remain there
>   *formato locho*...
>   to remain there, resurgent ΕΙΚΟΝΕΣ

And then a bit later, in 76, there's the full statement:

>   nothing matters but the quality
>   of the affection—
>   in the end—that has carved the trace in the mind
>   dove sta memoria

—Wherever the quality of the affection—Aphrodite—is strong enough to carve a trace in the mind, the past is preserved and its content, its images, rise up again and are renewed like the moon —Artemis—who renews herself each month. Or, since the crescent moon suggests growth, say that memories rise from the dark of the mind like flowers from the dark earth.

Memory, then, points to the existence of another kind of time that is not evil, seasonal time. For though it carries us to age and death, it holds everything and brings everything back in its perpetually self-renewing rhythm. But only when love is there. Hence, juxtaposing the two times, Pound writes:

> Time is not, Time is the evil, beloved
> Beloved the hours βροδοδάκτυλος

"Beloved," and *brododaktulos*, rose-fingered, Sappho's epithet for the moon. How gentle the words are. Aphrodite and Artemis: Love and Time...

Perhaps we are almost ready to start reading our passage from Canto 81. We have found how to move inside it fairly freely and let other passages from the poem flow into it. We have found words to say about it and help us understand... Or perhaps only to evade it?

> Zeus lies in Ceres' bosom

The sacred marriage of heaven and earth, someone said, prefigured by the fertility rites in Cantos 39 and 47. Fine, that's the kind of thing Poundian critics are expected to say. Yet what do we know of sacred marriages and fertility rites as we sit here this afternoon in a room in Boston and listen to the traffic go by? Are we simply deceiving ourselves with big words?

X   But you said yourself that the passage doesn't exist in isolation. The first line, for instance, has been... prepared for.

—That's true, yes. One of the special beauties of the *Pisan Cantos* is the way an incomplete phrase is so to say planted and emerges later on, still incomplete, and grows silently in the dark of the poem to emerge eventually in its perfect form.

Q   You mean like "of sapphire, for this stone giveth sleep..."

D   ...which nine pages farther on reappears in part, "for this stone giveth sleep..."

X   ...and then after twenty-four pages emerges fully grown in the couplet that closes a lyrical meditation:

> Her bed-posts are of sapphire
> for this stone giveth sleep.

—What is happening to us this afternoon? It is as though...the poem were taking over, and guiding us. As though we had learned to be silent and let the poem speak through us.

G   Are we supposed to be able to remember single phrases for pages on end?

—Poets do expect this, yes. Not just Pound—Dante, for example. At the beginning of the *Purgatorio* he stands at the foot of the mountain and looks over the southern sea on which no man sailed and afterward returned. And Virgil girds him with the reed of humility, *com'altrui piacque,* as Cato willed. But this same phrase was used earlier on in another context. We remember the great scene in the *Inferno* telling how Ulysses sailed on that sea and how his heroic, arrogant voyage ended in disaster when the waters closed over him, *com'altrui piacque,* as *God* willed. Dante counts on our recalling and juxtaposing the two scenes. So does Pound, though his repeated phrases work differently. They grow in the dark while we aren't watching.

What about the first line of our passage: Zeus lies in Ceres' bosom? X, you said it had been "prepared for."

X   Well, not exactly, but in Canto 77, page 470, there's the line

> so kissed the earth after sleeping on concrete

and then something about Demeter, which is Greek for Ceres. I don't know if that helps.

—I think it does. When Pound first came to the Pisan detention camp they put him in a cage with a concrete floor. After three weeks of this he broke down and was moved to a tent in the medical compound. And in gratitude he kissed the earth. This surely is a humanly understandable gesture, something that any of us might do if we were overwrought and faced with that sort of situation. It is not outside our range, as the sacred marriage is. But then Pound realizes the significance of what he has done and he leaves a space to show that he is moving into a different kind of experience. He blocks it out with one of his verbal ideograms:

> bel seno   Δημήτηρ   copulatrix
> thy furrow

In Italian first, because the fair breast or bosom of earth he has kissed is Italian and must be addressed in her own tongue. Then he gives earth one of her sacred names, the name of the great goddess Demeter. And because sleeping on earth means sleeping *with* earth, if you have that way of looking at things, he adds "copulatrix." This is a mystery—"connubium terrae . . . mysterium," he writes later on—and the mysteries can't be uttered openly; they need their sacred languages which in the West are Greek and Latin.

What about "thy furrow"?

X   There is a line not far from our passage in 81, near the end of Canto 80:

> Demeter has lain in my furrow

—And just before that?

X   with a smoky torch thru the unending
>   labyrinth of the souterrain
>   or remembering Carleton let him celebrate Christ in the grain

—The whole poem, as we've said so often, is governed by the seasonal rhythm of fall and rise, descent and ascent. The lines you have just read are obviously part of an ascent, a ritual that culminates in an ascent. The initiates must pass through a tortuous underground passage, a kind of testing, and at the end they emerge into the light and celebrate the god who has risen in the grain. Pound rather unexpectedly calls him Christ here. From the grain, bread, the fruit of Demeter. Hence Dolores in the next passage can say to her child, "Come pan, niño." And Pound here adds "Demeter has lain in my furrow" because it is the sacred marriage with the earth goddess which makes this possible and grants men the continuing gift of bread.

H   But why *my* furrow? Surely the marriage is between Demeter and Zeus—Zeus lies in Ceres' bosom?

—In his usual way Pound gives us the elements separately, so that we may put the rite together for ourselves. Perhaps it would help, though, to have the whole scenario all in one piece. Where might we hope to find it?

(*D nods a question toward a book he has brought with him*)

Yes, in the work that was so important to Pound and his generation, *The Golden Bough*. A note in my margin says that the passage we want is in chapter 12, near the start of the section called "The Marriage of the Gods." Can you find it for us?

D   This must be it. "In the great mysteries solemnised at Eleusis in the month of September the union of the sky-god Zeus with the corn-goddess Demeter appears to have been represented by the union of the hierophant with the priestess of Demeter—"

—Hence

> Demeter has lain in *my* furrow

The poet is the hierophant who stands in for the god. As hierophant, he shows the sacred event to us, *to hieron.*

D   "The torches having been extinguished, the pair descended into a murky place—"

—Hence

> with a smoky torch thru the unending
> labyrinth of the souterrain

Pound has changed the details a little.

209

D   "...while the throng of worshippers awaited in anxious sus-
pense the result of the mystic congress, on which they believed
their own salvation to depend."

—Mark the detached, scholarly tone of voice. Frazer couldn't
have guessed that fifty years later this primitive belief (should we
call it?) would come to new life in a modern poem. Or perhaps
with part of his mind he would have understood.

D   "After a time the hierophant reappeared, and in a blaze of
light silently exhibited to the assembly a reaped ear of corn, the
fruit of the divine marriage."[11]

—Hence

> let him celebrate Christ in the grain,

remembering of course that corn is British for wheat.
    So this is what Pound is presenting in the lines from Canto 81
and in all the other passages that lead into and prepare for them.
He starts, triumphantly,

> Zeus lies in Ceres' bosom

with the divine union which the rite mimes. It is only *because*
Zeus lies in Ceres' bosom, under Cythera or Aphrodite who is
now at one with the moon-goddess, Artemis: love and time
reconciled in the seasonal rhythm of nature, nature's divinity
recovered and celebrated under the twin signs of love and returning time. It is only *because of* the sacred union of heaven and
earth that Dolores can say, "Come pan, niño." Only now do we
understand what her words mean, all they mean. We had...for-
gotten that to eat bread is to take part in a great mystery. And
yet it is the most homely, everyday thing there is.

P   That's why he calls Demeter Ceres here. Ceres, cereal...

G   Wouldn't it have seemed more everyday to us if he had put it
in English?

—Pound puts it in English too. It has to go in Spanish, to his way of seeing, because it is only in Catholic cultures that traces of the old rites have been preserved and he was always very much concerned with the process of preservation, of transmission. Hence Elizondo's two statements are necessary: Elizondo who had understood what lies behind the Christian sacraments and knew how to distinguish what endures and what recurs from what passes away.

Zeus lies in Ceres' bosom, "Come pan, niño," and the lines between and everything that leads into them from elsewhere: a single sentence enacting the recovered rite, the central mystery "venerable and articulate and complete."

So that's it, then; it all coheres. Everything is perfectly clear. Or perhaps not; perhaps nothing is clear. Perhaps we haven't got it at all. I come back to the question I raised just now: What can the mysteries Pound tries to revive *mean* today? We make our classroom response. Can we do anything more? So much of our work in class, with the older texts specially and Pound's at its best is as ancient as any, is a matter of pretending to respond to things that are altogether outside our experience.

If it were easy to understand what these things mean, Pound would not have had to write the *Cantos*. A great deal stands in our way. "2 thousand years, desensitization" he called it at the end of Canto 92 (and just before that he spoke of "the degradation of sacraments"): two thousand years during which the mysteries meant almost nothing. The Catholic church preserved a trace of them, he thought, but in today's world they are mere mumbo jumbo. We'd be embarrassed even to mention them out of class. So students of the *Cantos* have been forced to take Pound's gods and myths as simply part of the machinery of the poem, matters we suspend disbelief in while we get on with the business of reading, like the vegetation ceremonies that provide part of the machinery of *The Waste Land*.

For Pound they had always been very much more, though perhaps it is only with the *Pisan Cantos* that we see how much more. When these cantos came out in 1948, people who had been ignoring Pound's work for decades were reluctantly forced to admit that he did exist. They even found something there they could latch onto. It is mostly very obscure, they said, but at least he is writing personal poetry, that being the only kind poets are now supposed to write. The Pisans are personal poetry and they aren't, but what is beyond question is that Pound's own tragedy put him at the center of the poem—the center of consciousness—as never before.

D   Can we quite say *tragedy*?

—I think so, by this time, though it's a good question.

D   If he hadn't fallen for Mussolini . . .

—In a desperate time men are driven to desperate measures and a man of Pound's kind may make mistakes that smaller people like ourselves would avoid. I don't think there's any doubt that he was following what he believed to be the good. In any event, there is not much use fighting yesterday's battles.

As I was saying, what his tragedy or disaster meant above all was that his beliefs were tested as never before. In his book-lined study at Rapallo he had said, "I assert that the Gods exist." He had affirmed the life-giving powers of the mysteries, the saving rhythm of descent and ascent. In Canto 47 he had written:

> Falleth,
> Adonis falleth.
> Fruit cometh after.

Now it was Pound who had fallen—into a very convincing, quite unliterary hell. Would he rise again? Does fruit come after? Are the mysteries strong enough to lift up a man on whom the shadow of death has fallen? Do the gods exist or are they simply part of a poet's fancy baggage?

The answer, we may say, is in the 120 or so pages of the *Pisan Cantos*, in the sense that they record a great human victory. Pound does come through. We may put this down to his own personal toughness, an irreducible pigheaded heroism. God knows, I wouldn't want to underrate this. Pound is a great poet, I believe; he was also a very brave man. At the same time what these cantos show is that Pound won through because he felt himself sustained by the powers he had always believed in. He himself went down into the unending labyrinth of the souterrain, a dark night of the soul that left no room for "poetry," for make-believe. And he came up, to look on the eternal elements and a nature once again brilliant with divinity. The army gave him a

patch of ground to lie on and he found Demeter there and celebrated the marriage of Heaven and Earth. It must be the most
astounding breach of military discipline since Coleridge joined
the 15th Dragoons.

And that is not all. The fact that when the test came Pound's
"pagan" beliefs did literally work points to something very
important about these beliefs: they were always strangely, dis-
concertingly literal. We may have stumbled on a feature of his
work which has put so many people off and perhaps holds the
key to it.

You were offended earlier on, R—you're Catholic, I take it—
when you found an analogy to the sacrament of Communion in
Dolores' words about bread. Pound honors the Church for preserving traces of the mysteries, but it is the mysteries themselves
he believes in. The Church has lost their true meaning, their true
form, and that is what Pound wants to recover. The trouble with
Communion, he would say, is that the Church has left out the
sacred marriage! He would say, I believe, that when the founder
of Christianity declared that "except a grain of wheat fall into
the ground and die, it abideth alone; but if it die, it bringeth forth
much fruit"—saying that, Christ was reducing what had been a
sacred truth, the truth of Eleusis, to a mere metaphor, a figure.
Christian poets continued to use the myth of seasonal death and
rebirth as a figure for man's spiritual rebirth. Both Dante and
Milton so use the myth of Persephone. But it is only a figure, not
the literal truth. Hence for the last two thousand years poetry
has had to be polysemous, as Servius said of Virgil and Dante
said of himself and critics say admiringly of every important
modern author except Pound.[12] Poetry has had to point away
from the first, literal level to deeper levels of meaning, to "that
which is signified by the letter," as Dante puts it. The thing,
however concretely rendered, always "stands for" something
else supposedly more important. But Pound is not polysemous;
his first level doesn't point beyond itself. He is therefore not
"complex" and in our critical language this means that he is a
simpleminded fellow, despite the surface complexity of his cultural allusions, though of course he writes very good verse. "The
Cantos are never really difficult," Mr. Alvarez announces, confident that no one in his vicinity will correct him. Pound "says
what he wants very skilfully, and he never has anything very
difficult to say."[13]

Readers have in fact found the Cantos difficult, but the diffi-

213

culty that first confronts them—that surface complexity of cultural allusion—is not the real problem. The allusiveness of *The Waste Land* has not kept people away. I don't want to be facile and say that what is difficult about Pound's poem is its simplicity and yet in a sense this is true. We feel something is missing there; the whole reverberating dimension of inwardness is missing. There is no murmurous echo chamber where deeps supposedly answer to deeps. Not merely does the thing, in Pound's best verse, not point beyond itself: scandalously, *it doesn't point to us.* The green tip that pushes through the earth does not stand for or symbolize man's power of spiritual renewal. And in no way has it been created or half created by man—"processed into an object of consciousness,"[14] so that it becomes part and parcel of a subjective mental activity. It is really there. Later Pound said of another natural phenomenon: "Leaf is a LEAF / that is enough / it has infinite implications. LOOK at it, look at the leaf / dont try to make it into a symbol of something ELSE."[15] The green tip is not symbolic and it's not polysemous. Pound's whole effort is *not* to be polysemous but to give back to the literal level its full significance, its old significance, I would say. That green thrust is itself the divine event, the fruit of the marriage at Eleusis. Persephone is in that thrusting tip, and if man matters it is because he too has a share in that same power, he too is part of the seasonal, sacred life of nature. But only a part.

Meant as literally as Pound means it, this is very hard to take. Not only does it offend against the ways we have been taught to read literature; it is an offence against the great principle of inwardness or internalization that has put man at the center of things and laid waste the visible world.[16] It gives back to the visible world—a world "out there" which is not of our construction nor dependent on our collaboration—an importance it hasn't had for centuries. And in so doing it drastically reduces our importance.

Pound was praised for the new humility he reveals in the *Pisan Cantos*, by critics not specially noted for that virtue. But his humility goes beyond anything they have in mind. Take the passage in Canto 83 where he watches Brother Wasp building his mud house. To say that there is nothing remotely *de haut en bas* about his attitude doesn't sufficiently make the point. What is disconcerting is that Brother Wasp in no sense derives his significance from the inner world of the human observer and is quite as important as he is, rather more so indeed since he is closer to the divine sources, to what Pound calls the process. Listen to the way he celebrates the infant wasp's descent to the earth:

The infant has descended,
from mud on the tent roof to Tellus,
like to like colour he goes amid grass-blades
    greeting them that dwell under XTHONOS   XΘONOΣ
OI XΘONIOI;   to carry our news
        εἰς χθονίους   to them that dwell under the earth,
begotten of air, that shall sing in the bower
    of Kore,   Περσεφόνεια
and have speech with Tiresias, Thebae

Donald Davie in an excellent passage speaks of Pound's "reverent vigilance before the natural world."[17] But there is more here even than that, a solemnity of accent which no other poet, perhaps, could have found for so seemingly humble an occasion. The little creature has been entrusted with the poem's central movement or theme, the Odyssean descent to the underworld to bring up new sources of strength.

Compare if you like Lawrence's poem "Snake." A fine poem. Lawrence is certainly respectful enough yet he is very self-conscious about it and has to assure us he "felt so honoured" that "one of the lords of life" had come to drink at his water trough. The effect is to direct attention to Lawrence, and away from the snake. Whereas Pound can simply disappear. He doesn't tell us what he felt or try to persuade us of the wasp's importance. He lets the solemnity of his verse do that. Unlike Lawrence again, he can honor the nonhuman without feeling the need to rail at his "cursed human education." On the contrary, having celebrated the magnificence of Brother Wasp he at once goes on to celebrate another magnificent act in the distinctively human field of high culture: "Uncle William"—Yeats—composing a poem as "perdurable," as free from the bonds of mortality, as the wasp's building activities. Brother Wasp and Uncle William confront each other, ideogrammatically, and together make a statement that could be put in no other way.

I read you a sentence from Alvarez just now, a typical enough piece of criticism, about Pound never having anything very difficult to say. Alvarez goes on to make his point by contrasting Pound and Eliot. "Ash Wednesday," he says, is obscure (unlike the *Cantos,* that is) "because it demands so much of the reader; preconceptions and obfuscations have to be stripped away in order to follow the delicate unfeigned shifts of feeling and argument." Sometimes it's a help when a critic manages to get things completely back to front. You have all read "Ash Wednesday," I imagine. Apart from the difficulty for the non-Christian reader of having to take Christianity seriously, did the poem make demands on you greater than modern poetry normally does? Didn't you take those delicate unfeigned shifts of what not entirely in your stride? They are almost the minimal requirement of any good writing today. Eliot's poem is "difficult," I suppose, but it's the kind of difficulty we enjoy. It flatters our self-esteem. Pound's simplicity is chastening.

What our weekly conversations have surely shown is that the *Cantos* demand enormously more of us, a departure from our normal ways of thinking about ourselves and the world more radical than most of us are prepared or even able to make. Century-old preconceptions and obfuscations have to be stripped away before one can understand what Pound is saying. To read the *Cantos* means, in his own words, to recover "a lost kind of experience," a lost unity of experience within which the elements that have been separated come together again. So that to eat bread is once more to take part in a great mystery, the marriage of heaven and earth.

Years ago Pound himself put it like this. Writing to a friend about the entrepreneurial activities that consumed so much of his time, he said: "I desire to go on with my long poem; and like the Duke of Chang, I desire to hear the music of a lost dynasty."[18]

Well... What I wanted to do this afternoon was read, and read, a single representative passage in such a way that what at first sight looks a muddle becomes entirely lucid—a lucidity not of our contriving nor imposed on the text by arbitrary interpretation but there *in* the text, waiting for us. Perhaps all I have succeeded in doing is to demonstrate that the *Cantos* are even more impenetrable than you were told when you signed up for this course. Or perhaps not. I can't tell from your patient, polite faces what you are really thinking. There's a way to find out, though. Why doesn't someone read the lines from Canto 81 just once more, and then we'll call it a day.

G   I have a question. If Pound's poetry isn't polysemous, what justification is there for taking those croissants to signify Artemis and the moon?

—You are an invaluable man, G. You have just given us our first topic for next week. And now, who is going to read the lines?

X   Me again?

—You again, yes, I want to hear if you are assisting at a sacred event.

X   Zeus lies in Ceres' bosom
             Taishan is attended of loves
                       under Cythera, before sunrise
             and he said...

BIOGRAPHICAL NOTE

Quotations are from *The Cantos of Ezra Pound* (New York, 1970).

VIII

THE SCANDAL OF NECESSITY

... as far as I can see, we are all very like men forced into
guerrilla tactics—we operate in a terrain over-run by the
enemy—and pretty efficiently administered by him. And
whether we are the kind of chaps who feel inclined to plan
this or that local coup, or whether we feel we must go to
earth with the yellow-skirted Fayes, that the nipping of
our cultural December is a little too much, that a very private and secret labyrinthine life is indicated—in either
case, the words of Professor Ker's *Dark Ages* may be remembered: "But the gods who are defeated, think that
defeat no refutation.'

David Jones[1]

1

Literature speaks of what until yesterday seemed unchanging in
human existence. By literature I mean the whole Western tradition, old and new. Literature today speaks from today's new circumstance and yet the best work of this century still carries the
old message and it is a modern poet who says:

> And whether in Argos or England
> There are certain inflexible laws
> Unalterable, in the nature of music.[2]

Unlike other animals, man is born to no world and must constantly build a world in which he feels at home. Literature is one

of the means by which he builds his world. What agriculture does or once did on the material level, humanizing the earth with patient collaborative toil until alien nature is transformed into the rich works of men, in Homer's phrase, so literature (with the other arts) does on the spiritual level. Greek poetry peoples the empty spaces of earth and sea and air with a company of sacred beings, so that every aspect of the natural world is embodied and named. Dante's similes and incidental descriptions, and before him those of Virgil, combine with the serene vistas against which the painters set their madonnas and saints to create the civilized landscape of Italy where human and natural exist in perfect harmony. Literature, the tale of the tribe in Pound's phrase, records the deeds of the ancestors, their adventures and triumphs, their lamentable falls. It tells us about the place where we live, and the terms under which we live. Constantly it asserts the great polar distinctions through which we have made our sense of things: night and day, life and death, heaven and earth, man and god, man and woman, youth and age, the city and the wild. Mapping our condition, literature speaks of what bounds man's action, necessity (in Greek, ἀνάγκη); it does so even when it is playing and forgets necessity, as in fairy tale or romance. It affirms necessity no less when man is shown violating it as when he is seen humbly or proudly accepting it. Greek poetry, celebrating necessity's final line, ceaselessly reminds man that for all his greatness he is the mortal one.

Literature's old role, its central function in the human artifice, is threatened today because the world of which it speaks seems almost to have vanished. With the enormous increase in man's power, the bounds of necessity have been pushed back so far that much of the time they are hardly discernible. In the West at least, we assume that there should always be enough to eat and a constant supply of more or less drinkable water. Convenient switches turn night into day, provide heat against winter's cold and cool against summer's heat. The natural world has been tamed and policed until it is not much more than a park for the various leisure industries, raw material for the agribusiness. We have almost conquered space, for the automobile, the plane, and now the machines that are putting the nearer planets within our grasp are abolishing distance, as we like to say,[3] and information can be transmitted instantaneously from one end of the world to the other. Time is still intact and so is death, but that terminal

219

event can be significantly if as yet not indefinitely postponed, while the troubles that attend the later stages of our journey to death can be mitigated by a variety of devices, from the hospital's million-dollar technology down to a couple of aspirins. It is true that the full rigor of necessity still prevails in the experience of great pain or great grief, but these are wordless, incommunicable states that take place in private and hence cause no public scandal. Only occasionally does the scandal of our continuing subjection to necessity have to be publicly acknowledged. When a hurricane gathers and advances on the works of men, then for a little we are back in the world of the fathers. Yet even here we are not helpless, for our instruments plot the great beast's progress step by step so that we are ready for him when he strikes. And we are sustained by the thought that he survives only on sufferance. Before long, science will be able to seed the storm clouds and put a stop to the nuisance. Such acts of God as still disrupt the human course of events are felt to be anachronisms.

If the last vestiges of earthly existence as man has always known it disappear, our classic texts old and new will become meaningless. Literature will join nature and necessity on the great scrap heap of history. In the introduction to *The Human Condition* Hannah Arendt touches on some decisive events in the modern world (space travel, automation, science's abandonment of human language for a language of mathematical symbols) and sees them as constituting "a rebellion against human existence as it has been given, a free gift from nowhere (secularly speaking), which [modern man] wishes to exchange . . . for something he has made himself." If there really is such a desire, and much suggests that there is, it may be realizable, given science's seemingly limitless powers. It may be possible to change the human condition almost entirely, modifying man genetically and creating an artificial environment where he will live on his own terms—skinned round by a protective envelope, perhaps, as though on some alien planet. It may prove possible to banish necessity for good and all.

Quite recently, however, there have been a few straws in the wind suggesting that we are not after all heading for the new, man-made future that to many looked so promising, to a few so oppressive. In my first essay I mention the odd appearance in the public realm of the philosopher's word *finite.* It appears that our resources are not, as we had supposed, limitless and that the infinite growth of material consumption in a finite world is not on the cards. Another curious word has turned up, one formally associated more with the religious background to the *Oedipus Tyrannus* than the morning news: *pollution.* It seems that nature will not support us in the expensive life-style we have grown used to and may be preparing to resist, even strike back at, her conqueror. Quite suddenly the great modern project, man's dream of absolute dominion, is showing signs of strain. Take the supposed abolition of distance. One still reads, though not quite so often as one once did, grandiose claims like these: "Men now live in an earth-wide continuous whole where even the notion of distance . . . has yielded before the onslaught of speed."[4] True enough. The Concorde will take you from London to New York in three hours, if you happen to have the price of a first-class ticket. There are faster and faster means of travel but since the cost rises steadily fewer and fewer people are going to be able to use them. One after another the technological easements that were supposed to flow effortlessly into human life, like air and sunlight, are becoming unmanageably expensive. Even a simple nineteenth-century convenience like a cheap, rapid postal service may soon be a luxury that later twentieth-century America can no longer afford.

The joker in the pack is energy. Our entire enterprise depends on a constant, moderately priced supply of primary energy, and it looks as if this life-giving stream is going to dry up. And yet energy is what permits all our triumphs. Until a few years ago we would have taken it for granted that, should one source of energy run out, science in its clever way would provide us with new ones. We are not quite so sure nowadays about the benefactions of science, but all the same we must have more energy and are prepared to risk devastating the planet to get it. First things first. How can we live the good life without enough gas to drive to the end of the road and then back? What else will give us our daily fun?

2

Human conceit leads people to think of the age they live in as especially momentous. All the same there are momentous ages when great structures that seemed proof against time sag and collapse, and there are indications that our society may be heading that way. "We civilizations know now that we are mortal," Valéry wrote at an earlier phase of the modern crisis. "We sense that a civilization is as fragile as a life. The circumstances that would send the works of Keats and Baudelaire to join those of Menander are by no means inconceivable. They are in the newspapers."[5] A few years ago this would have been dismissed as doomsday talk, but the spreading cracks in our fabric discovered and discussed every day suggest that there may be something in it. Despite our almighty powers, we are no longer quite sure that we are going to make it. There is however another possibility that is more important because there is more that we personally can do about it. In the later 1960s when the counterculture was in full swing we heard a lot about the exodus from the big cities; every day, it seemed, pilgrims were setting out for the wilds to discover radical innocence in the sweat of their brows and the shortest possible time. The whole movement was shallow and overpublicized and most of the pilgrims are now back on the nine-to-five circuit. Some remained, though, and the remoter regions of New England are scattered with exiles from megalopolis, making do as best they can. It may be that the countercultural exodus was by way of a trial run, a step in the right direction but a premature, insufficiently thoughtful step: that may still have to be taken. For the discontents that prompted it have not gone away. A good many people are quietly resigned to the thought that the roles society offers them (or denies them, the job market being what it is) are simply not worth playing. It is more than a crisis of confidence. To such people even the notion of confidence in today's society is out of the question, and though they are sympathetic to this or that reform they suspect that matters may have gone too far for reformation. Outwardly conforming to the rules of a society that violates all their best instincts, they have withdrawn allegiance and gone into inner exile.

Inner exile is a lonely, unsatisfying condition that suffers from its essential negativity. It is a movement away from rather than *to* anything, and it leaves the exiled person at the mercy of every passing spiritual prank. What these exiles need, what we all need, is a direction or directive to focus our discontents. Perhaps we might find one in these words from E. F. Schumacher's heartening book, *Small is Beautiful*:

The task of our generation . . . is one of metaphysical reconstruction. It is not as if we had to invent anything new; at the same time, it is not good enough merely to revert to the old formulations. Our task—and the task of all education—is to understand the present world, the world in which we live and make our choices.[6]

We cannot, it seems to me, understand the present world from a position inside it. We need to contemplate it at a certain distance, a distance greater than inner exile will grant. Or than our official system of schooling can provide, for directly or indirectly it is the servant of the mass society. Even at its best, metaphysical reconstruction—what Plato calls a turning about (*periagōgē*) of one's whole being—was hardly what the academy had in mind, and today we see it at its worst, financially threatened and still suffering from the crisis of confidence of the later sixties. The large questions that were then raised, questions about the *purpose* of a liberal education, are no longer much discussed but they have not been answered; they have simply been shelved. Few predict a long future for the university as we know it today. Some even wonder if it deserves to have a future at all.

Among the large numbers still in college, whether teachers or taught, there exists a small all-important minority, an elite, who genuinely care about learning (which is not the same thing as scholarship). Many of the younger teachers have jobs they expect to lose; others are unemployed and likely to remain so. Those who are students realize that what they are being given is for the most part not good enough and that a true education is to be had only between the cracks of the institution. These are the people I had mainly in mind when I spoke of inner exiles. College has provided them with a refuge of sorts, somewhere to pursue their interests and meet their own kind. It looks as though this refuge is now failing them and the question is: What are they going to do? They can submit passively to eviction and dispersal. Or they can join forces and create their own learning places.

I spoke just now of two possibilities. The first, which is too large for our minds really to grasp, is that from whatever combination of causes society as we know it disintegrates. The second possibility is that even if our social contraption does somehow hang together, becoming steadily more intolerable, serious-minded people decide they have had enough and opt out. (Getting out a little ahead of time, it may be.) If they are simply running away from a life they find unworthy, there is little hope for them. They must be going *to* something, something that does not exist and that they themselves must create: a place of learning, a place where learning is also a way of living. One can imagine various such groups inspired by very different programs. I propose in what follows to try to picture the fortunes of a set of people for whom the Schumacher passage I quoted makes sense and who see themselves not as dropouts or escapists (a word our society uses to keep its sheep from straying) but rather as what Schumacher calls "home-comers." This may sound too romantic, less so if one recalls what homecoming means in the *Aeneid*. These are people

> who are deeply convinced that technological development has taken a wrong turn and needs to be redirected. The term "home-comer" has, of course, a religious connotation. For it takes a good deal of courage to say "no" to the fashions and fascinations of the age and to question the presuppositions of a civilization which appears destined to conquer the whole world [or appeared so until very recently]; the requisite strength can only be derived from deep convictions. If it were derived from nothing more than fear of the future, it would be likely to disappear at the decisive moment. The genuine "home-comer" does not have the best tunes, but he does have the most exalted text, nothing less than the Gospels.[7]

We need the right text, certainly, but perhaps not the one that Schumacher offers. I would propose texts of the kind that have occupied me in this book, those that speak of what is unchanging in earthly existence and the certain inflexible laws that govern it. This is to say: high culture (the work studied to so little effect in the academy) is today called on to play a most paradoxical role. Once the adornment of privileged leisure, it must now help to preserve man's essential nature. The mysteries, driven out from all their other sanctuaries, have taken refuge there. The arts, Heidegger says, shelter the growth of that which saves.[8]

But if it is to do anything of the sort, high culture must first be understood differently.

3

Suppose that a group of people who individually withdrew their allegiance from society some time ago have taken the decisive step and, jointly withdrawing their persons, have created a small *collegium in agris*, so far as possible self-supporting and minimally dependent on the economy of the mass society. Academically, the group might at first be conventional in structure to the extent that degrees were granted and that students were paid something to learn and faculty paid something to teach. As times grew harder the initial structure would be likely to dissolve and the college might turn into a community where people simply learned and lived together, permanent residents and those who came for a few months at a time. Or it might take this form from the start—a community of resistance, to borrow a term that the religious have been using.[9] The task is absurdly large and yet quite simple. The members of the community want to find out what human life is about, minus the additives. More formally, they want to discover or recover what they take to be the permanent facts of human existence. They want to do this not from any innate craving for austerity, but because they have come to suspect that, as Hannah Arendt put it, "man cannot be free if he does not know that he is subject to necessity."[10]

The community must brace itself for criticism. Abstaining where they can from the handy devices that a supposedly neutral technology puts at everyone's disposal, from the outside they will resemble what Kingsley Amis once called the homemade pottery crowd. They must expect to be told that they have dropped out of the dialogue, the intellectual forum where new ideas and positions are tested. They will be accused of selfishly withdrawing from a world of poverty and injustice in order to save their own souls. Others will dislike their tendency to see themselves as *les purs* confronting a fantasy world of *les corrompus*. The question of their physical survival will also be raised. Will these bookish people make it, out there in the woods? And perhaps there is a question about their political survival. As the later sixties showed, a frightened society that has gone badly off course does not take kindly to its critics and another Nixon may crawl out of the sewers to lead the hard hats against the pointy heads.

But they face a more fundamental challenge, one both practical and philosophical. The community I am trying to picture is made up of people of the book. They need their texts not for scholarship or aesthetic pleasure but for their essential sustenance, to propose models of a reality other than the reality enforced by our society and as a defense against the values of that society. They need time for their texts, time to practice the almost lost art of reading. And yet how are they going to find the time, out there in the woods? High culture has always been grounded in leisure, leisure that once was provided by servants, by a whole structure of social privilege. What leisure remains is provided by technology, by the huge technological apparatus that (their argument is) has overlaid the facts of earthly existence and must be used as sparingly as possible. Moreover, they aim to be self-supporting, growing their own food and attending to the maintenance of their settlement. What fag end of time will be left for their studies after a day spent in virtuous self-reliance?

It looks as though they have run into a fatal contradiction. The studies we still call liberal, *studia liberalia*, were originally so called because they were open only to the *liber*, the free man as opposed to the slave, the man who was to some extent free from the yoke of necessity because others bore it for him. And yet here they are proposing once again to take on that harsh yoke, believing that man cannot be free unless he acknowledges his subjection to necessity.

Since the English word necessity is no more than a token equivalent of Greek ἀνάγκη, we had better try to hear what the Greek word says. In the *Metaphysics* (Δ1015a20 ff.) Aristotle distinguishes three kinds of necessary things (*anangkaia*): (1) the necessary as a condition of existence (I must eat in order to live) or as the condition of some desired good (I must drink this medicine to get well); (2) the necessary as compulsion or force majeure, that which thwarts or constrains one painfully, such as sickness or an act of God (I take it that most kinds of work belong in this category); and (3) the necessary as that which cannot be otherwise and is thus necessarily as it is. It is from (3), Aristotle says, that the other kinds of necessary things are somehow derived. And yet despite this derivation, it seems that for Aristotle there is a real difference between necessaries (1) and (2), and (3). That which cannot be otherwise is necessity itself, the final line of things, the nature of reality even, the contemplation of which should be our highest and most constant endeavor. Necessaries (2) and to some extent (1), on the other hand, obstruct this contemplation and must be satisfied or overcome before it can begin. Today, however, the relationship of these three forms of the necessary may have changed. We live in a world that Aristotle in his frugal, technologically primitive

226

Greece could not have imagined, one where the constraining, if not yet the conditional, necessaries have been so far reduced that necessity itself is being obscured. Technology, which in its humbler phases sought to do no more than provide man with an adequate supply of what he needed to live, has now given him such almost superhuman powers that "that which cannot be otherwise" appears to be subject to his will and indefinitely modifiable. Of course no sensible person really wants to bring back the oppressions of the necessary; mankind has been struggling to get that burden off its back from the beginning of time. We may nonetheless have to assume this burden again as the only way of reinstating necessary (3), for when primary necessity is lost to sight we live at best in a fool's paradise, at worst in a fool's hell.

The members of this little community propose, then, to get the necessaries back into the curriculum, and in so doing they look as though they have run into a fatal contradiction. The most pressing, permanent form of the necessary is work, and this is what faces them, since they intend to be as far as possible self-supporting. They also intend to pursue their studies, with a seriousness they have found to be no longer possible in the academy exposed to the distractions and corruptions of the mass society. As they are well aware, handwork and mind work have traditionally been kept separate, for a very sensible reason: to allow mind to contemplate in some sort of tranquillity the things that are and the great creations of men's minds which reveal the things that are, while the handworkers look after the shop and keep the human artifice going.[11] The outward form of this convenient Greek division of labor (more convenient for mind workers than handworkers, to be sure) persisted until our own time. It is well within living memory that the scholar sat in the quiet of his book-lined study while the servants went respectfully about their business. I am not concerned with the social and political upheavals that have brought about the collapse of this arrangement nor with the threat to high culture (as we have known it) which that collapse poses, but rather with the fact that the reasons, the justification, for the mind's privileged freedom changed or failed long before the social and political changes that made it no longer possible. For Greece and, with altered emphases, for medieval Christendom, mind needed its freedom from the constraints of the necessary in order to contemplate the

227

unchanging truth of being or God. (Hence the superiority of the contemplative to the practical life. I should say that I am including among contemplative activities the study of literature and the arts.) The great shift came in the seventeenth century when mind ceased to take as its highest task the contemplation of an unchanging reality and turning itself into an instrument of attack directed its energies *against* that reality. Drawing handwork into its service and in due course providing it with powers vastly greater than man's, mind set out on the radical transformation not only of the human condition but of what was formerly thought of as the changeless, divine order of nature.

For this kind of mental activity, the scientist's, freedom from the distracting constraints of the necessary is as much required as ever. It is up to the scientist to find means of preserving his privileged seclusion. For the contemplative mind, however, whether philosophical or literary, the old seclusion has become a mockery. Once it needed its relative freedom from the necessary to contemplate unchanging reality: that which cannot be otherwise, necessity. But what happens when the boundaries of the necessary have been pushed back so far that necessity itself is almost disappearing? The reality offered to its attention (one can scarcely speak of contemplation) is little more than a human fiction or confection that changes from day to day. The old seclusion is no longer needed, nor is it justified: it is crippling. Mind alone cannot recover the dimension in which it once moved. The hand will have to go out again, hand working alongside mind, exploring, testing, laboring, to discover what remains and start building again. Thinking will have to be joined to making and doing; the necessary accepted again and necessity reinstated as the final line of things. Necessity, our old enemy, is coming to look like a new friend, an ally against the monstrous man-made structure that balloons us round, and a pointer to the permanent facts of earthly existence and divine, unchanging nature.

4

The contradiction between mind work and handwork, though it remains a contradiction or conflict on the practical level, must then be accepted. Theoretically, however, the members of the community are beginning to see why these two kinds of work have to be brought together. They also see that bringing them together calls for a rethinking of the whole structure of "liberal" education and beyond that a redefinition of high culture. A *re-definition*, not a last-ditch attempt to hold on to what remains of high culture in the form we have hitherto known it. It is this essentially conservative position that seems to me the weakness of Philip Rieff's powerful cultural polemic, *Fellow Teachers*, a work that in its spirit if not in its disorderly gait bears some resemblance to the *Laws*. Like Plato, Rieff reacts to the decay of our inherited fabric of beliefs and the consequent social and intellectual disarray by seeking to give the failed cultural norms a religious sanction. The primary forms of high culture, for Rieff, are not the arts and sciences but the "interdicts," the graven Hebraic thou-shalt-nots that compel our obedience because they are enforced by what he calls the "god-terms." The god-terms, we are told, "will not be treated as mere heuristic devices.... [They are] neither 'functional' nor 'mythic': they are truths."[12] Society at all events cannot get on without them and Rieff is resolved to bring them back. But once failed, where are they to come from? Despite many compelling pages, *Fellow Teachers* does not offer a hint of an answer, hence much of it amounts to no more than a moving, angry attempt to conserve "what remains of our received culture."[13] To a lesser extent George Steiner's important paper, "Text and Context," is open to the same criticism. Steiner vividly pictures the former conditions of high culture, "the compacted privacy, the investments of silence, required by serious reading": "Self-bestowal on a text, the vertigo of attention which bends the scholar's back and blears the eye, is a posture simultaneously sacrificial and stringently selfish. It feeds on a stillness, on a sanctuary of egotistical space, which excludes even those closest to one."[14] These conditions have now gone and Steiner ends by proposing that we must once again start to teach reading, from the ground up. We will have to create "houses of reading."

But is this enough? Can we recover high culture *in the form we have known it?* To flourish again, will it not have to take new forms? It may have to expand until it becomes culture in the full or the old sense, *cultura agri* as well as *cultura animi*. The virtue that in my first paper I called literacy and defined in bookish, intellectual terms may have to expand until it is no longer merely a *forma mentis* but a way of living. I suspect that a number of people are finding themselves driven unwillingly to think along these lines. Nothing could have led us even to contemplate so radical a departure, one so alien to most of our inclinations, except the sense that it is time to move beyond critiques of our multiple disorders and start thinking about what happens next, about what can be *done*. We should, as Steiner says in criticism of Rieff, "take the risk of positive contrivancies." A call for a return to the thwarting constraints of the necessary, in a world where for most people these constraints are grindingly present, comes awkwardly, I realize, from someone who has never been exposed to their rigor. I am conscious, too, of the agonizing, almost insuperable, difficulties of welding into a community a handful of atomized individuals unused to accepting any rule that they have not spun out of their own innards. This desperate problem may nonetheless provide a point from which to look ahead, beyond the obstacles to the prospects, beyong the difficulties to the possibilities.

If the settlement is to be more than a place where a few dissatisfied people come to do their thing for a while and then drift away, it must have a discipline; it must acknowledge some principle of authority. Distasteful words. We have been taught to look back disapprovingly at the days when students came to school and college to do what they were told. And yet we know the farce of an educational system where authority is lacking: the authority of the teacher and, more serious, of the subject or discipline, the authority of learning itself and of the past.[15] Steiner is correct when he says that the "text" (shorthand for literacy and the whole art of reading) "flourishes in a context of authority."[16] Rieff puts it more bluntly: "The disciplines of the intellect that constitute higher schooling are inherently undemocratic and need both long preparation and regular exercise in a protected institution uniquely unchanging in its object."[17] Unpleasant again, but then finding a way out of our libertarian wastelands is not going to be pleasant.

Where is this principle of authority to come from? Could it come from the texts themselves, the community's guide to and in the wilderness? But how could a principle of authority come from something so uncoercive as a set (even a canon) of texts? It may help to rephrase this question and ask: In what sort of community can such powerless authority be binding? The answer is then seen to be: in a monastic or quasi-monastic structure. William Mullen writes in a letter: "Monastic structures seem to have been designed precisely to reduce the difference between power and authority to a minimum. Power requires force to back itself up, whereas authority is able to influence action only to the extent that it has renounced force as a means of making action occur." Education in the West began in such places; it may have to return there. In the Dark Ages, a historian writes, "the monastic cell, with its self-contained economy, [was] capable of survival in the oddest places and the worst times, like a seed in the winter detritus of Nature.... Every cell was independent. If one perished, others survived. If all but one perished, the system could yet be re-created from one survivor."[18] It is an uncomfortable model, but we may be heading for uncomfortable times.

This attempt to answer the question about the source of authority has however only pushed it back one step. The monastery derived its authority from the fact that it was peopled by men bound in obedience by religious faith. What comparable binding principle can we hope to derive from a set of literary texts?

Perhaps it will help to imagine a scene, a moment in the life of the community. It might come at a time of need or distress. Or a time of joy, when a day is set aside to celebrate the fifth anniversary of the founding or the birth of the first child there. A poem is chosen for performance before the whole company, "The Tutelar of the Place" by David Jones. It is a prayer addressed by those who dwell in a loved, threatened place to their tutelar or protectress, "a rare one for locality," the poet calls her. Part of the poem is spoken; other parts are sung or chanted by several voices in unison; some passages are danced. It begins quietly, scored for a single, speaking voice ("She that loves place, time, demarcation, hearth, kin, enclosure, site, differentiated cult..."), moves through a variety of tones, mingling verse and prose, the prose often sounding more "poetic" than the verse, drawing on a wide range of diction and composed in larger, freer rhythmical units. Sometimes it swells out, the tone growing fuller and the accent becoming liturgical:

> Queen of the differentiated sites, administratrix of the demarcations, let our cry come unto you....
>
> When they proscribe the diverse uses and impose the
> rootless uniformities, pray for us.

When they sit in *Consilium*
to liquidate the holy diversities
        mother of particular perfections
        queen of otherness
        mistress of asymmetry
patroness of things counter, parti, pied, several
protectress of things known and handled
help of things familiar and small
        wardress of the secret crevices
        of things wrapped and hidden
mediatrix of all the deposits
        margravine of the troia
empress of the labyrinth
        receive our prayers.

The words become more tender, more lyrical, as they invoke "the diversities by which we are, by which we call on your name, sweet Jill of the demarcations." A few more lines of invocation are followed by a snatch of prose (should one call it?) which modulates into something that must be danced:

In the December of our culture ward somewhere the secret seed, under the mountain, under and between, between the grids of the Ram's survey when he squares the world-circle. Sweet Mair devise a mazy-guard
in and out and round about
double-dance defences
countermure and echelon meanders round
the holy mound. . . .

When the technicians manipulate the dead limbs of our culture as though it yet had life, have mercy on us. Open unto us, let us enter a second time within your stola-folds in those days—ventricle and refuge both, *hendref* for world-winter, asylum from world-storm.[19]

Hendref, Jones tells us, means both ancestral dwelling and winter quarters. A useful word. And Jones is a useful poet (*utilis urbi*, as poets once were) who provides the community with some of its necessary verses. His sense of locality and limit, of place and the piety of place, of *Bodenständigkeit*, "homesteadi-ness," makes his work a corrective to Pound's ecumenical spread and offers an alternative to the empty universalism that is only another word for homelessness, grounded as it is in our common subjection to a technology that everywhere destroys the diversities by which we are.

The community has made poetry part of its life all along and there is nothing, in the performance and reception of Jones's poem, of the holy hush that makes the usual poetry reading so embarrassing. As the lovely words are translated into sound and gesture, a strange thing happens. The poem takes possession of the listeners and brings into the open something they are beginning to feel: the sense of attachment to a particular place, *this* place. In the mass society we live like vagrants, hopping from spot to spot, pausing only long enough to ruin. The settlement is revealing the possibility of a different way of living on earth, nearer to what Heidegger means by *dwelling:* "to cherish and protect, to preserve and care for."[20] This is what the poem (like many older poems) is saying but only now can they understand it. In the classroom, Jones's tutelar and the place she guards would have to be taken as metaphors; here they are on the way to becoming literal. As they "pray" to this "goddess" they are still in the mode of play, but it is serious playing and may in time become something else.

And still in the mode of play, they find that they are *doing* things that formerly were possible only within the distanced sphere of the poem. In a clearing a little way from the field where they grow their food someone has inexpertly scratched on a stone the Latin words that occur a number of times in the *Cantos:* ARAM NEMUS VULT. A self-conscious gesture, but the words look right there and surely Pound would not have objected to his poem being used in this way. All the same, the inscription will not do as it stands. The clearing may in some sense "want" an altar, but an altar is a raised stone upon which offerings are placed and we have no gods to receive our offerings. So he adds three more words: SED NUMINA ABSUNT. Play is starting to point beyond itself, for the inscription now raises the matter proposed for thought by the fragment of dialogue in Pound's 113th Canto:

> The Gods have not returned. "They have never left us."
> They have not returned.

This resembles the dialectical movement of Hölderlin's enigmatic phrase, the god's absence or default helps. The gods who have not returned and yet never left us are neither present nor absent.

Or, if absent, it is a pregnant absence that may become presence again. The task is to remain close to this absence and cherish it until, in a time not of our choosing, the gods may return.

A meager yield, in no way comparable to the binding principle that held the monasteries together? No, but it is enough, because there is nothing else.

5

The texts are authoritative because they are charged with knowledge that we once had and may retrieve; they preserve the "deviant knowledge" that constitutes the center of resistance where the community makes its stand. The texts are authoritative because they are the last remaining witnesses to a reality other than the reality enforced by the mass society. The principle of authority they provide is vested mediately in those who interpret them and teach tomorrow's interpreters. The authority of the teachers, the leaders of this community devoted to learning, derives from the texts. It is not in their own right that the texts possess this authority but by virtue of what they bear witness to, a witness in constant need of interpretation. The circle should be tight enough to hold.

But the nagging question still remains. How much time can the community reasonably expect to devote to these texts of theirs? Mind cannot flourish until the body's primary needs have been met; it cannot function at all after a day of monotonous, backbreaking labor. In resubmitting to necessity and its attendant necessaries, have they bitten off more than they can chew?

I spoke just now of the community as a quasi-monastic structure, and it is worth glancing at what we know of the life led in such places. In the medieval Benedictine monastery a five-hour working day was established; this work was accepted, in Lewis Mumford's phrase, "not as a slave's curse but as part of a free man's moral commitment."[21] A monastery could be agreeably small; twelve members were sufficient to form one. And since the Benedictines had intellectual interests, enlightened use was made of laborsaving devices like the horse-powered mill, the water mill and later the windmill. "The monks sought," Mumford writes, "to avoid unnecessary labor in order to have more time and energy for meditation and prayer.... Though they themselves were disciplined to regular work, they readily turned over to machinery those operations that could be performed without benefit of mind."[22] There should be something to learn here.

Five hours of physical work (or perhaps four, making selective use of the less vicious power tools) is not too daunting a prospect, once one had learned to see it not as time stolen from one's proper pursuits but as part of full *cultura.* Life in the settlement would still be rugged, of course, and as we sit in our well-appointed living rooms we are bound to wonder if intellectual activity would be possible there at all. These fears do us little credit. The great reaches of the mind were not achieved by those lapped in *tous les conforts modernes.* In the long run our studies would only benefit from being conducted in conditions of material austerity. Irksome at first, a radical simplification of the human artifice would bring its own satisfactions and release new energies. We have put on too much fat.

And there is too much fat on our library shelves. Certainly there would be less time for reading, out there in the woods, and fewer books to read. But then those who still read now read far too much—reading, often, as a defense against the surrounding society. And we spend too much time on the wrong kind of books, the books—too numerous to absorb and rapidly becoming too expensive to buy—that one must at least have looked at in order to keep up. What a relief if the whole parastructure of commentary and critique and much of what passes for scholarship were to fall away into silence: a silence out of which the few, primary, texts could speak.

6

Fewer books, then, but *what* books? And to speak in academic terms, what *subjects* might figure in the curriculum of this community devoted to learning? Clearly there could be no attempt to construct miniature, purer versions of the academy as we have it today, a more harmonious orchestration of all the voices of our present world of discourse. The coacervation of intellectually discordant people which we call a university is not proving a happy arrangement. The community, being small, would be far more unified in its interests and guided by a more definite sense

235

of ends. Education would have to become simpler and more radical than it has been for centuries. Its first task might be to teach us about the relation between man and what is not man.[23]

The members of the community broke away from the mass society in order to create a life more in tune with the permanent facts of earthly existence. Gradually they come to see that their task is far larger—far too large for them, of course, but someone has to make a start somewhere. What they find they are aiming at, on the smallest of scales, is nothing less than a new founding, another instauration. Inevitably they are led to think of the previous instauration, the one associated with Francis Bacon in the seventeenth century when mind turned from the contemplation of an unchanging reality and transformed itself into an instrument of attack. Bacon's aim, in drafting his program for the advancement of natural science, was to restore "to its perfect and original condition...that commerce between the mind of man and the nature of things"[24] which the long catalogue of human errors had blocked. By commerce Bacon meant that the mind must "exercise over the nature of things the authority which properly belongs to it." If asked about the source of this authority he had simply to say God,[25] an amenable deity who had agreed to get out of man's way. The answer is less clear today and indeed the question is not often asked. We exercise our authority over the nature of things because we have the power to do so. To ask about the "source" of this power sounds like a piece of foolish metaphysics. We should ask rather about its end and this is at once seen to be beneficent. It is, in another of Bacon's famous phrases, the relief of man's estate.[26] This is supposed to settle everything. It does so only if man's estate matters more than anything else and only if it can be relieved at no matter what cost to everything else.

From inside the world that Bacon predicted, the *regnum hominis* governed by science and technology which we inhabit today, every assertion seems axiomatic and unquestionable. Only from some extraterritorial vantage point can questions be asked, and this is of course the position the community is struggling to reach. The act of breaking away has in itself given them a fresh perspective since they find themselves looking back, with something like revulsion, at the promised land to which Bacon so confidently looked forward. That a few dissatisfied people should question the constitution would be no more significant than a worm's misgivings about the wisdom of the bulldozer's progress were it not that they have been led out, or let out, by something larger than themselves, something still quite vague and perhaps quite small though it seems to be growing. Call it simply a doubt about the whole course we are set on. Since it is science, more than anything else, which sets our course, what is primarily in question is science's ability to provide the one valid map of reality.

So they decide to take Bacon as their first author for study and discussion. The approach to his work is simplified by the way he so often says the same thing, concentrating his thought in a single pregnant saying that leads out into and sums up a great many other passages. For instance: "The End of our Foundation is the knowledge of Causes, and secret motions of things; and the enlarging of the bounds of Human Empire, to the effecting of all things possible."[27] Bacon was much concerned with enlarging bounds or limits and it is no accident that he so often reverts to the figure of the mariner passing beyond the Pillars of Hercules into uncharted seas, the emblem he chose for the title page of his *Novum Organum*.[28] Probably he was not thinking of Dante's Ulysses, but we can hardly help recalling that archetypal limit-breaker who ventured beyond the marks set up *Acció che l'uom più oltre non si metta* (*Inferno* 26.109), "that man should not pass beyond." For Dante's Christian thinking, there was no doubt about the limit that Ulysses was transgressing. He was re-enacting the primal sin of pride, of disobedience caused by pride, which drove Adam out of paradise and Satan out of heaven.[29] This Christian veto has lost most of its force today. Greek thinking about transgression (*huperbasia*) may still be useful, however, since it is more complex and recognizes the ambivalence of the drive—at once our greatest glory and the high road to ruin—rather than simply handing it over to the devil. Within Western culture, certainly, one is forced to recognize this ambivalence if large parts of our enterprise are not to be written off as an aberration. From this point of view, Bacon's instauration and the conquest of the world by Western science and technology to which it has led can be seen as the latest and most successful expression of an old Western ambition. Disguised in various ways, the *libido dominandi* is deeply inscribed in our tradition; the drive to mastery is still in us and we cannot disown our past, setting up overnight as meek Hindus. But can we continue mindlessly on the same course, enlarging one bound after another because there is always a new bound to enlarge? Surely what we need above all else is to recover a thinking that recognizes limit, to find the limits set on permissible action.

Since limit cannot be arbitrarily imposed but must seem in some sense given by the nature of things, and since yesterday's limits cannot be resurrected, it is not at all clear how we are to set about looking for limits. Perhaps the first large question the community set itself, the relation between man and what is not man, might provide some indications. That very large numbers of animals should every year be tormented to madness and death in order that some superfluous commercial product may be certified as safe: it is not too hard to see this as illicit, once the relevant facts are pointed out.[30] The matter becomes more difficult when one asks how many animals can justifiably be tortured in order to bring about an improvement in human health. Is there some sort of equation? For instance, is it proper for a thousand rats to die excruciating deaths that I may be cured of a skin disease, whereas only if my life is in question should a million rats so die? Or is there no equation, is man so uniquely valuable that the whole animal creation could properly be exterminated to benefit or save one human life?

This however may not be the best place to look for the limits of permissible action since we can fairly easily be led to regret what we do here by our dislike of inflicting pain on creatures that suffer as we do. What provides the check is our celebrated humanitarianism, or in other words a man-oriented virtue that can be extended only so far beyond the human sphere. It may be more fruitful to think of our relation to things, what in Greek are called *ta phusei onta*, things or beings that are by nature.[31] Are there any limits to what we can properly do to a tree or a landscape? Here again the danger is, inveterate humanists that we are, of falling back on a man-oriented virtue that in this case is no more than enlightened self-interest. It is mere prudence, though a prudence still only halfheartedly accepted, not to ruin *our* environment and endanger the continuing supply of *our* resources. What is wanted is something that would stop us devastating the natural world, even if it could be done safely, an instinct or attitude that might in time lead to a principle: that while man can dispose as he wishes of the things he has made, he has no such absolute rights over what is by nature, not by man. Since he is driven to create his polis, he must use the things the earth provides. But why not do so respectfully, sparingly, like someone asking his neighbor for help, not like a tyrant coercing his slaves? Perhaps *respect* is the word that describes such an attitude to the things we share the earth with, what Heidegger calls *Wesenlassen eines Wesenden in seinem Wesen*,[32] the readiness to let a thing be in its essential nature, to let things rest in their peace unless our proper purposes compel us to disturb them.[33] There is more here than respect, though, something that deserves to be called piety and might in time lead man to see that the things that are by nature are not his property and are even, in their unknown life out there, in some sense sacred. In still further time, the qualifying phrase "in some sense" might be dropped, and the light of the sacred begin to shine again in all that is.

Education of this sort could not take place in the academy. It could happen only in a place where learning was also a way of living, through a stumbling, resolute dialogue between the members of the community and the land they worked on, the daily tasks they performed, the books they read, the thoughts they tried to think through. So far as the human interlocutors are concerned, it would be very important that a scientist be of their number or at least join them now and then. Not only to let these humanists—or people of the book, as they prefer to call themselves—see the full weight of what they are up against but because if science is ever to be led back within its proper boundaries and taught to abandon its claim to provide the ultimate map of reality, then it must be science that undertakes the task. Not of course that science is being asked to stand repentantly in a corner by itself. The humanist has hardly less to repent, for so much of his treasured record is scarred by the same drive to mastery. He has merely been less successful in reaching his goal. We are all in it together, called on to renounce a presumption that may be as old as the race but which our new powers have made monstrous. Such an undertaking would probably be quite impossible were it not for the signs that before very long our powers are going to be withdrawn anyway.

7

In the final section of *The Symbolism of Evil* Ricoeur speaks of the hermeneutic project of revivifying philosophy through contact with "the fundamental symbols of consciousness."[34] Does this mean that we are to go back to a primitive naïveté, he asks, and replies: "Not at all. In every way, something has been lost, irremediably lost: immediacy of belief. But if we can no longer live the great symbolisms of the sacred in accordance with the original belief in them, we can, we modern men, aim at a second naïveté in and through criticism," or hermeneutics. It will be clear by now what I am trying to do, what I have been aiming at throughout in my reading of the poets. I am trying to take what Ricoeur would certainly regard as an illicit short cut to something like his primitive naïveté. This may well be impossible. The dreams of replenishment and restoration which haunt the modern world may be incapable of realization in waking life. And yet man is a creature of circumstance, and if circumstance were to change radically, might man not change with it? A change of thought, a change to a different kind of thinking, might be brought about by something other than thinking: by events in the public realm.[35] We can no longer live and believe the great symbolisms of the sacred, Ricoeur says. No, but suppose that from choice or necessity we ate food we had grown ourselves, instead of getting it from an anonymous pipeline for cash down. Suppose that, the transportation network having failed so that no other source of food was available, the grain we had planted was long and anxiously awaited and then, miraculously, its fruit was granted. Might not the symbolisms of the sacred then seem something more than a professor's fancy talk? As things stand, the green tip that thrusts through the earth is for the literary person a metaphor, for the agribusinessman a figure on the production chart, for the philosopher a symbol he may hope to interpret hermeneutically. In the world I am imagining, might it not again, in time, be a divine event, fruit of the marriage at Eleusis?

> Zeus lies in Ceres' bosom . . .

The poets have been saying this all along, but for centuries we were unable to take them seriously.

Suppose further that, first from choice and then from necessity (our new, frightening friend), we had to stay put in one spot, vagrants no longer since the gas that whisked us over the face of the earth had run out and the highways had buckled and half vanished as grass returned to cover the scars of that self-inflicted wound. Suppose that our lives were spent in homes where the mysteries of birth and death had occurred, instead of being handed over to sterilized non-places called hospitals, and that our work was done near the hallowed ground where our dead lay. Suppose that we had to live according to the rhythms of day and night, the magic juice that disrupted those rhythms having long since been priced off the market by the utilities companies. Might not the symbolisms of the sacred which have withered in the *regnum hominis* start to take hold again? None of these changes is impossible to conceive, unless we are so mesmerized by the size and noise of the man-locked set all around us that we think it indestructible. Is it impossible or illicit to imagine the change of heart and mind which might in time go with these material changes?

Too much supposition, too many questions, and yet what can we do but question, humbly, earnestly, in a kind of desperate hope? To me at least this seems the direction in which hope should reach. One should act as though these things might be so, and in the meantime prepare the ground and build for this future, scouting around for the necessary building materials and holding on to whatever has survived and might prove useful again. The poets, I have tried to show, can help us; they are the pointers to where we should go, they could do much to guide us when we get there. Perhaps our founding poet will provide an image to end on, one final pointer to a new foundation. After he escaped from Kalypso's enchantments and had suffered shipwreck, Odysseus swam for days till at last he came to land on Phaiakia. He covered himself with leaves and fell sound asleep near the shore, regaining strength to begin the journey home after his long exile. Homer uses a simile to describe this:

> As a man in a distant field, no neighbors near,
> hides a glowing log in the dark embers,
> saving the seed of fire—

> ὡς δ᾽ ὅτε τις δαλὸν σποδιῇ ἐνέκρυψε μελαίνῃ
> ἀγροῦ ἐπ᾽ ἐσχατιῆς, ᾧ μὴ πάρα γείτονες ἄλλοι,
> σπέρμα πυρὸς σώζων—

241

NOTES

PREFACE

1. Introduction to Roger Munier's translation of Heidegger's *Humanismusbrief, Lettre sur l'humanisme* (Paris, 1964), 20.

2. *The Empty Space* (New York, 1969), 42.

3. Francine du Plessix Gray, in *New York Times Book Review*, June 19, 1977.

CENTER OF RESISTANCE

1. Philip Larkin, "Church Going," in *The Less Deceived* (Hessle, Yorkshire, 1955), 27.

2. One could do so in ancient times too: "Ceterum unum studium vere liberale est; quod liberum facit" (Seneca, *Epistulae Morales*, 88.2).

3. *Epoch and Artist* (New York, 1959), 140.

4. *Fellow Teachers* (New York, 1973), e.g., 83n. A very serious book which, since it rejects much liberal dogma, has been studiously ignored.

5. Hans-Georg Gadamer, *Truth and Method*, trans. anon (New York, 1975), 496. The rest of the paragraph presents a simplified classroom summary of central elements of Gadamer's hermeneutic.

6. "Hérésies artistiques: L'art pour tous," *Oeuvres Complètes*, Pléiade ed. (1965), 257.

7. *Dombey and Son*, ch. 6, *ad init*. In ch. 15 (Penguin ed., p. 290) Dickens subtly notes the way the immemorial rhythms of

nature were effected by this expression of human power: "There was even railway time observed in clocks, as if the sun itself had given in."

8. See for instance the essay "Belief and Suspension of Disbelief" by M. H. Abrams in the volume edited by him, *Literature and Belief* (New York, 1958). Mr. Abrams very ably examines passages from Keats, Dante, and Wordsworth, and by allowing for the complex ways in which the beliefs of writer and reader do and do not enter into the creation and experience of the literary work leaves one with the comfortable feeling that the problem, if not exactly soluble, is at least not actively troubling. *Tamen usque recurret.*

9. *Between Past and Future* (New York, 1968), 94.

10. *The Birth of Tragedy*, §23.

11. *Museum without Walls*, trans. Stuart Gilbert and Francis Price (New York, 1967), 72.

12. In "Aletheia," *Vorträge und Aufsätze* (Tübingen, 1967), III.53 ff. See, e.g., p. 56: "Das Bemühen beschränkt sich darauf, näher am Wort des heraklitischen Spruches zu bleiben. Dies könnte dazu beitragen, ein künftiges Denken in den Bereich noch ungehörter Zusprüche einzuweisen."

13. *The Scope of Anthropology*, trans. S. O. Paul and R. A. Paul (London, 1967), 47.

14. Compare Hugh Kenner on Pound: "The *Cantos* scan the past for possibilities, but their dynamic is turned toward the future" (*The Pound Era* [Berkeley and Los Angeles, 1971], 325).

15. Heidegger, *On the Way to Language*, trans. Peter D. Hertz (New York, 1971), 38.

16. In his introduction to the French trans. of Heidegger's *Vorträge und Aufsätze, Essais et conférences* (Poitiers, Vienne, 1969), xi.

17. See "Die Frage nach der Technik," in *Vorträge*, I.22.

18. Walter F. Otto, *The Homeric Gods*, trans. Moses Hadas (Boston, 1964), 7.

19. *Beyond Culture* (New York, 1968), 108. The useful word "extraterritorial" is, I believe, the property of George Steiner.

20. *Earth House Hold* (New York, 1969), 133.

21. See for example the description of Raveloe, "a village where many of the old echoes lingered," in the first two chapters of *Silas Marner* which point constantly to the survival of the pagan pieties. Or the passage in ch. 12 where Eliot speaks of "the gods of the hearth." In Hardy's *The Woodlanders*, Giles Winterborne (note the name) is at times unmistakably the Green Man of medieval carving and occasionally appears in still older forms

("He rose upon her memory as the fruit-god and wood-god in alternation..." [ch. 28]).

22. *Guide to Kulchur* (New York, 1970), 299, 126.

23. See Norman Austin, *Archery at the Dark of the Moon* (Berkeley, Los Angeles, London, 1975), 67.

24. The first sentence is found in *Guide to Kulchur*, 191, the second in "A Visiting Card," reprinted in *Selected Prose, 1909-1965*, ed. William Cookson (New York, 1973), 320.

25. *Ezra Pound: Poet as Sculptor* (Oxford, 1964), 222.

26. See Gadamer, *Truth and Method*, e.g., p. 87: "Is there to be no knowledge in art? Does not the experience of art contain a claim to truth which is certainly different from that of science, but equally certainly is not inferior to it? And is not the task of aesthetics [a task which traditional aesthetics cannot perform, as Gadamer convincingly shows] precisely to provide a basis for the fact that artistic experience is a mode of knowledge of a unique kind, certainly different from that sensory knowledge which provides science with the data from which it constructs the knowledge of nature, and certainly different from all moral rational knowledge, and indeed from all conceptual knowledge, but still knowledge, i.e. the transmission of truth?"

27. *A Rumor of Angels* (New York, 1969), 7. I draw on the fuller treatment of this concept by Berger and Thomas Luckmann, *The Social Construction of Reality* (New York, 1967).

The quotation on p. 28 is from Pound's 112th Canto (*The Cantos of Ezra Pound* [New York, 1970], 790). I do not care to tag this line.

WEAVING WITH POINTS OF GOLD:
PINDAR'S SIXTH OLYMPIAN

1. *Pindar* (Berkeley, 1945), 129.

2. I have in mind Hannah Arendt's remarkable discussion of this topic in *Between Past and Future* (New York, 1968), 41-48.

3. Line numbers refer to the Greek text. Though cut into line lengths for convenience, my translation makes no claim to be verse. I have to thank Janet Lembke for letting me steal an occasional phrase from her version of the ode, as yet unpublished.

4. Subsidiary myths occur in a few other odes and their functions vary. The best example is at the end of *Pythian 9*, a complete narrative in little on the same theme as the main myth. In *Olympian 9* the main myth is introduced by a brief tale about Herakles, which Pindar declines to continue, and is followed by a short myth about Patroklos.

5. *Cosmos and History* (New York, 1959), 22, 38.

6. C. S. Lewis, discussing Spenser's *Epithalamion*, "the most Pindaric thing we have," in *English Literature in the Sixteenth Century* (Oxford, 1954), 373.

7. In *Nemean* 4.49 f. Pindar uses a related word, *phaennos*, to mean white, calling Leuke (White Island) *phaennan nason*. For what it is worth, Philostratos many centuries later says that Amphiaraos's horses were white (*Imagines* 1.27, noted by Gildersleeve; see B. L. Roscher, *Lexicon, s.v.* I.297, col. 1). "The Departure of Amphiaraos" on the magnificent Corinthian krater of circa 575 B.C. shows the pole horses black, the more prominent trace horses white. (See E. Pfuhl, *Malerei und Zeichnung der Griechen* [Rome, 1969], III, pl. 179.)

8. *The Works of Pindar*, 3 vols. (London, 1932), II, 43.

9. See pp. 57 ff.

10. "Leda and the Swan" ("Did she put on his knowledge with his power / Before the indifferent beak could let her drop?") and the exquisite third stanza of "Lullaby" which complements and corrects the terror of the earlier version. Pound, in Canto 5, as it were sets the scene, with the bride (Danae) "awaiting the god's touch," but it is only at the end of Canto 39, after the fertility rite that "made the spring," that the mystery takes place: "Dark shoulders have stirred the lightning / A girl's arms have nested the fire, / Not I but the handmaid kindled / Cantat sic nupta / I have eaten the flame."

11. "Die Sage selbst ist im Grunde das nämliche Peloponnesische Märchen vom ausgesetzten und wunderbar erhaltenen Kinde, von welchem die eine Form, die von Asklepios, oben behandelt ist" (*Isyllos von Epidauros* [Berlin, 1885], 177).

12. With Farnell, who translates "her girdle of purple and saffron hues," and John H. Finley, *Aeschylus and Pindar* (Cambridge, Mass., 1966), 115.

13. For honey and prophecy, see the Homeric hymn to Hermes, IV.558 ff., where the Thriai, hag priestesses who transform themselves into bees or are bee-winged, "flit hither and thither feeding on honeycomb and bringing all things to pass. When they are inspired by eating yellow honey they speak the truth willingly." See also *Pythian* 4.60, where Pindar calls the Delphic priestess *Melissa* (bee). For honey and poetry, see the pretty hagiographic detail in the ancient life of Pindar which tells how as a boy he once slept on Mount Helikon and a bee alighted on his lips and made honey there (*Scholia*, I.1).

14. Despite the long and short iotas which would not have troubled Pindar, who derives "Ιαμος (Ῑ) from ἴον (ῐ).

15. The three words "to our eyes" need stressing or we turn Pindar into the lucky simpleton of the undivided consciousness. Paul Ricoeur writes of the mythmaking faculty: "This intuition of a cosmic whole, from which man is not separated, and this undivided plenitude, anterior to the division into supernatural, natural, and human, are not *given* but simply *aimed at*. It is only in intention that the myth restores some wholeness; it is because he himself has lost that wholeness that man re-enacts and imitates it in myth and rite. . . . If mythmaking is an antidote to distress, this is because the man of myths is already an unhappy consciousness" (*The Symbolism of Evil*, trans. Emerson Buchanan [Boston, 1969], 167).

16. Compare R. C. Jebb on ἀρτίπους (Sophocles, *Trachiniae* 58): "With *opportune foot* (ἀρτίως καὶ ἡρμοσμένως τῷ καιρῷ, schol.)."

17. Compare, e.g., Bacchylides 13.199 ff.: "Let all who are not subdued by envy praise the victor. Yet men must censure every act. (βροτῶν δὲ μῶμος πάντεσσι μέν ἐστιν ἐπ᾽ ἔργοις.) Truth will nonetheless prevail."

18. At *Isthmian* 4.80, for example, Pindar speaks of shedding (*epistazōn*) *kharis* on the victor, and at *Olympian* 10.98 ff., more lavishly, of bathing (*katabrekhōn*) a whole city in honey. In Greek this may be more nearly "normal" poetic diction than it seems to us, given passages like *Odyssey* 6.235, where Athene pours (*katekheue*) *kharis* on Odysseus's head and shoulders.

19. Leonard Woodbury shows that the uncompounded form of this verb "is often used of the movement of forces that affect man but are not under his control," and he takes *proserpei* here to mean "comes over him . . . in power" ("The Tongue and the Whetstone," *Transactions of the American Philological Association*, 86 [1955], 38 f.). For the sense of the passage as a whole I have leaned heavily on an article by Carl Ruck ("Marginalia Pindarica," *Hermes*, 96 [1968], 132 ff.) which seems to me to take account of the linguistic facts and to make poetic sense. Following one of Ruck's suggestions I understand *akonas* as an appositional genitive: the *doxa* or thought is itself, consists of, or is like a whetstone.

20. I take *piomai* to be present, not future.

21. Cf. Carl Ruck and W. H. Matheson: "The poet's thought in this ode repeatedly returns to the significance of the poetizing process" (*Pindar: Selected Odes* [Ann Arbor, 1968], 82). Their reading of *Olympian* 6 is imaginative and, since it in some ways resembles my own, strikes me as very sound.

22. For the Arkadian cult of Hera as Maiden, Wife, and

Widow, see Pausanias, 8.22.2. In the next line I take *alathesin logois* ("by words told true") as instrumental dative, not as it is usually understood, "in very truth," which seems rather empty. It thus refers to the truthfulness of the poet's praise of Hagesias, forceful enough to prevail against any disparagement of Boiotian bards, just as *endikas apo glōssas* ("from truthful lips," 12-13) certified to the truthfulness of Adrastos's praise of Amphiaraos in the protomyth that corrected any tendency to grudge the victor is due tribute of song.

23. See David C. Young, "Pindaric Criticism," *Pindaros und Bakchylides*, ed. W. Calder and J. Stern (Darmstadt, 1970), 40 n. 89. Young shows that the name Aineias was not confined to Arkadia but was used in various parts of Greece. We know from *Nemean* 3.3 ff., e.g., that Pindar used local choruses, but it is perfectly possible that sometimes at least he assigned the rehearsal and performance of an ode to a visiting professional he knew and trusted, and Aineias may have been such a man.

24. Rumpel, *Lexicon Pindaricum, s.v. leukippos,* provides an attractive detail. The adjective is used "quod simulacrum Proserpinae vernis sollemnibus, quae dicebantur ἀνακαλυπτήρια, curru albis equis iuncto vehebatur per urbem."

25. Compare, e.g., *Olympian* 8.28 f.: ὁ δ᾿ ἐπαντέλλων χρόνος / τοῦτο πράσσων μὴ κάμοι, or *Isthmian* 7.39: ὁ δ᾿ ἀθανάτων μὴ θρασσέτω φθόνος.

26. Amphitrita's stately epithet, literally "with golden distaff," is not "decorative," but it serves to cast a glow over the water Hagesias must traverse. Ruck and Matheson (*Pindar: Selected Odes*) attractively translate: "Thou mate of Amphitrite, / Who spins the sea to gold."

27. According to the Cornford-Nilsson view which is in danger of becoming orthodox, Persephone came up not in spring but in the fall. Her descent supposedly occurred after the June harvest when the grain was stored in subterranean chambers or in large jars stored in the earth, her ascent in October when some of the grain was sown for the next year. Against this view is the direct testimony of the Hymn to Demeter, II.401 ff., whose latest editor, N. T. Richardson, accepts the traditional view: "There can be little doubt that the *Hymn* here represents what was from very early times felt to be the significance of the myth: the absence of Core corresponds to the winter, when corn and other plants are under the earth, her return to the spring-time when the earth is again covered in flowers, and the corn is growing" (*Homeric Hymn to Demeter* [Oxford, 1974], 284). Apart from the evidence of the Hymn, it is a mistake to read a great myth as the mere transcription of a technological arrangement. Men

rejoiced at the return of Persephone long before they thought of building vaults to store her yield.

28. Compare Farnell, *Works of Pindar*, II, 43: "In [*Paian* 2.49] the same epithet φοινικόπεζα is applied to Hekate and is merely conventional; we may therefore suspect it is so here." He goes on to admit: "On the other hand, we may attach a special significance to the epithet λεύκιππος, for we cannot say that this was a conventional epithet for any goddess."

29. Compare Wilamowitz, *Isyllos von Epidauros*, 183: "φοινικόπεζα kann nur auf die Farbe des Schuhes gehen; viele Tonfiguren, die thronende Göttinen darstellen, haben die roten Schuhe." See also C. M. Bowra, *Pindar* (Oxford, 1964), 43: "Though it is tempting to see in Demeter's adjective . . . an imaginative invention for the goddess who treads on the ripe ears of corn, the same epithet is applied to Hekate . . . and seems to be derived from the painted feet of statues."

30. Compare A. Boeckh, *Pindari Opera* (Leipzig, 1811-1819), 163: "Recte Ceres ob segetis maturae colorem illo epitheto ornata ab interpretibus dicitur: sic apud Virg. Georg. I.297, seges matura est *rubicunda Ceres.*"

31. Slater, *Lexicon, s.v. phuteuō*, distinguishes between the senses "plant" for trees and "beget, be born" for human beings. The stated aim of his lexicon is *Pindaron ek Pindarou saphēnizein.* A good aim, but is this the way to go about it?

DEIANEIRA'S DARK CUPBOARD:
A QUESTION FROM SOPHOCLES

1. *Supplices*, 201-202.

2. G. S. Kirk finds "no specific evidence" for this traditional view of Herakles in *The Nature of Greek Myths* (Penguin Books, 1974), 204. It is hard to see what else Sophocles had in mind when at *Trakh.* 1011 ff. he made Herakles reproach the Greek bystanders for not helping him, although "I have destroyed myself in purging your country of pests by sea and land." When Pindar speaks of the pillars that "the hero-god set up as marks of furthest seafaring; he destroyed monstrous beasts in the sea and discovered the currents of the shallows . . . and made the land known" (*Nemean* 3.22 ff.), he is surely speaking of the hero's cultural services.

3. *The Symbolism of Evil*, trans. Emerson Buchanan (Boston, 1969), 348.

4. Though the image of woman as ploughed field is of course common and usually neutral, it sounds more like an affront at

Antigone 568-569 when Ismene asks Creon, "Will you kill your own son's bride?" and he answers grossly, "There are plenty of other fields for him to plough."

5. The straits are those of the Black Sea, one extreme point of the known world, the pillars Herakles set up at Gibraltar the other. See Hugh Lloyd-Jones in *Classical Quarterly*, 4 (1945), 91-93.

6. To save a reader anxiety let me remark that I am aware of another way of interpreting lines like these, in the light of which my way will seem wasteful ingenuity. What the chorus wants to say, it may be held, is "Where is Herakles?" They decorate this simple question (though the language of Greek poetry is complex and brilliantly stylized, the thought is usually quite straightforward) in a purely conventional way by asking the sun to tell them. (The sun sees everything, *Iliad* 3.277.) No less conventionally they go on to locate Herakles somewhere between the two farthest points of the known world. (Greek polar thinking.) So far as it goes, this approach is perfectly correct but there will always be those who believe that a great poet requires us to go a good deal further.

7. See P. E. Easterling, "Sophocles, *Trachiniae*," *London University Institute of Classical Studies Bulletin*, 15 (1968), 59, and de Romilly, *Loss and Modification: Time in Greek Tragedy* (Ithaca, 1968), 90.

8. Cedric H. Whitman, *Sophocles: A Study of Heroic Humanism* (Cambridge, Mass., 1971), chap. 6.

9. τὸ γὰρ νεάζον ἐν τοιοῖσδε βόσκεται
χώροισιν αὑτοῦ, καί νιν οὐ θάλπος θεοῦ,
οὐδ' ὄμβρος, οὐδὲ πνευμάτων οὐδὲν κλονεῖ,
ἀλλ' ἡδοναῖς ἄμοχθον ἐξαίρει βίον
ἐς τοῦθ', ἕως... (144-148)

10. There may be a similar distancing of too personal emotion in her words at 547 ff. (see p. 72, below).

11. At 1168 Lewis Campbell notes that "Dodona and not Delphi is the fountain of revelation in the *Trach*, because Herakles is not to receive oracles from any one less than his father Zeus."

12. Of the verb Deianeira uses ("risen") the scholiast notes: ἀνασχὸν δὲ ἀναφανέν, ἀνατεῖλαν ἐκ μεταφορᾶς τοῦ ἡλίου.

13. Following Kitto and, less directly, Jebb rather than Kamerbeek and Mazon, who take *phronein* in the sense of *sōphronein*: "d'autant qu'elle est seule à se dominer." But surely the girl's self-control is not to the point here?

14. It is more complicated than this, though. She is in a muddle and by the end of the scene cracks are showing in her mag-

nanimous front. She tells Likhas, on his way to rejoin Herakles, to wait while she decides on gifts to "match" those he sent her. Her verb, *prosarmozein*, means "to fit, attach closely to," and is oddly used here. (She again employs the simple form of the verb oddly, at 687, when she speaks of "applying" the love charm to Herakles' robe.) She seems already to be thinking of the robe that is to win back his love by magic, little knowing how closely it will attach itself to Herakles' body. Her final words to Likhas are also loaded, though here the irony is personal, not dramatic: "It isn't right for you to return empty-handed when you come with this whole troop," the troop of captive women which includes Herakles' new mistress Iole.

15. E. R. Dodds, *Plato: Gorgias* (Oxford, 1971), 477b.

16. ὁρῶ γὰρ ἥβην τὴν μὲν ἕρπουσαν πρόσω,
τὴν δὲ φθίνουσαν· ὧν ἀφαρπάζειν φιλεῖ
ὀφθαλμὸς ἄνθος, τῶν δ᾽ ὑπεκτρέπει πόδα.

17. See, e.g., C. M. Bowra, *Sophoclean Tragedy* (Oxford, 1944), 147 f.

18. "The Women of Trachis," pt. 2, *Arion*, 2/2 (Summer 1963), 118.

19. *The Greeks and the Irrational* (Berkeley, Los Angeles, London, 1971), 192.

20. θαυμαστῶς δὲ βρώματα πρίονος εἶπεν τὸ πρίσμα. τρόπον γάρ τινα ἐσθίων τὸ ξύλον ὁ πρίων ἐκεῖνο τὸ λεπτὸν ἀποβάλλει.

21. E. R. Dodds, introduction to his edition of the *Bacchae*, 2d ed. (Oxford, 1966), xii.

22. *Phainesthai* (to appear) and related words may have a stronger sense in earlier Greek than we usually allow, standing as we do on the other side of the great divide after which appearance dwindled into mere appearance, not full presence. Athene's dreadful or wonderful eyes do not simply appear to Achilles in *Iliad* 1.200 (δεινὼ δέ οἱ ὄσσε φάανθεν), nor does the rose-fingered dawn-goddess simply appear (φάνη) to mortals. They burst forth in radiance. For Plato, still, beauty is *ekphanestaton*, that which most completely appears (*Phaedrus* 250d). Heidegger writes: "*phainesthai* means [to the Greeks] that a being assumes its radiance, and in that radiance it appears" (*On the Way to Language*, trans. Peter D. Hertz (New York, 1971), 38.

23. *The Life and Work of Sophocles* (London and New York, 1953), 78.

24. It is used of quick, wriggling things like snakes and worms; of changeable things; of shining things, like bronze armor; of night with its shimmering or flickering stars; of discolored, mottled flesh.

25. προστετακὼς φάσματι· προσκεκολλημένος τῷ ἰῷ τῆς ὕδρας.

26. *Life and Work of Sophocles*, 78-79.

27. *Inferno* 25.58-63. "Ivy was never so rooted to a tree as the fearful beast enwound its limbs about the other's. Then they stuck together, as though they had been hot wax, and mingled their colors, nor did the one nor the other seem what he was before."

28. Hugh Lloyd-Jones, "Greek Tragedy: Sophocles' *Women of Trachis,*" in ed. Lloyd-Jones (Penguin Books, 1965), 114.

29. Whitman, *Sophocles*, 119.

30. So far as I am concerned, the observation comes from William Arrowsmith, in conversation. No doubt it occurs somewhere in the literature.

31. No doubt commentators are right to take *tuphlos* as passive here (Kamerbeek) and to translate "unseen" (Jeb) rather than "blind." (Though Mazon is content to write "détruit par un désastre aveugle.") Nonetheless it is unwise to press discriminations of this sort, which belong to the classroom and not to the intense experience of poetry. Try pinning down a word in Shakespeare to one meaning only. It works no better with Sophocles. Lewis Campbell long ago warned us not to approach his language "with alien preconceptions and view it through the foreign medium of a grammar-laden consciousness" (preface to his edition of Sophocles, I.xiv).

32. H. D. F. Kitto, *Greek Tragedy*, 2d ed. (London, 1971), 293.

33. Sophocles' Philoctetes uses the same word of his pains at 745.

34. ἐμοὶ γὰρ ἦν πρόφαντον ἐκ πατρὸς πάλαι,
πρὸς τῶν πνεόντων μηδενὸς θανεῖν ποτε,
ἀλλ᾽ ὅστις Ἅιδου φθίμενος οἰκήτωρ πέλοι.
ὅδ᾽ οὖν ὁ θὴρ Κένταυρος, ὡς τὸ θεῖον ἦν
πρόφαντον, οὕτω ζῶντά μ᾽ ἔκτεινεν θανών.
φανῶ δ᾽ ἐγὼ τούτοισι συμβαίνοντ᾽ ἴσα
μαντεῖα καινά, τοῖς πάλαι ξυνήγορα,
ἃ τῶν ὀρείων καὶ χαμαικοιτῶν ἐγὼ
Σελλῶν ἐσελθὼν ἄλσος ἐξεγραψάμην
πρὸς τῆς πατρῴας καὶ πολυγλώσσου δρυός,
ἥ μοι χρόνῳ τῷ ζῶντι καὶ παρόντι νῦν
ἔφασκε μόχθων τῶν ἐφεστώτων ἐμοὶ
λύσιν τελεῖσθαι· κἀδόκουν πράξειν καλῶς.
τὸ δ᾽ ἦν ἄρ᾽ οὐδὲν ἄλλο πλὴν θανεῖν ἐμέ.
τοῖς γὰρ θανοῦσι μόχθος οὐ προσγίγνεται.

35. In Sophocles, *lampros* is used in the literal or near literal sense of "splendidus, illustris" or, metaphorically, "de rebus insignibus et magnificis" (Ellendt, *Lexicon Sophocleum, s.v.*). He uses the word, e.g., of the sun's light (*El.* 17, *Ant.* 416), of lightning (*Aj.* 257), of Oedipus's once bright eyes now dimmed forever (*OT* 1483), of Orestes' brilliant appearance in the chariot race (*El.* 685), of the chorus's brilliant words in praise of Athens (*OC* 721).

36. The vagaries of Pound's *Women of Trachis* are for the most part unilluminating, since they are not governed by any clear grasp of the statement the play is making. As a workshop study of the formal and stylistic problems Greek tragedy poses for translation, problems we have hardly yet started to face, his version is of the greatest interest.

37. Cf. *OT* 1403-1405 where Oedipus, calling on his father's marriage bed and his own, says: "You gave me birth and then sent forth the same seed again" (ἀνεῖτε ταὐτὸν σπέρμα) —Laios's and his own.

38.   ...χάλυβος
    λιθόκολλητον στόμιον παρέχουσ᾽,
    ἀνάπαυε βοήν, ὡς ἐπίχαρτον
    τελέουσ᾽ ἀεκούσιον ἔργον.

39. *Sophocles and Pericles* (Oxford, 1954), 2.

40. Although, as Kamerbeek points out (5-6), Deianeira is presented *more tragico* in a dithyramb of Bacchylides (16 in Bruno Snell's Teubner, ed.) which seems to have points of resemblance to the *Trakhiniai.* We do not know, however, which work was written first.

41. Pausanias 10.4.7.

42. *Pericles*, 38.

43. *The Greeks and the Irrational*, 193.

44. *Greek Myths*, 203, 206 ff.

45. *Khoephoroi* 585 ff.: "Many things earth breeds, dreadful, fearful, and the arms of the sea swarm with hateful beasts." And *Ajax* 669 ff., with Jebb's comment.

46. W. K. C. Guthrie, *A History of Greek Philosophy* (Cambridge, 1969), III, 18.

47. It so happens that Greek expressions of this theme seem to be preserved only in later literature, e.g., in Aratos 110 f., Oppian, *Halieutika* 1.354 ff., *Anthologia Palatina* 9.29 (Antiphilos). Horace's powerful statement on the impiety of navigation in *Odes* 1.3 must, however, surely reflect earlier, Greek thought: "In vain has God severed land from land by the estranging sea if impious ships cross the waters that should not

be touched. Bold to dare all things, humankind ruins through forbidden sacrilege" (*Audax omnia perpeti / gens humana ruit per vetitum nefas*).

48. Pindar uses a similar verb (*tarassein*) of the heroes in the Isles of the Blest who "do not disturb the earth with their strong hands or the sea for a narrow living" (*Olympian* 2.63-65). In Ovid's Golden Age the earth, "unwounded by ploughshares" (*nec ullis saucia vomeribus*), of herself gave all things freely (*Metamorphoses* 1.101-102). Note the more anthropocentric stress in Genesis where the Fall is seen not in its effect on nature but on man ("In the sweat of thy face shalt thou eat bread").

49. For the two views on the advance of civilization, see E. R. Dodds, *The Ancient Concept of Progress* (Oxford, 1973), 7-8.

50. *Between Past and Future* (New York, 1968), 42.

51. *Poetae Melici Graeci*, ed. D. L. Page (Oxford, 1962), fr. 581:

ἀεναοῖς ποταμοῖσ' ἄνθεσι τ' εἰαρινοῖς
ἀελίου τε φλογὶ χρυσέας τε σελάνας
καὶ θαλασσαίαισι δίναισ' ἀντία θέντα μένος στάλας.

52. *Ibid.*, fr. 531.

53. This aspect of Sophocles has been fully and finely studied by Bernard M. W. Knox in *The Heroic Temper* (Berkeley and Los Angeles, 1966). See also his *Oedipus at Thebes* (New Haven, 1957), 159.

54. See Edward B. Irving, Jr., *A Reading of Beowulf* (New Haven and London, 1968), 98.

55. *Beowulf*, trans. Edwin Morgan (Berkeley and Los Angeles, 1952).

56. *The Prose Edda of Snorri Sturluson: Tales from Norse Mythology*, trans. Jean I. Young (Berkeley and Los Angeles, 1964), 66.

57. Irving, *A Reading of Beowulf*, 90, notes "verbal parallels connecting the two creative acts."

58. More literally lines 112-113 read: "Ogres and elves and monsters, giants that fought with God."

59. Some knowledge of the poem may have entered the Greek tradition via Hesiod. See chap. 2 of Peter Walcot, *Hesiod and the Near East* (Cardiff, 1966).

60. Tablet I, 21 ff., in *Ancient Near Eastern Texts*, trans. E. A. Speiser, ed. James B. Pritchard (Princeton, 1955), 60 ff.

61. *Poetics* 1450a18-19. In context it may be better to take "the end," *to telos*, not as I take it here, following the Budé trans., but as "the end of the story" (Else) or dramatic fable.

62. Trans. James Strachey (New York, 1961), 36.

63. Trans. James Strachey (New York, 1962), 65-66.

64. *Beyond the Pleasure Principle*, 32.

65. Eric Weil, "Wisdom, Revelation, and Doubt: Perspectives on the First Millennium B.C.," *Daedalus* (Spring 1975). I draw the picture in far bolder, cruder terms than the contributors to *Daedalus* who, to my mind, unduly muffle their important theme by an excess of scholarly caution.

66. For a full discussion of the two terms, see Victor Ehrenberg, "Polypragmosyne: A Study in Greek Politics," *Journal of Hellenic Studies*, LXVII (1947), 46 ff. My greatly simplified discussion ignores, among other things, the political dimensions of the debate.

67. Introduction to Arrowsmith's translation [*The Birds* (New York, 1961), and in his "Aristophanes' Birds: The Fantasy Politics of Eros," *Arion*, n.s.1/1 (Spring 1973).

68. Fr. 594 in *Poetae Melici Graeci*, ed. Page. Since only four certain words of Simonides are embedded in a passage from Plutarch, it is not in fact quite certain what the thrust of the lines is. I follow H. Fränkel, *Early Greek Poetry and Philosophy*, trans. Moses Hadas and James Willis (New York, London, 1975), 305.

69. *Truth and Method*, trans. anon. (New York, 1975), 494.

70. A pervasive theme in Heidegger, but see especially: *Platons Lehre von der Wahrheit* (Bern, 1947); "Die Zeit des Weltbildes," in *Holzwege* (Frankfurt, 1963), e.g., 80 ff.; "What are Poets For?" in *Poetry, Language, Thought*, trans. Albert Hofstadter (New York, 1971), 110 ff. For Heidegger's thinking on technology, see "Die Frage nach der Technik," in *Vorträge und Aufsätze* (Tübingen, 1967), I.5 ff.

71. Gadamer, *Truth and Method*, 262-263.

72. "The largest of the remaining natural areas left on this planet to succumb to man's insatiable hunger for power and domination, or to civilization's alleged material needs, is the vast Amazon region with its great, yet extremely fragile, rain-forest ecosystem" (Dr. Harald Sioli, director of the Max Planck Institute of Limnology in West Germany, preface to R. J. A. Goodland and H. S. Irwin, *Amazon Jungle: Green Hell to Red Desert?* (Amsterdam, Oxford, New York, 1975).

73. *Notes from Underground*, trans. anon. (New York and Toronto, 1961), 114.

74. See Philip Rieff, *Freud: The Mind of the Moralist* (Garden City, N.Y., 1961), 375.

75. "Building Dwelling Thinking," in *Poetry, Language, Thought*, 150-151.

76. *Ibid.*, 147.

DANTE ANTAGONISTES

1. *Dante Studies 2: Journey to Beatrice* (Cambridge, Mass., 1958), v (= *Studies 2*).

2. Quotations from *Studies 2*, 8, 93, and from "The Vistas in Retrospect," *Modern Language Notes*, 81 (1966), 58 (= "Vistas").

3. *Dante Studies 1: Elements of Structure* (Cambridge, Mass., 1954), 77 (= *Studies 1*).

4. "Dante," in *Selected Essays, 1917-1932* (London, 1932), 244, 257, 243.

5. "Vistas," 60.

6. *Dante's Drama of the Mind* (Princeton, 1953), 7.

7. *Basic Questions in Theology* (New York, 1971), 109-110.

8. *The Lion and the Honeycomb* (New York, 1955), 226.

9. *Prefaces to Renaissance Literature* (Cambridge, Mass., 1965), 44.

10. *Dante Alighieri: The Divine Comedy*, trans., with commentary, by Charles S. Singleton, 6 vols. (Princeton, 1970-1975).

11. *Studies 1*, 1-2.

12. *Three Philosophical Poets* (Cambridge, Mass., 1910), 115-116.

13. *Milton's God* (London, 1965), 34.

14. *Studies 1*, 28.

15. *Wahrheit und Methode*, 2d ed. (Tübingen, 1965).

16. In *Mythic-Symbolic Language and Philosophic Anthropology*, ed. David Rasmussen (New York, 1971), 135-150.

17. Theodore Kisiel, "The Happening of Tradition," *Man and World*, 2, 3 (1969), 366.

18. *Wahrheit und Methode*, 289 f., 356 f., 374 f.

19. Nathan A. Scott, Jr., *The Wild Prayer of Longing: Poetry and the Sacred* (New Haven and London, 1971), 25.

20. In *The Doctrine and Discipline of Divorce*, Milton censured the Christian who "would fain work himself aloof these rocks and quicksands, and thinks it best to conclude that God certainly did dispense, but by some way to us unknown, and so to leave it. But to this I oppose that a Christian by no means ought rest himself in such an ignorance; whereby so many absurdities will strait reflect both against the purity, justice, and wisdome of God."

21. "Notes toward a Supreme Fiction," Part 1, III, in *The Collected Poems of Wallace Stevens* (New York, 1972), 383.

22. Quoted by Douglas Bush in *John Milton* (New York, 1967), 153.

23. Croce's reservations about the language and style bear mainly on the opening cantos: "I primi canti dell'*Inferno* sono, in generale, i piú gracili; o che appartenessero a un primo abbozzo, poi ritoccato e adattato . . . , o che ritenessero dell'incertezza di tutti i cominciamenti, accresciuta in questo caso dalla difficoltà di costruire e mettere in moto una macchina così grande. Specialmente il primo canto dà qualche impressione di stento. . . . I legamenti qui e nei canti prossimi seguenti sono fiacchi, con titubanze artificiate a risposte che vanno di là dalla domanda . . . lo stile stesso, il ritmo, la terzina hanno poca pienezza e tengono sovente del prosaico" (*La poesia di Dante* [Bari, 1952], 67-68). Even if Croce's critical understanding of the poem was defective, we can grant him a sense of the Italian language not inferior to that of Dante's Anglo-Saxon admirers.

24. *Studies 1*, 24.

25. *De doctrina christiana* I.4, quoted in *Studies 1*, 24-25.

26. From the end of the first book of the *Secretum* where Augustine complains of Petrarch's inconstancy: "tuque inops consilii modo huc modo illuc mira fluctuatione volvaris, nusquam integer, nusquam totus" (*Francesco Petrarca: Prose*, Ricciardi ed. (Milan and Naples, 1955), 68.

27. *Studies 2*, 7.

28. *Wahrheit und Methode*, 370.

29. *The Empty Space* (New York, 1969), 42.

30. *On the Way to Language*, trans. Peter D. Hertz (New York, 1971), 163.

DARK WITH EXCESSIVE BRIGHT:
FOUR WAY OF LOOKING AT GÓNGORA

1. *The Solitudes of Don Luis de Góngora*, trans. into verse by Edward Meryon Wilson (Cambridge, 1965).

2. *The Solitudes of Luis de Góngora*, Spanish text with English trans. by Gilbert F. Cunningham (Baltimore, 1968). See also Cunningham, *Luis de Góngora y Argote: Polyphemus* (privately printed, 1965).

3. The quincentenary of Ariosto's birth saw two versions of the *Furioso*, a prose translation by Guido Waldman (London, Oxford, New York, 1974), and a translation of Cantos 1-23 in workaday verse by Barbara Reynolds (Penguin Books, 1975). W. C. Atkinson's prose *Lusiads* (Penguin, 1952), being concerned with "the substance, not the form, of the original," leaves out the mythology and much else that makes the poem a poem.

Leonard Bacon's *Lusiads* (New York, 1950) is in very dull verse but the book is useful and suggests a genuine dedication to Camoëns. Joseph Tusiani's *Gerusalem Delivered* (Rutherford, 1970) sticks closer to the literal sense than Fairfax's Tudor version but is quite lifeless. H. M. Priest's *Adonis* (Ithaca, 1967), in the blankest blank verse, provides the "sense" of selected passages from Marino's vast poem. There is a very free virtuoso rendering of the famous stanzas on the nightingale, from Canto 7, in Ian Fletcher's *Motets* (Reading, 1962). Some distinguished translations from Scève's *Délie* by Edwin Morgan appeared in *Nine*, III.2 (1951), reprinted in *Fifty Renascence Love-Poems* (Reading, 1975). More recently Nicholas Kilmer has interestingly tried to find a modern manner for Petrarch and Ronsard in some versions published in *Arion*, n.s., 2/3 (1975); 3/2 (1977).

4. I am aware that Milton studies are now a flourishing academic enterprise, but this Milton revival is very unlike the Donne revival with which it has been compared. It sometimes seems that those who write on Milton do not so much like his poetry as regard it as a splendid field for scholarly research.

5. "As a crimson flower languishes and dies, cut down by the passing ploughshare, or as a poppy overburdened by rain droops its head in the garden. So, the color draining from his face, Dardinello's life fails. It fails, and with it fail the spirit and courage of all his men" (*Orlando Furioso*, 18.153).

6. 'Noble and harmonious, Maria, while all day long the rose of dawn shines on your cheeks, Phoebus in your eyes, and on your forehead, day; and while the wind with soft discourtesy ruffles that flying mane, whose gold was hoarded in the veins of Araby and coined by Tagus's sands; before Phoebus is eclipsed by age and clear day turns to somber night, let dawn fly from the mortal cloud; before the blond treasure that now is yours outdoes the whiteness of white snow, enjoy, enjoy! the color, the light, the gold."

7. "The Noble Rider and the Sound of Words," in *The Necessary Angel* (New York, 1951), 8-9.

8. "Claridad y belleza de las 'Soledades,'" in *Estudios y ensayos gongorinos* (Madrid, 1960), 74.

9. *Language and Poetry* (Cambridge, Mass., 1961), 31.

10. *Revaluation* (London, 1936), 49-50, 56.

11. I express what I take to be a common attitude to Milton's verse. It is very far from my own.

12. *Elizabethan and Metaphysical Imagery* (Chicago and London, 1965), 61.

13. *Mallarmé* (Chicago and London, 1962), 254.

14. "La retina de Góngora es sensible como la de ninguno,

pero sus ojos son antiguos como la humanidad: antiguos y sabios." I borrow this sentence, and a good deal else, from Alonso's brilliant essay of 1927 on the *Soledades*, "Claridad y belleza," republished in *Estudios...gongorinos*, 71.

15. I draw freely on the admirable commentaries by Alonso (*Góngora y el "Polifemo"*) and Antonio Vilanova (*Las fuentes y los temas del Polifemo de Góngora* [Madrid, 1957]).

16. There is an even more startling example near the end of the *Soledades*, finely analyzed by Alonso, though he does not make this particular point. Falcons, *at rest* on the falconers' gloves, are called "los raudos torbellinos de Noruega" (the tempestuous whirlwinds of Norway) which they resemble *in flight*.

17.   Donde espumoso el mar sicil'iano
el pie argenta de plato al Lilibeo
(bóveda o de las fraguas de Vulcano,
o tumba de los huesos di Tifeo),
pálidas señas cenizoso un llano
—cuando no del sacrílego deseo—
del duro oficio da. Allí una alta roca
mordaza es a una gruta, de su boca.

Guarnición tosca de este escollo duro
troncos robustos son, a cuya greña
menos luz debe, menos aire puro
la caverna profunda, que a la peña;
caliginoso lecho, el seno obscuro
ser de la negra noche nos lo enseña
infame turba de nocturnas aves,
gimiendo tristes y volando graves.

De este, pues, formidable de la tierra
bostezo, el melancólico vacío
a Polifemo, horror de aquella sierra,
bárbara choza es, albergue umbrío.

18. Wilson translates the last two lines: "Sweet apples, that in Atalanta's way / Had been a rein of gold." This brilliantly and perhaps unintentionally out-Góngoras Góngora, since not long before we have had a reference to the *rain* of gold ("la pluvia luciente de oro fino") by means of which Zeus took Danaë. Though Góngora does not himself connect the two myths, it is quite in his way to keep a mythological allusion covertly at work, as for instance at 1.579 where the description of a rock surrounded by narcissi is followed a little later by a veiled reference to the story of Narcissus (585 ff.).

19. Compare for instance the passage in *Pythian 9*, 97-100:

πλεῖστα νικάσαντά σε καὶ τελεταῖς
ὡρίαις ἐν Παλλάδος εἶδον ἄφωνοί
θ᾽ ὡς ἕκασται φίλτατον
παρθενικαὶ πόσιν ἦ
υἱὸν εὔχοντ᾽, ὦ Τελεσίκρατες,

20. In his poem "Arachne" Empson writes: "But oh beware, whose vain / Hydroptic soap my meagre water saves" (*Collected Poems* [London, 1956], 23).

21. "The Poetic Unity of the *Soledades* of Góngora," *Bulletin of Hispanic Studies* (October 1954).

22. *The Ladder of Vision* (New York, 1962), 49.

23. "Stephane Mallarmé: Sonnet in 'ix,'" *Delos*, 4 (1970), 27, reprinted in *Traducción: literatura y literalidad* (Madrid, 1971).

24. L. J. Woodward in the April 1962 issue. Woodward allows that though Guillén is not to be trusted on the substance of Góngora's poetry, "on structure and rhythm . . . there is everything to be learned from this practising poet."

25. "The falcon-gentle, with his claw a ray, / His feathers lightning" (Wilson).

26. "And while one sweetly his own death foretold / In reeds and greenery, / Another led her cygnets to the sea" (Wilson).

27. Frank Kermode, *Wallace Stevens* (Edinburgh and London, 1960), 109. A good deal of what Kermode says of Stevens in this vivid little primer might be said of Góngora too, e.g., on "nature" in Stevens's poetry (p. 112): "It is a nature full of the squawk and clatter of birds, of unique flowers, of the excitement of changing seasons, of unexpected persons welling out of the *fonction fabulatrice*, of resemblances, of irrational transitions. It gives us pleasure because of the way we are and because of where we are; because it satisfies our desire to convert our *Lumpenwelt*, the irrational needs of our sensibility."

28. Trans. R. J. Hollingdale (Penguin Books, 1961), 102.

29. *Between Past and Future* (New York, 1968), 30.

30. *Milton's God* (London, 1965), 254-255.

31. Empson remarks: "Much has been said in recent times of the marvellous intellectual completeness of the religion, based securely upon its profound paradoxes; but they are a matter of jamming together all available contradictions with the standard solution 'Heads I win, tails I burn you alive'" (*ibid.*, 252-253).

32. "Vieles kann ich ertragen," *Venetian Epigrams* number 66 (*Die Gedichte der Ausgabe letzter Hand, dtv-Gesamtausgabe* [Munich, 1961], vol. 4, 207). The last word of the poem, as Goethe wrote it, is "Christ" (Christians, or Christ?). Most editors substitute a cross.

33. *Nietzsche*, trans. C. F. Wallraff and F. J. Schmitz (Tucson, AZ, 1965), 320 f.

34. *Nietzsche* (Meridian Books, 1965), 311, 312.

35. "Esthétique du Mal," in *The Collected Poems of Wallace Stevens* (New York, 1972), 315-316.

LEOPARDI: THE POET IN A TIME OF NEED

1. Foreword to the first edition of Iris Origo's *Leopardi* (London, 1935), v.

2. The most serviceable edition, by N. Gallo and C. Gàrboli (Turin, 1962), has a full but not excessive philological commentary.

3. Leopardi held the Italian canzone to be the formal equivalent of the Greek choric ode (*Zibaldone* I.814-815).

4. I translate where translation is helpful or possible. Here it is neither.

5. "Once the streams were the home of the white nymphs, tranquil home and mirror were the lucid streams. Strange dances of immortal feet shook the headlong peaks and the steep woods (today, lonely haunt of the winds)."

6. "Now the tired shepherd followed by his weary flock seeks the shade and stream and thickets of the shaggy wood-god. No breeze wanders along the quiet bank" (Horace, *Odes* 3.29).

7. Götzen-Dämmerung, "Was ich den Alten verdanke," in *Werke in drei Bänden*, ed. Schlechta (Munich, 1966), II, 1027.

8. "And the shepherd boy, who was leading his thirsty lambs to the glancing noontide shades and the flowery brink of the rivers, heard the piercing song of rustic Pans along the banks, and saw the water tremble and marveled, for, not revealed to his eyes, the quivered goddess was going down into the warm current and cleansing the dust of the bloodstained chase from her snowy flank and virginal arms."

9. Achilles, when Athene appeared to him during his quarrel with Agamemnon, was amazed, θάμβησεν (*Iliad* 1.119).

10. Though the point is often made (e.g., by Bickersteth, 51, 64-65), it has never to my knowledge been adequately demonstrated. We need a stylistic study of the *Canti* and perhaps of the *Operette Morali* showing how Leopardi, a great Latinist in Latinate Italy, achieved in his best work a Greek ease and fluidity. Of a passage from "A Silvia" Bickersteth remarks, I think justly, that "it might be Sappho herself writing Italian." In a line like "che tra gli spenti ad abitar sen giva" ("Amore e morte," 61) and

261

in parts of "Sopra un bassorilievo antico sepolcrale" there is the perfect gravity of Sophocles. Countless pages of *Zibaldone* show Leopardi's profound knowledge of the Greek language and his sensitivity to its slightest nuances.

11. "From the summit of the ancient tower, solitary thrush, you go on singing to the countryside until day dies, and the harmony wanders through the valley. All around spring shines in the air and exults through the fields, so that gazing on it the heart is moved to tenderness. Listen to the bleating flocks, the herds lowing! The other birds, content, race each other in wheeling flights through the open sky, they too celebrating their best season. You, pensive and apart, gaze at it all; no companions, no flights—you care nothing for pleasure, avoid their games. You sing, and in this fashion spend the loveliest flower of your life and of the year."

Alas, how like your ways to mine! Pleasure and laughter, young life's sweet companions, and you, close kin to youth, love, the sharp regret of our later days—this somehow I care nothing for. Instead I almost fly from them; almost a hermit, a stranger to my native place, I pass my life's springtime. This day which is now yielding to evening our little town always celebrates. Listen to the sound of bells through the clear sky, listen to the thunder of gunshot which keeps reverberating in the distance from hamlet to hamlet. The young people of the place in their holiday best leave their homes and scatter through the streets, to see and be seen, and grow glad in heart. I, solitary, going out to this remote part of the countryside, put off all delight and joy to some other time. And meanwhile against my glance, stretched into the golden air, the sun strikes as after the clear day it sinks between distant hills, and seems to say that blessed youth time fails.

You, lonely little bird, when you have reached the evening of the span that the stars will give you, for sure you will not grieve at your course of life, for all your desires were nature's fruit. As for me, if it is not granted me to shun the hated threshold of age —when these eyes will be mute to every other heart and the world a void for them and the day to come more wearisome and gloomy than the day at hand—how will this choice of mine appear then? How will these years appear, and I myself? Alas, I shall repent and often, comfortlessly, look back.

12. "Dialogo di Tristano e di un amico," *Le poesie e le prose*, I.1026.

13. "Intorno alla poesia romantica," *Le poesie e le prose*, II.479.

14. E.g., *Zib.* I.395-396, 1210.

15. E.g., "Di vanità, di belle / fole e strani pensieri / si comonea l'umana vita" ("Ad Angelo Mai," 115-117). Cf also "Le ricordanze," 7.

16. "You went dancing forth. Joy shone on your brow, shone in your eyes that sure imagination, that light of youth."

17. Letter of Nov. 22, 1817, in *The Letters of John Keats,* ed. M. B. Forman (Oxford, 1952), 67.

18. *Zibaldone* I.184-185.

19. "Dialogo di Timandro e di Eleandro," *Le poesie e le prose,* I.987.

20. *Zibaldone* I.223-224.

21. *Ibid.,* I.85.

22. *Le lettere,* 440, June 1823.

23. "Intorno alla poesia romantica," 514.

24. "Era già l'ora che volge il disio / ai navicanti e 'ntenerisce il core / lo dí c'han detto ai dolci amici addio; / e che lo novo peregrin d'amore / punge, se ode squilla di lontano / che paia il giorno pianger che si more" (*Purgatorio* 8, 1-6). Strictly, there are two figures here, a traveler who leaves home by ship and a pilgrim who leaves, presumably by land, on a different mission. Leopardi does not require us to make this distinction.

25. *Vorlesungen uber die Ästhetik,* in G. W. F. Hegel, *Werke in zwanzig Bänden* (Frankfurt am Main, 1970), XIV, 128 f.

26. There is no reference in *Zibaldone* to Hegel, whose influence was not felt in Italy until the 1830s and 1840s. (See Mario Sansone, "Leopardi e la filosofia del settecento," in *Leopardi: Introduzione all'opera e antologia della critica,* ed. N. Borsellino and A. Marinari [Rome, 1973], 176.) Leopardi's few references to Kant and German philosophy of the period are unappreciative and suggest no depth of knowledge.

27. "Tasso e il suo genio familiare," *Le poesie e le prose,* I.880.

28. "There he looks on the open sea, here on the blond wheat waving in the sunburnt valleys" (*Orlando Furioso* 28.92). An Italian Keats would have wanted the word *aprico* when he wrote of "the deep-delvèd earth, / Tasting of Flora and the country-green, / Dance and Provençal song, and sunburnt mirth." An Italian Stevens would have needed it for the fourth section of "Credences of Summer." The entrancing word *apricot* is said to come, by a false derivation, from *in aprico coctus* ("cooked in the sunburnt air").

29. Compare "Tu pria che l'erbe inaridisse il verno" in "A Silvia," "Pur tu, solinga, eterna peregrina" in "Canto notturno," and "E tu, lenta ginestra" in the poem of that name.

30. *Zibaldone* I.738.

31. In a prose note for an uncompleted poem on girls caught in a storm, Leopardi first writes "Ahi! povere fanciulle" (poor girls), then at once translates it into aulic Leopardian, "Ahi! triste donzellette" (pp. 432-433 in the Gallo and Gàrboli edition of the *Canti*).

32. *Le lettere*, 601.

33. *Ibid.*, 836. The February letter is on p. 827.

34. I do not know if it has been noticed that a fragment of this meter does in fact appear in "Alla primavera," just after the epiphany of Diana: "Vissero i fiori e l'erbe, / vissero i boschi un dí" (39-40). These are the *settenari*, the first *piano*, the second *tronco* or catalectic, found in lines two, three, and four of each half strophe of "Il risorgimento." That is to say, the sprightly measure in which Leopardi had once celebrated the old vital nature returned to his mind when he experienced nature's rebirth.

35. "With my returning life the field and wood and mountain live; the spring speaks to my heart, the sea talks to me."

36. M. H. Abrams, *The Mirror and the Lamp* (New York, 1958), 67.

37. In addition to "Il passero solitario," see lines 17 and 30-31 of "La sera del dí di festa": "questo dí fu solenne" (Latin *solemnis*, i.e., festive), "Ecco è fuggito / il dí festivo"; from "A Silvia," "né teco le compagne ai dí festivi / ragionavan d'amore," 47-48; from "Le ricordanze," "se a feste anco talvolta . . ." 158 ff.; from "Il sabato del villaggio," "or la squilla dà segno / della festa che viene," 20-21, and also 7, 12, 47, 50.

38. "Now the bell announces the coming festa, and at that sound you would say that the heart grows glad again."

39. In the poem from which I quote, by a somewhat artificial refinement of pessimism Leopardi asserts that only the *anticipation* of the festa is joyous.

40. "But now day breaks! I waited and saw it come, and what I saw, the holy be my word."

41. See *Hölderlin: Werke und Briefe*, ed. F. Beissner (Frankfurt, 1969), II.33-35.

42. "But friend, we come too late. The gods are alive, yes, but up there above us in another world. There they are endlessly active and seem to pay little heed to whether we live or not, so sparing of us are the heavenly ones. For not always can a fragile vessel contain them; only at times can man sustain the divine plenitude. Henceforth life has become a dream about them. Yet error helps, like sleep, and need and night make us strong, until enough heroes have grown in the brazen cradle, hearts become,

as they once were, like the heavenly ones in strength. Then they will come in thunder. Meanwhile it often seems to me better to sleep than to be so companionless, to wait like this, and what to do or say in the meantime I do not know, nor why poets in a destitute time. But, you say, they are like the holy priests of the wine-god who traveled from land to land in holy night."

43. *Le lettere*, 1033, May 1832.

44. *Ibid.*

45. *Pensieri*, lxviii, *Le poesie e le prose*, II.42.

46. *Zibaldone*, I.181.

47. *Ibid.*, I.195-196.

48. Leopardi wrote in 1819: "I was terrified to find myself in the midst of nothingness, myself a nothing. I felt as though I were suffocating, reflecting and feeling that all is nothing, solid nothing" (*Zibaldone* I.112). Four years later he wrote in a letter: "Pendant un certain temps j'ai senti le vide de l'existence comme si ç'avait été une chose réelle qui pesât rudement sur mon âme. Le néant des choses était pour moi la seule chose qui existait. Il m'était toujours présent comme un fantôme affreux" (*Le lettere*, 439).

49. *Zibaldone* I.253-254.

50. "I gazed on the clear sky, on the golden paths and gardens, and here on the distant sea, there on the mountain. Mortal tongue cannot tell what I felt in my heart."

51. Translated by John Heath-Stubbs:
> Before the winter's cold withered the grass,
> Assailed and conquered by a hid disease
> You died, poor gentle child.

52. *Oeuvres*, Pléiade ed. (1965), I.651.

53. In Leopardi's *Argomenti di idilli* (1819) there is a note beginning: "Shadow of the sheds. Morning rain as in my father's drawing. Rainbow as the sun rose. Moon fallen as in my dream" (Gallo and Gàrboli ed. of *Canti*, 432).

54. "Listen, Melisso, and I'll tell you about a dream I had last night. It comes back to me as I look at the moon. I was standing by the window that gives onto the meadow, gazing up when all of a sudden the moon came loose. And it seemed to me that coming nearer and nearer as it fell it looked bigger, till at last it landed smack in the middle of the meadow. It was big as a bucket and spewed out a cloud of sparks that hissed like a live coal when you plunge it into water and put it out. That was how the moon went out—just as I've told you—in the middle of the meadow. Slowly it turned black and all the grass around it started smoking. Then I looked up at the sky and saw that there

was still a kind of glimmer there, or a trace—no, a kind of pocket where it had been torn out. I froze with fear and still don't feel quite easy."

55. In *Poetry, Language, Thought,* trans. Albert Hofstadter (New York, 1971), 93. The quotations that follow are from the early part of the essay.

56. For my purposes I translate the phrase given in German more literally than Hofstadter, who writes "a divine radiance."

THE MUSIC OF A LOST DYNASTY:
POUND IN THE CLASSROOM

1. "In a Station of the Metro," in *Personae,* 5th ptg. (New York, 1926), 109.

2. See Herbert N. Schneidau, *Ezra Pound: The Image and the Real* (Baton Rouge, 1969), 62 ff.

3. Boris de Rachewiltz, "Pagan and Magic Elements," in *New Approaches to Ezra Pound,* ed. Eva Hesse (Berkeley and Los Angeles, 1969), 194.

4. Reprinted in *Ezra Pound: Selected Prose, 1909-1965,* ed. William Cookson (New York, 1973), 125.

5. *The Letters of Ezra Pound, 1907-1941,* ed. D. D. Paige (New York, 1950), 303.

6. Siegfried Giedion, *Mechanization Takes Command* (New York, 1969): "The bread of full mechanization has the resiliency of a rubber sponge ... the bread is half-masticated, as it were, before reaching the mouth" (198); "The changed characteristics of bread always turned out to the benefit of the producer. It was as if the consumer unconsciously adapted his taste to the type of bread best suited to mass production and rapid turn-over" (201); "The question, 'how did mechanization alter bread?' cannot be put off and no doubt can remain about the answer. Mechanization has devaluated the constant character of bread and turned it into an article of fashion for which new-found charms must ever be devised" (207). Pound would say: It is not mechanization that has devalued bread but usura. In his old age he discovered that usura was only the symptom, not the cause, of our troubles: "The cause is AVARICE,"—which Petrarch defined as *rerum temporalium appetitus* (foreword to *Selected Prose*).

7. The story is told by E. R. Dodds in his edition of the *Bacchae* of Euripides, 2d ed. (Oxford, 1966), 104-105.

8. *The Pound Era* (Berkeley and Los Angeles, 1971), 171-172.

9. The word "haruspicating" is Kenner's (*Era,* 450); Kenner

thus describes Pound's approach to Chinese ideograms: "Follow the crib, and when it flags, haruspicate the characters." (*Haruspex*: the priest who scrutinized the entrails of sacrificial victims for signs.)

10. *The Barb of Time* (New York, 1969), 280 n. 49. See also the end of Canto 112:

neath

luna 🌙

11. James George Frazer, *The Golden Bough*, abr. ed. (New York, 1971), 165.

12. *Polysemus*, πολύσημος, "having many significations." Dante said of the *Comedy*: "...istius operis non est simplex sensus, immo dici potest polysemos, hoc est plurium sensuum; nam primus sensus est qui habetur per literam, alius est qui habetur per significata per literam" (letter to Can Grande).

13. "Craft and morals," in *Ezra Pound: Perspectives*, ed. Noel Stock (Chicago, 1965), 52-53.

14. The expression is Hannah Arendt's, discussing Descartes (*The Human Condition* [Chicago and London, 1969], 282).

15. *Some Letters of Ezra Pound*, ed. Louis Dudek (Montreal, 1974), letter 54.

16. See C. S. Lewis: "...that great movement of internalisation, and the consequent aggrandisement of man and dessication of the outer universe, in which the psychological history of the West has so largely consisted" (*The Discarded Image* [Oxford, 1964], 42).

17. *Ezra Pound: Poet as Sculptor* (New York, 1964), 175-177.

18. *Letters of Ezra Pound*, ed. Paige, 128.

THE SCANDAL OF NECESSITY

1. *Epoch and Artist* (New York, 1959), 106.

2. T. S. Eliot, *The Family Reunion* in *The Complete Poems and Plays, 1909-1950* (New York, 1971), 271.

3. A reporter in the *New York Times* for November 14, 1976, hailing the twentieth birthday of America's interstate highway system, described it as the citizen's "liberation from the bonds of geography."

4. Hannah Arendt, *The Human Condition* (Chicago and London, 1969), 250.

5. "La crise de l'esprit" (1919), in *Oeuvres*, Pléiade ed. (Paris, 1965), I.988. Tough-minded people often warn us against this

sort of attitude. Frank Kermode, in *The Sense of an Ending* (New York, 1967), observes how common millenarian panic has been through the ages and discovers that even the Babylonians suffered from it: "There is nothing at all distinguishing about eschatological anxiety; it was, one gathers, a feature of Babylonian culture" (95). "One gathers" is excellent, but of course the Babylonians are no longer with us.

6. *Small Is Beautiful* (New York, 1973), 101.

7. *Ibid.*, 156.

8. *Vorträge und Aufsätze* (Tübingen, 1967), I.35.

9. "Community of Resistance" is the title of the last section of *The Raft Is Not the Shore* (Boston, 1975), a series of conversations between Daniel Berrigan and Thich Nhat Hanh. See esp. 121 f.

10. *Human Condition*, 121.

11. Here I am ignoring here the Greek political justification for leisure, namely, the need to devote one's full time to the demands of the polis.

12. *Fellow Teachers* (New York, 1973), 67 f.

13. *Ibid.*, 107.

14. "Text and Context," *Salmagundi* (Winter 1975), 179.

15. A mathematician researching into "math anxiety" found that some students suffer from their perception of math as an "authoritarian" and teacher-dominated discipline (*New York Times*, Oct. 3, 1976, "The Week in Review").

16. "Text and Context," 182.

17. *Fellow Teachers*, 125.

18. Hugh Trevor-Roper, *The Rise of Christian Europe* (New York, 1965), 88.

19. David Jones, *The Sleeping Lord and Other Fragments* (London, 1974), 59-64.

20. *Poetry, Language, Thought,* trans. Albert Hofstadter (New York, 1971), 147.

21. *The Myth of the Machine* (New York, 1967), 264.

22. *Ibid.*, 269.

23. I am imagining a group composed for the most part of what we loosely call humanists. As the academy disintegrates, there are likely to be other groups organized in different ways and inspired by different aims, united only in their search for alternative educational forms.

24. Proem to *The Great Instauration*, in *Selected Writings of Francis Bacon*, ed. Hugh G. Dick, Modern Library ed. (New York, 1955), 423. The following quotation comes from the preface to the same work (428).

25. "Only let the human race recover that right over nature which belongs to it by divine bequest, and let power be given it; the exercise thereof will be governed by sound reason and true religion" (*Novum Organum* I.cxxix, 539).

26. Men should seek knowledge because it is "a rich store-house, for the glory of the Creator and the relief of man's estate" (*The Advancement of Learning*, 193).

27. *The New Atlantis*, 574.

28. For example: "that which is question is kept question, so as the columns of no further proceeding are pitched" (395); "for why should a few received authors stand up like Hercules' Columns, beyond which there should be no sailing or discovering" (222). For further passages in the same vein, see 428, 440; and for a general expression of Bacon's "Faustianism" see, for example, *Novum Organum* I.xlviii, 473.

29. In the equivalent canto of the *Paradiso*, 26.115 ff., Adam tells Dante that his offense was not the eating of the forbidden fruit but solely *il trapassar del segno*, the transgressing of the bound.

30. See Peter Singer's carefully documented *Animal Liberation: A New Ethics for Our Treatment of Animals* (New York, 1975), 49-50: "Another major field of experimentation involves the poisoning of millions of animals annually. Often this too is done for trivial reasons. In Britain it is known that over 23 percent of the 5 million experiments performed annually are mandatory tests of drugs and other materials required by law. In the United States no figures are available, but the Food and Drug Administration requires extensive animal testing of new substances before they are released. While it may be thought justifiable to require animal tests of potentially life-saving drugs, the same tests are done for products like cosmetics, food colorings, and floor polishes. Should hundreds [*sic*] of animals suffer so that a new kind of lipstick or mouthwash can be put on the market?"

31. The phrase is Aristotle's and applies of course to animals, fauna, as well. I am arbitrarily restricting it to flora.

32. *Erläuterungen zu Hölderlins Dichtung* (Frankfurt am Main, 1963), 99.

33. Respect for natural things is found in other cultures, e.g., in this Kwakiutl Indian prayer to a young cedar: "Look at me, friend! / I come to ask for your dress. / For you have come to take pity on us; / For there is nothing for which you cannot be used, . . . / For you are really willing to give us your dress . . . / I am going to make a basket for lily roots out of you. / I pray you,

friend, not to feel angry" (quoted in *American Indian Prose and Poetry*, ed. Margot Astrov [New York, 1962], 281). This prayer, though moving, is culturally too remote to be directly useful to us. No less respectful and within our Western orbit is Pindar's parable of the Oak: "If a man with his keen axe-edge / lops the branches of a great oak tree, / defiling the beauty that men wondered at— / it will not put forth again, yet / it bears witness to itself, / whether it comes in the end to winter's fire / or pressed down on its master's pillars / does sad labor in a stranger's house, / its own place left desolate" (*Pythian* 4.263 ff., after C. M. Bowra's trans.).

34. *The Symbolism of Evil*, trans. Emerson Buchanan (Boston, 1969), 351.

35. Hannah Arendt suggests that on one momentous occasion this did happen: ". . . the eventual victory of the [Christian] concern with eternity over all other [i.e. Greek] kinds of aspiration toward immortality is not due to philosophic thought. The fall of the Roman Empire plainly demonstrated that no work of mortal hands can be immortal" (*The Human Condition*, 21).

INDEX

Abrams, M. H., 244n (see p. 10)
Aeneid (Virgil), 224
Aeschylus, 2, 25, 27, 39, 77, 92, 106
Alberti, Rafael, 151
Alonso, Damaso, 139, 141, 143, 144, 149, 150, 151, 155, 166
Alvarez, A., 213, 215-216
Amis, Kingsley, 225
Anaxagoras, 91
Antony and Cleopatra (Shakespeare), 81
Aquinas, Thomas, 120, 128
Arendt, Hannah, 11, 33, 93-94, 101-102, 111, 160, 220, 225, 245n (see p. 31), 270n; quoted 221, 267n
Ariosto, Ludovico, 66, 136-138, 145, 183; *Orlando Furioso*, 134
Aristophanes, 105
Aristotle, 15, 80, 101, 226-227
Armstrong, Neil, 14
Arnold, Matthew, 2, 3
Arrowsmith, William, 105, 252n (see p. 81)
Aubigné, Agrippa d', 134
Auerbach, Erich, 20
Augustine, Saint, 127
Austen, Jane, 9
Austin, Norman, 21, 245n

Bacchylides, 59, 247n
Bacon, Francis, 104, 236-237, 269n (see p. 236)
Baudelaire, Charles, 222
Beaufret, Jean, 15
Bembo, Pietro, 139
Beowulf, 32-33, 96-99, 101, 102, 111-112, 114, 136, 158
Berger, Peter, 24, 245n
Bible, The: Old Testament, 18; Micah, 22; Hebrews, 126; Psalms, 178; St. John, 213; Genesis, 254n
Bickersteth, Geoffrey L., 182, 192, 261n
Blackmur, R. P., 118, 119
Boccaccio, Giovanni, 117, 127
Boeckh, A., 249n (see p. 56)
Boswell, James, 10
Botticelli, Sandro, 22
Bowra, C. M., 60, 249n (see p. 56), 270n
Brandeis, Irma, 153
Brook, Peter, 130
Browne, Sir Thomas, quoted, 136
Bultmann, Rudolf, 118
Bundy, Elroy L., 43
Burckhardt, Jacob, 135
Burton, R. W. B., 58
Bush, Douglas, 118

271